KEY CONCEPTS  TURE

D1427568

:ey Concepts

.y Concepts provide an accessible and comprehensive range of
saries at undergraduate level. They are the ideal companion to
:extbook making them invaluable reading to students through-
)urse of study and especially useful as a revision aid.

s in Accounting and Finance
s in Business Practice
s in Criminal Justice and Criminology
s in Cultural Studies
s in Drama and Performance (second edition)
s in e-Commerce
s in Human Resource Management
s in Information and Communication Technology
s in International Business
s in Language and Linguistics (second edition)
ts in Law (second edition)
ts in Leisure
ts in Management
ts in Marketing
ts in Operations Management
ts in Philosophy
ts in Politics
ts in Public Relations
ts in Psychology
ts in Social Research Methods
ts in Sociology
ts in Strategic Management
ts in Tourism

y Concepts: Literature

tors: John Peck and Martin Coyle

ts in Contemporary Literature
ts in Creative Writing
ts in Crime Fiction
ts in Medieval Literature
ts in Modernist Literature
ts in Postcolonial Literature
ts in Renaissance Literature
ts in Romantic Literature
ts in Victorian Literature
ns and Criticism (third edition)

s are in preparation
ekeyconcepts.com

Concepts
ng Order
–3210–7

h America only)

ve future titles in this series as they are published by placing a
r. Please contact your bookseller or, in the case of difficulty, write
ddress below with your name and address, the title of the series
quoted above.

vices Department, Macmillan Distribution Ltd
asingstoke, Hampshire RG21 6XS, England

Key Concepts in Postcolonial Literature

Gina Wisker

First published 2007 by
PALGRAVE MACMILLAN

Palgrave Macmillan in the UK is an imprint of Macmillan Publishers Limited, registered in England, company number 785998, of Houndmills, Basingstoke, Hampshire RG21 6XS.

Palgrave Macmillan in the US is a division of St Martin's Press LLC, 175 Fifth Avenue, New York, NY 10010.

Palgrave Macmillan is the global academic imprint of the above companies and has companies and representatives throughout the world.

Palgrave® and Macmillan® are registered trademarks in the United States, the United Kingdom, Europe and other countries.

ISBN-13: 978 1-4039-4448-1
ISBN-10: 1-4039-4448-2

This book is printed on paper suitable for recycling and made from fully managed and sustained forest sources. Logging, pulping and manufacturing processes are expected to conform to the environmental regulations of the country of origin.

A catalogue record for this book is available from the British Library.

A catalog record for this book is available from the Library of Congress.

Printed and bound in Great Britain by
CPI Antony Rowe, Chippenham and Eastbourne

Contents

General Editors' Preface	viii
Acknowledgements	ix
General Introduction	x

1 Contexts: History, Politics, Culture | **1**
Introduction	1
Imperial and colonial periods and terms	3
Aboriginal/indigenous people	9
Anti-colonialism	10
Apartheid	11
Cannibal	16
Caribbean	17
Colonialism and imperialism	17
Commonwealth	22
Decolonisation	23
Diasporan writers	26
Difference and dialogue	36
Discourse	39
Fanon, Frantz (1925–61)	43
Independence	44
Land rights	47
Nation and nationalism	49
Neocolonialism	51
Pan-Africanism	52
Postcolonial discourse	53
Postcolonialism and feminism	56
Resistance	59
Rewriting history	60
Settler societies	62
SS Empire Windrush	65
Terra Nullius	68
Tricontinentalism	68

2 Texts: Themes, Issues, Concepts | **71**
| Introduction | 71 |
| Aboriginal literature | 74 |

Aboriginal writing: testimony, tale-telling and women's
  experience   79
Anti-apartheid political writing   80
Challenges to empire   87
Colonial status and cultural inequalities   89
Cultural change   91
Diaspora   92
Forms of writing – identity and subjectivity   100
Gender and convention: African women's novels   101
Language, discourse, culture and power: reclaiming/rewriting
  language and power   107
Literature and politics   109
Mother Africa, Mother India, motherhood, mothering   112
Myths of adapting and replaying   117
Nation language   120
Nationhood and women's equality   123
New literatures in English   127
New views of indigenous people – questioning the record   127
Oral-based literature, oral literature   130
Patriarchy and colonised women   135
Performance poetry   138
Postcolonial Gothic   147
Postcolonialism and feminism   155
Postcolonial settler writing   156
Recuperating and rewriting history   159
Semi-fictionalised autobiography   164
The last outpost of colonisation: rewriting the coloniser's
  homeland, from the inside   168

3 **Criticism: Approaches, Theory, Practice**   **171**
Introduction   171
Some of the major issues   174
Carnival   176
Colonial discourse   177
Commonwealth literature   178
Cosmopolitanism   179
Critical issues: location and difference   182
Essentialism   184
Fanon, Frantz (1925–61)   185
Global citizenship and cosmopolitanism   186
Hobson, John A. (1858–1940)   189
Hybridity   189

Mimicry	192
Nation language	193
Négritude	194
Postcolonial Gothic	197
Postcolonial theory	200
Said, Edward (1935–2003) and Orientalism	201
Speaking about or for Others	204
Spivak, Gayatri Chakravorty (1942–)	206
Chronology	208
References	230
General Index	239
Index of Works Cited	245

General Editors' Preface

The purpose of **Palgrave Key Concepts in Literature** is to provide students with key critical and historical ideas about the texts they are studying as part of their literature courses. These ideas include information about the historical and cultural contexts of literature as well as the theoretical approaches current in the subject today. Behind the series lies a recognition of the need nowadays for students to be familiar with a range of concepts and contextual material to inform their reading and writing about literature.

The series is also based on a recognition of the changes that have transformed degree courses in Literature in recent years. Central to these changes has been the impact of critical theory together with a renewed interest in the way in which texts intersect with their immediate context and historical circumstances. The result has been an opening up of new ways of reading texts and a new understanding of what the study of literature involves together with the introduction of a wide set of new critical issues that demand our attention. An important aim of **Palgrave Key Concepts in Literature** is to provide brief, accessible introductions to these new ways of reading and new issues.

Each volume in **Palgrave Key Concepts in Literature** follows the same structure. An initial overview essay is followed by three sections – *Contexts*, *Texts*, and *Criticism* – each containing a sequence of brief alphabetically arranged entries on a sequence of topics. 'Contexts' essays provide an impression of the historical, social and cultural environment in which literary texts were produced. 'Texts' essays, as might be expected, focus more directly on the works themselves. 'Criticism' essays then outline the manner in which changes and developments in criticism have affected the ways in which we discuss the texts featured in the volume. The informing intention throughout is to help the reader create something new in the process of combining context, text and criticism.

John Peck
Martin Coyle

Acknowledgements

It has been a fascinating exercise writing this book, and many thanks are due to my students over the years for asking the questions, indicating the kinds of need for clarification, and engaging with the arguments that led to many of the entries. I should like to thank Michelle Bernard most profusely for her tireless work on finding sources, tidying and editing the script, and Charlotte Morris for research and tidying at earlier stages. I started the book while working at Anglia Ruskin University and would like to thank the English department for their investment of RAE money in my work. I finished it while working at the University of Brighton and would like to thank senior colleagues who supported the time taken by its completion. My knowledge of ideas and texts would have been so much thinner without the guidance of a range of postcolonial scholar friends and colleagues in Australia, New Zealand, the Caribbean, South Africa and the UK, including Carole Ferrier, Ian Conrich, Pauline Dodgson-Katiyo, Mervyn Morris, and Clarke's Bookshop in Cape Town. Thanks to colleagues at Palgrave Macmillan for their continued support, and to John Peck and Martin Coyle for support and advice at crucial moments. Finally, thanks to my sons for putting up with the typing, and the trips abroad.

Gina Wisker

We would like to thank the following rights holders for permission to publish extracts from their works:

Bloodaxe Books for the extract from Jean Breeze's poem 'Brighteye' and Jackie Kay's 'Mummy and Donor and Deirdre'.

Selina Marsh Tusitala for her poem 'Statued [stat you?] Traditions'.

Every effort has been made to trace all copyright holders, but if any have been inadvertently overlooked the publishers will be pleased to make the necessary arrangement at the first opportunity.

General Introduction

The study of postcolonial literatures and the development of postcolonial literary critical practices are well established across the world, most particularly in the ex-British (and other) colonies. The writing from these is the main focus of this book, although there are many other postcolonial contexts relating to a diversity of powers who were also colonisers or imperial rulers. Also of interest is who has written back after the colonisers' rule has ended, by which I mean they have engaged with issues of power and representation which confront some of the established views. American writing in one sense is postcolonial, insofar as it is written after and against British colonial rule, while internationally there is a variety of postcolonial writing against and after a host of other periods of colonial rule.

According to noted postcolonial critics Bill Ashcroft, Gareth Griffiths and Helen Tiffin (2000), postcolonial studies more broadly seeks to examine the experiences, processes and effects of European colonialism, and reactions to it, from the sixteenth century up to and including the contemporary responses of neo-colonialism. While many of the terms which appear in this book – such as 'nation', 'other', 'Orientalism' and 'hybridity' – would also appear in a book which focused on postcolonial studies in the broadest sense, the focus of this book on key concepts is on postcolonial literature which has been and is produced and written as a political, ideological engagement with the experiences of colonisation and imperial rule. Critic Stephen Slemon defines postcolonial literature as a 'category of literary activity which springs from a new and welcome political energy going on within what used to be called 'Commonwealth' literary studies (Slemon, 1994, pp. 16-17). In this book, we are looking in the main at literature, and at the key historical contexts and key concepts which inform and underpin that literature.

More specifically, the study of postcolonial literatures and critical practices has flowered in Britain, USA, Australasia and around the world since the 1980s, initially inspired by both the political resistance within once-colonial countries and by writers from those countries. These writers needed to explore and create literary expressions about their own and others' positions, histories and experiences as people who had lived under colonialism or imperialism and who were now able to assert or reassert their own world-views and positions in their own expressive forms. The study of postcolonial literatures also developed as part of a postmodernist fundamental questioning of the established literary canon. This has been followed by recognition from the literary establishment, as well as the general public and college and university staff and students, of the literary and cultural worth of work by postcolonial writers and also by those who produce and perform oral literature from a range of cultural backgrounds. This recognition extends to a need for literary scrutiny of colonial and other texts, using postcolonial critical practices.

Much postcolonial writing springs from forms of questioning of, or opposition to, the established literary canon (in English literature, for example, this would include Shakespeare, Wordsworth and those other writers whose work appears on most literature syllabi). This is largely because of the ways in which many canonical texts imposed a version of worlds-views, values, perceptions and forms of writing which largely ignored, neglected or excluded the different experiences of colonised people and those under imperial rule. As readers and students, it is important to recognise that many people come to postcolonial literature from reading works from the canon. Links with and reactions against canonical writers make a useful initial bridge for readers. Indeed, such links are made in this book for a definite purpose. The interpretation of the word 'postcolonial' suggests both *after* colonialism and imperialism, and *in opposition to* colonialism and imperialism. However it is important to recognise that not *all* postcolonial writers are Black or Asian, and that those who have suffered under colonialism and imperialism also include the Irish and settlers from many different origins. Also, not all writers who write postcolonial-inflected texts, texts with postcolonial views, have themselves been colonised peoples. Writers who write some of the earliest literature with postcolonial elements often do so, as they do now, from their own established literary reputations (sometimes they, too, are part of that literary canon), as an enlightened and ideologically engaged reaction to the silencing and inequality caused by colonialism and imperialism. Recognising such critical attacks on the worldviews, mindsets and behaviours which established and maintained colonial and imperial rule, this book makes some initial links with modernism and those writers who are early postcolonial writers and (not exclusively but in the examples here) are English, European, or Irish, but who genuinely have a postcolonial viewpoint and arguments. Because a writer writes from a nation of imperialists and colonisers it does not mean they support that nation's oppressive practices; many have criticised from within. A number of writers really pave the way for a questioning of colonialism, and among them are some of the literary modernists (experimental writers from the 1880s to around 1945) who also criticised the staleness of pre-modernist writing.

Postcolonial writing is a very rich, fascinating and ever-growing area of writing, and one gaining popularity for reading and study. However, appreciating postcolonial literature does require a certain amount of contextual, cultural and critical work on the part of the reader. As a field, or subject area of literary study, postcolonial literature involves readers in finding out about historical and cultural contexts in order to be able to read postcolonial texts with some insight about why they were produced, how, where and to what ends, what they might be arguing, why they are exploring or arguing about those issues in those ways, and even the forms which the texts themselves take.

A focus on postcolonial literatures raises issues about the differing ways in which literatures produced by writers from very different cultural backgrounds, geographies, religions and literary traditions can be classed together under the same identifying words. Our reading of the literatures of settler nations such as Canada, Australia, New Zealand, South Africa, ex-British colonies now nations, or independent republics such as Cyprus, Singapore, Jamaica, Pakistan, India, Nigeria and Ireland, will inevitably differ in relation to the different histories, geographies and contexts in which the writers write (or perform, or declaim) and are published, read, taught (or not). Some of these issues are picked up in the discussion of the different terms – Commonwealth literature, new literatures in English, post-colonial and postcolonial – in this book.

There are, however – surprisingly perhaps – some common themes which we might find across the works of writers from such different contexts, and these themes can serve to unite our explorations; they include identity, nationhood, finding a language, a discourse both creative and critical, issues of relations to the ex-colonial power, engagement, re-engagement, renewal and recuperation. Some of these themes focus on the development of different forms of expression, language and imagery, and emphasise writing that was in forms which were marginalised, devalued or even illegal under colonial or imperial rule. They are present in any kind of literary production moving on beyond being 'mimic' men, an idea developed by the critic Homi Bhabha, in which people are destined forever, somehow and always, to reference the colonial past.

The critical perspectives and frameworks which inform the reading of postcolonial texts are also many, including psychoanalysis (issues about identity formation; speaking out from oppression; and silencing), linguistics (the forms the writing takes; language and structure choice), feminism (ways in which women are represented; women's worldviews expressed, specifically female-oriented forms of expression and language; a focus on constructions and representations of masculinities), queer theory (identification and rejection of the 'Othering' of those whose sexuality and sexual orientation does not fit categories and forms of heterosexual views, which question normalcy and see it as a construction and an imposition), Marxism (relating literary production and expression to modes of labour; relationships of power socially and politically in history; people in their historical and social context) and post-structuralism (recognising the constructedness of all representations and expressions; opportunities or otherwise for choices of expression and view).

These differing critical stances intersect with and inform each other in our reading from a postcolonial critical perspective, so that there could be said to be many postcolonialisms in terms of literary critical practices. You will no doubt settle on the approaches and interests which appeal to your own critical, analytical, informed views about ways of appreciating, reading and understanding literature and writing. Since the term postcolonialism is so widely used, we will use it here to include the whole range of perspectives and influences on our reading and to identify writing and oral production produced both in opposition to and after colonialism. Those other critical practices (feminism and Marxism – as above) inform as they intersect with the postcolonial in our reading.

There are very many postcolonial writers whose names are well known for their groundbreaking work, and there are others, many of whom are women writers, whose names are less well known. This book provides a critical introduction to the established, the lesser known and some of the emerging writers, to the writers who have won Nobel prizes and Booker prizes, such as V.S. Naipaul (Trinidad), Derek Walcott (St Lucia), Wole Soyinka (Nigeria), Salman Rushdie and Anita Desai (India) and Margaret Atwood (Canada), and those whose work is only now beginning to appear on reading lists or who have only recently gained an audience, such as Australian aboriginal writers including Sally Morgan and Doris Pilkington, or other writers who write with cultural perceptions and insights unfamiliar even to avid readers of postcolonial literature who have grown up reading Salman Rushdie and J.M. Coetzee. This might well include, for instance, writers famous in their own lands but often less well known on international literary class booklists, such as the Maori writers Patricia Grace and Witi Ihimaera, or writers from the Fiji islands such as Konai Helu Thaman and Vilsoni Hereniko. Indeed, in addition to introducing some of the very wide range of postcolonial writers whose work is rarely mentioned in other critical texts, there are in this book more women writers than one finds in some other more conventional postcolonial critical texts. This, I would argue, is part of a reinstatement of significant writers, in line with the arguments about avoiding cultural marginalising of writers (an argument made by well-known critics such as Gayatri Chakravorty Spivak).

One of the exciting elements of working with postcolonial literatures is the ways in which we can reconstruct, reinterpret and create a range of new readings and new interpretations through our deployment of postcolonial criticism in all *its* variety in our reading of postcolonial literatures in all *their* variety. A key point to remember is that it is better to be engaged, exploring and questioning than to be silenced. Here, I find some of the advice of feminist critics Gayatri Chakravorty Spivak, Sara Suleri and Sneja Gunew most helpful, not only in giving us rights to engage with and appreciate that with which we are normally unfamiliar, decoding our own origins, but in generally indicating that *not* to so engage because of fear of ignorant blundering would be yet another form of silencing, a fate experienced by much precolonial and then anti-colonial writing (colonialists and imperialists frequently suggested that neither of these forms of writing, the precolonial or the anticolonial a) existed nor b) had any worth). In other words, the postcolonial critic's job has been to unearth and recuperate, re-read and revalue works which provide us with a rich sense of life, values and different world-views before colonialism. These critics also bring to a reading public the critical responses of early postcolonial writers, who criticised the suppression and misinterpretation which occurred under colonialism and who at the time were thought to be dangerously subversive.

Many of our established reading practices are challenged and recon-stituted by reading postcolonial literatures which might deploy tradi-tional literary forms to express experiences not usually found in these forms. For example, while a writer such as Derek Walcott might choose to use the classical forms of an English educated literary man, informed by the cadences of the Romantic poets and the well-established metre of iambic pentameter which runs throughout Milton, Shakespeare and Wordsworth, he will also transport his readers to a Caribbean context. In the poem 'The Schooner Flight' (1987), for instance, he creates the Caribbean islands, sensual relations and personal exploration in context, growing from his own origins and his English-educated, Caribbean-oriented journeying, while at the same time exploring a kind of epic journey itself influenced by the West, through the quests for origins and values explored in works inspired by classical Greek myths, notably Homer's *The Odyssey* and *The Iliad*.

Such a deliberately postcolonial text reflects the many influences of the Western coloniser and the literatures and values which earlier critics and some contemporary readers believed to be the *only* ways of seeing and expressing personal and cultural responses. It adopts, adapts and translates them, both in terms of what is written about and how it is written. What Walcott does, in other words, is use the literature of Western Europe to provide him with a way of exploring Caribbean cultural differences.

More radically, as Edward Kamau Brathwaite has shown (*The History of the Voice,* 1984), other writers, such as the Caribbean oral perfor-mance poets, work with the oral influences of their origins and the sounds and experiences around them, so that while 'the hurricane does not roar in pentameters' (p. 19), the capturing of its roar, rather than the glow of Wordsworth's daffodils, is a major project.

This book also considers issues of context and history and the cultural perspectives through which we read and interpret postcolonial texts. Language is a key issue here. There could be a problem for postcolonial writers in terms of the language in which they express themselves. If they use the language of the coloniser, they are speaking perhaps of their own experiences but in someone else's imposed language. If they use the language of their origins, they cannot engage directly with the coloniser, nor can they find a wider audience outside their own language community. Perhaps this does not matter; in fact, it can be argued that the most important issue is to write of your life and country in the language of your own people because this is empowering, and so postcolonial writers might write using their own language to their own friends, family and country folk and by so doing establish the importance of the use of 'nation language' (as Caribbean performance poets such as Louise Bennett – 'Miss Lou' – term the use of the language of your origins). Indeed, the whole issue of writing or oral literature is raised here, especially in countries where the passing on of wisdom, the making of comments about life and the weaving of myth and stories is conducted in an oral rather than a written form, but also where written literary language rarely appears.

The issue of language is not just one of orality and valuing forms of expression – it is specifically concerned with cultural identity and world-view. Discourse, it is now accepted, relates to power, sex, identity and the way we see the world and ourselves in it. If a writer writes in his or her own language, it is possible to use traditional forms but necessary also to ask how far they have now been merged with or affected by those of the coloniser. It might not actually be possible to produce a response which ignores the influence of the coloniser and re-creates anew the years before colonial influence. Even writing in the mother tongue will be affected by events. Ngugi Wa Thiong'o (1938–, Kenya) chooses to write in the very specific language of his home, and by doing so engages with complex literary thought to be expressed in his own language, moving it from the language of the merely day-to-day. The price is the potential loss of an audience beyond the language group, the achievement one of asserting nationhood, as indeed is the case when one chooses to write in Welsh, for instance, where readership is confined to those who understand Welsh.

Another key area about postcolonial literatures concerns when they are written and in what contexts. Are they written during the rule of the coloniser? Or after it? In opposition to it during this rule? Or celebrating its end? Is this a temporal construct or one of reactive or proactive change? This is an issue contested in postcolonial literature and criticism. In this book we have chosen the broader description of postcolonial, that is, identifying it as both a radical critique during colonisation (which would include contemporary Maori writing, and E.M. Forster's *A Passage to India* [1924], for instance), and a critique after the end of imperialism and colonial rule. In this broad view we also need to take into consideration both new expressions of post-colonisation and the continuing effects of colonisation, for example, the influence of multi-nationals and any maintenance of racial and religious prejudices and hierarchies.

The choice of what postcolonial writers write about is always crucial. Perhaps they write about the colonisation process and a need to speak against it, seeking out and creating a sense of identity as they do so. If this is the writers' choice, they might well be re-playing at the level of their expression and exploring the kind of articulation of the imagination and mind which has held them and their forebears in a kind of colonised loop, unable to see beyond or express themselves beyond the constraints of the mind sets, languages and forms of the colonial masters. The writers lived and breathed these impositions and they had become embedded as part of their way of life. Whatever the choices, postcolonial writers and readers are engaged in constructing, expressing, interpreting, enjoying and debating ways in which text is produced by, reflections and comments on the contexts from which they spring, and in wrestling with ideologically infused issues such as identity, nationality, nationhood, language, power politics and human relations. The choices are many and the decisions difficult. Some of these choices and decisions the tensions, the contradictions and the possibilities – form part of this study of postcolonial literatures.

Contexts: History, Politics, Culture

Introduction

> Where are your monuments, your battles, martyrs?
> Where is your tribal memory? Sirs,
> in that gray vault. The sea. The sea
> has locked them up. The sea is History.
> ('The Sea Is History', Walcott, 1987)

> History, to the defeated
> May say 'Alas', but cannot help or pardon.
> ('Spain 1937', Auden, 1977)

Derek Walcott sums up ways in which the history of colonised peoples has been obliterated in the past, but at the same time, he begins to re-establish it in his own writing. W. H. Auden's poignant and painful comment defines part of the project of postcolonial peoples to reassert and recuperate a history which is not merely that of the coloniser or imperialist, a history from which frequently they are absent, the ignored if not the defeated – and usually both.

This section explores some of the crucial historical moments, the political movements, developments and the cultural differences that have influenced postcolonial literature. Initially it mentions very briefly, if available, the pre-colonial and pre-imperial contexts, followed by a record and discussion of some of the key moments which established colonial and imperial rule, beginning with the first landing, colonising, settling and establishing of imperial rule (depending on the country). It then moves on to mention briefly key political, religious and other moments when colonial rule was challenged: the wars, mutinies, rebellions and imprisonments, the dates of independence and other significant moments. In historical terms, in the main, our focus here is on the questioning of and revolts against colonial and imperial rule, the movements for independence and other key political, religious or cultural moments insofar as we can see that they affect the production and

1

reading of literary work – both oral and textual. Importantly, the section locates the moments when colonisation and imperialism formally ended, that is, when the country, nation or state under discussion formally gained independence, and the issues which have arisen as a result.

We need to be aware of historical and political moments in understanding the development of postcolonial literatures. Certain points of uprising or revolution, such as the Indian Mutiny or First War of Independence in 1857, or the Irish uprising (1916), when colleagues of the Irish poet W.B. Yeats took over the General Post Office in Sackville Street, Dublin (explored in the poem 'Easter 1916'), are critical moments for those countries, nations and states, in making often-violent statements about the rejection of imperialism and colonial rule, as are those individual points of revolution, suffrage and independence which differ from country to country, continent and nation, state to state.

This section also considers issues of race and culture, in some instances involving religious differences. In the case of India and Pakistan, for instance, there is a dynamic and abrasive conflation of the moment of independence from Imperial British rule in 1947, and the bloody dividing up of the sub-continent on largely religious grounds. At this memorable moment, millions of Muslims fled from what was to become India, to what became Pakistan, while millions of Hindus, Sikhs and others fled from what became Pakistan, a Muslim country, to what became India. This transit, exodus and restlessness were caused by the precise drawing of a red line on a map by Earl Mountbatten, an Englishman, Muhammad Ali Jinnah from Pakistan and Jawaharlal Nehru from India. Anita Desai, in *Clear Light of Day* (1980), marks the bloodshed and the painful and often fatal trekking involved in this moment, as does Salman Rushdie in *Midnight's Children* (1981), where Saleem Sinai's birthday is the midnight of the transition, his ears filled with the cries of the dispossessed and confused caught up in this change.

Strictly speaking, if we use the word 'post' to mean 'after', then the history of postcolonial literatures begins following the end of colonial or imperial rule in each of the different countries or nations. However, as I point out in the *Criticism* section (Chapter 3), there is critical debate about the definitions of postcolonial writing in terms of whether it is ante-post-colonial and produced during colonial or imperial rule, or whether its specific characteristics are related to being produced after the end of colonialism and imperialism. With the former, the sense of resistance against imposed forms of belief, behaviour and writing is present, while with the latter, it could be that some forms of writing in the postcolonial period are still colonial and imperial in tone and influences.

Several critics (see the debates in Ashcroft and Tiffin 1989, 2000; John Thieme 1989, 1996; Robert Young, 2001) have commented that it is actually impossible to write about colonial and imperial influence in the postcolonial period because this influence, although altered since the removal of colonial or imperial rule, is still present in the impact of multinationals and the inherited legacy of forms of belief, language, education, law and infrastructure. Indeed, Robert Young notes (2001, p. 50) how Kwame Nkrumah highlighted the continued dependency of newly independent states. Borrowing money from the West, many new states ended up in financial thrall to those who were once their imperial masters. Others argue that continuing to represent postcolonial literary concerns and expressions as reflecting the concerns and conflicts of the past is an insidious perpetration of those very colonial influences; people have moved on beyond colonialisation and imperialism, and are not merely products of it.

In this first section of the book we will also be considering some contexts which relate to race, religion, gender and economics, and which converge with historical moments to stimulate literary response. This, however, does not attempt to be a history book and indeed there are some excellent histories of postcolonialism, of which Robert Young's *Postcolonialism: An Historical Introduction* (2001) is an example to turn to for detail of movements in history which underpinned/are expressed through the postcolonial. Because there is always some overlap between a concept and a context, some terms and points occur in more than one section. Apartheid, for instance, falls into all three sections of the present volume since it is an ideology of separation and hierarchy based on colour, while it is also a historically inflected context which ended when Nelson Mandela was freed on 11 February 1990, and came to power in 1991. The legacy of apartheid, however, like so many other events and belief-dominated practices in colonial and imperial contexts, despite government attempts to redress these imbalances, still lingers on in economic subordination and poor health and housing.

Imperial and colonial periods and terms

Imperial, colonial, settler and postcolonial are all contested terms and imply differing histories, different kinds of rule. Nor are the histories of some countries/nations/states simply definable as fitting into one of these terms rather than another.

Imperialism and colonialism seem always to have been with us. Probably the first large-scale empire we know of in history is the Roman Empire, which spread across Europe and beyond. America can now be said to have a large-scale empire and, like the influence of multinationals from Japan and Korea, has entered households and affected the worldviews of millions, an invasion fantasised and explored in, for instance, Gabriel Garcia Marquez's *One Hundred Years of Solitude* (1970); in this novel a travelling American discovers bananas in Macondo and sets about developing a banana republic from which the locals are excluded in terms of wealth and access and kept out by an electric fence, which fries the perching birds.

The first major postcolonial context is one with which we will in the main not, however, be dealing with here – that is, the continent of North America (excluding Canada, an ex-colony). The group of islands (broadly defined as the Americas) which used slave and indentured labour is, however, part of our concern. This includes parts of America, South America and the Caribbean islands, which were developed initially for their plantation economy, and were colonised by a range of internationally originated peoples. For many in the Caribbean, various parts of Europe – notably Britain, France, Spain and Portugal – are still viewed as homelands. In our focus, mainly on British postcolonialism, the work of Caribbean people is highlighted.

Just as all empires, colonies, and settler societies are not the same, neither are all postcolonial contexts and postcolonial texts in terms of their forms of control, their argument, message or expression. It would be a naive and culturally simplistic, essentialist assumption which ignored the very different geographical, historical, social, religious and economic contexts of the different ex-colonies. The locations of ex-imperialist and colonial rule are also varied in size and history. Apart from the Roman Empire (from 30 BC to AD 476) and the Austro-Hungarian Empire (from 1867 to 1918), which were historically large-scale empires, those empires established in the eighteenth and nineteenth centuries by European powers have had the most impact on world history. The British Empire was the largest of this kind. British rule in India, the so-called British Raj, is the main example of imperial rule in the eighteenth, nineteenth and twentieth centuries, a rule which was constituted by having an imperial power at a distance whose army and administrators ruled the subjugated country, imposing their infrastructure on that country and thereby enabling it to develop its own infrastructure, which itself remained a version of that of the imperial power, at least in the short to medium term.

Imperial India was vast; Australia, an ex-colony, is also vast, but some of the ex-colonies of the British Empire are small islands such as Cyprus, Malta and Singapore – chosen for their military locations and trading significances. Many Caribbean islands were British colonies, and gained independence during the second half of the twentieth century, becoming members of the British Commonwealth.

The history of ex-British colonies which are settler societies, such as Australia, Canada and New Zealand, differs somewhat from the many countries within Africa, and smaller islands, for example, Cyprus and Malta, which came under imperial or colonial rule. In the second category there was an imposition and/or reorganisation run from a distance, a government back in Europe which maintained a local version of itself in the country it was ruling. That country's ways of life were undermined and transformed by Europeans until it could reclaim independence, remaining within the Commonwealth or not as it chose. In settler societies, the colonisers settled on the land.

Colonial or imperial rule is a situation which, in terms of the relationships between indigenous peoples and the colonisers, means a consistently maintained distance and difference. Settlers, however, do just that, settle and stay, changing the overall rule and ways of life in the country in which they have settled, making it their own. There is identification in many instances of politically aware settlers with indigenous peoples, in terms of their perceived mutual subordination to the rule of the colonial or imperial powers elsewhere. This kind of identification legitimates the inclusion of their work. Writers frequently take up the variety of these issues: thus, for example, Margaret Atwood exposes the capitalist globalisation enterprise of Americans in Canada in her survival tales, *Surfacing* (1972), and the essay 'Survival', while Australian poet Les Murray celebrates both the coming to identity of mostly poor white Australians and the Aboriginals alongside whom they work and live, who are, despite being the first owners of the land, still treated as third-class citizens. In his poem 'The Mitchells', for example, two men putting up telegraph poles are seen as solid, hardworking, ordinary. Asked about their identities, one immediately says he is a Mitchell. The pause of the second man indicates his mixed race ancestry. He is a Mitchell, but also an Aboriginal. They work on together and eat lunch. As with many of Murray's poems, the landscape is important in helping people locate their identities and we see an appreciation of a changing cultural mix.

Following the end of colonial rule and the advent of independence, new governments could initiate improvements, new hope, or terrible disappointments. Corruption, violence, disease and a desire to recuperate history establish new ways of seeing and being, and jostle for power in postcolonial societies – the direct or indirect result of having been colonised. America was an early colony which achieved independence. However, Britain's oldest colony, Bermuda (see *The Tempest* and

Robinson Crusoe), rejected independence in 1995. Independence was not necessarily the greatest spur to writing; often opposition proved more inspirational. Recognition of cultural identity was also influenced by reactions against oppression, such as the organisation of the anti-Pass Law protests by the African National Congress (ANC), its army, Umkhontowe Sizwe, and its allies, the Pan Africanist Congress and the Communist Party, in South Africa (1952), students' revolts in Soweto (1976), the Vietnam war (1960s), the Biafran war (Nigeria, 1967), and the murder of Martin Luther King (1968). This latter coincided with student uprisings in Paris, sit-ins in the UK while changes continued with Australian Aboriginals gaining the vote (1973).

Not all writers focus on oppression or independence, some preferring to look at more small-scale issues. So R. K. Narayan looks instead at a local village and its concerns, in this case at the issue of acceptable birth control in *The Painter of Signs* (1976). Indian writer V.S. Naipaul is a fierce critic of the postcolonial world and deals with the difficulties of settling in *A House for Mr Biswas* (1961) while fellow Trinidadian Earl Lovelace focuses, in *The Dragon Can't Dance* (1979), on internecine and racial strife embodied in the clashes at carnival time and the opportunities carnival offers people to express themselves, perform, and/or be radical up on Calvary Hill (a violent, economically deprived suburb of Port of Spain, Trinidad). Lovelace's work looks at local conflicts and the potential, or otherwise, for change. Similarly, following powerful criticism of British colonialism and history, Nigerian writers Chinua Achebe and Wole Soyinka exposed the evil acts of native-born dictators and corrupt officials who came to power after independence.

The ending of colonial or imperial rule created a short-lived hope in many newly independent countries that a properly postcolonial era would mean that those living in the newly independent lands – indigenous peoples, or First Nations peoples, alongside the settlers in some instances – would govern according to their own values and rules, independent from their previous colonial or imperial masters. However, in many cases the infrastructure established by Western powers remained, as did the language – for the most part English and other European languages, while continuing Western economic, political, military and ideological influence predominated, labelled by Marxists as 'neo-colonialism'.

The project of globalisation can be used to put into a theoretical framework these issues of what remains and what changes in postcolonial societies. Globalisation refers to both an attempt by first-world powers (mainly USA, Britain and Australia) to identify the needs of, and redress economic imbalances in, Third World countries. And also, beyond what might well deteriorate into paternalism, to continue to fuel a sense of dependency and a certain disenfranchisement and disempowerment deriving from the Coca Cola-nisation, McDonaldisation, and the creeping of controls over natural resources, local economies and spending power, by multinational companies based in the richer, Western, First World. The economic effect of large multinationals and the existence of Third World debt ensure the maintenance of a version of economic colonial power over countries that are not themselves economically viable independently and are still therefore visibly or invisibly under the control of wealthier Western powers. How these wealthy powers do or do not empower their poorer ex-colonies is often dependent on the kind of aid offered. In the 2004 tsunami, aid agencies which had become embedded in and worked successfully with local skilled and trained people were able to act immediately and effectively at a local level because the decisions to be made – as well as the materials which were needed for clearing up and reconstruction – were interpreted and enacted at that local level instead of being imposed in a temporary and humiliating fashion by a grandiose force from outside. Relationships between ex-colonial, ex-imperial and postcolonial peoples need to take account of history and local knowledge to be sensitive about terms used.

Interpretations of postcolonialism often depend largely upon the speaking position of those defining it. I will attempt to represent the debate but also to state clearly how I interpret and use the term here in the book. Postcolonial writing here is taken to mean (far from unproblematically) writing which resists colonialism and its power politics, produced mainly after the colonial period. This book concentrates on British colonialism rather than, for instance, that of Latin America, the US or the rest of Europe, although it does mention other examples of colonial, imperial and postcolonial contexts, issues and texts to stress parallels, similarities or differences.

In *The Empire Writes Back* (1989), one of their range of significant books on postcolonialism, the notable postcolonial critics Bill Ashcroft, Gareth Griffiths and Helen Tiffin establish a very accessible but (in my view) possibly rather too broad interpretation of postcolonialism, identifying postcolonial or resistance impulses as far back as seventeenth-century settler societies. It is not so easy to recognise resistance writing as postcolonial because not all of it is concerned with colonial power issues such as establishing identity, family/kinship, motherlands, nationhood, and mother tongue. Nor is it valid to concentrate simply on writing produced from the moment of the official end of colonial rule, since not all such writing resists or criticises colonialism. Additionally, as several other critics have pointed out, much of this writing is tinged by neo-colonialism that is, it probably inevitably indicates how the various oppressions or (to a lesser extent) the opportunities of colonialism still affect people's lives, influence their thought processes and their self-respect, and also influence the language and meta-language in which they produce their literature. For instance, New Zealand writers argue that theirs is still very much a colonial country in terms of values and behaviours:

> For Maori women in a colonial setting (we avoid using the term post-colonial since we believe that this country remains very much colonial) much of ourselves has been denied, and hence, for many Maori women there is an ongoing struggle to centre ourselves, to deconstruct colonial representations and to reconstruct and reclaim knowledge about ourselves.
>
> Johnston and Pihama, 1994, p. 95.

Stephen Slemon sees the term postcolonialism as referring to a set of anti-colonial cultural practices, attitudes and behaviours, while McLintock puts forward a different view:

> [the term] locates specifically anti or *postcolonial discursive purchase* in culture; one which begins in the moment that colonial power inscribes itself onto the body and space of its others and which continues as an often occulted tradition into the modern theatre of new-colonialist relations.
>
> Slemon, in Tiffin and Adam, 1991, p. 3.

> A country can be postcolonial, i.e. independent, and yet also neo-colonial, i.e. still economically dependent on the relations and links with those who operate colonial rule over it. It is sometimes debatable that once colonised countries can be seen as properly postcolonial because the ideas and economies are still tied to the coloniser.
>
> McLintock, 1993.

In the rest of this book, for the sake of being straightforward, we are going to move beyond the exclusively historical construction of post-colonial, indicated in the use of the hyphen, which suggests 'after' (such as in post-war); instead we shall use the term postcolonial to indicate not only work produced following colonial and imperial rule – that is, a historical construct – but also work responding to it, rejecting it, resisting it and focusing in some measure on the debates around the effects of the postcolonial condition, issues of identity, nationhood, discourse and so on. Many of the terms which follow in this section are also contentious, so I will attempt to represent the debates around their use, and also to explore some historical moments in the ending of imperial and postcolonial rule and the development of postcolonial experience, suggesting as far as possible their intention and their impact.

Postcolonial writing is produced, then, in the main (but not exclusively, see the introduction) by writers from lands which have been under colonial or imperial rule. They can be indigenous or settler writers and to be considered postcolonial they write with a critical edge about, against, and mostly after colonisation.

Further reading

Ashcroft, Bill, Gareth Griffiths and Helen Tiffin, *The Empire Writes Back* (London: Routledge, 1989).

Atwood, Margaret, *Surfacing* (Toronto, ON: House of Anansi Press, 1972).

Auden, W.H., 'Spain 1937' in *The English Auden: Poems, Essays, And Dramatic Writings, 1927–1939* (Oxford: Oxford University Press, 1977).

Boehmer, Elleke, *Colonial & Postcolonial Literature* (Oxford: Oxford University Press, 1995).

Defoe, Daniel, *Robinson Crusoe* [1719] (New York: Signet Classics, 1998).

Desai, Anita, *Clear Light of Day* (London: Vintage, 1980).

García Márquez, Gabriel, *One Hundred Years of Solitude* (New York: Jonathan Cape, 1970).

Johnston, P. and L. Pihama, 'The Marginalization of Maori Women' in *Hecate,* 2, v.4, October 1994.

Lovelace, Earl, *The Dragon Can't Dance* (London: André Deutsch, 1979).

McLintock, Anne, 'The Angel of Progress: Pitfalls of the Term "Colonialism"', in *Social Text,* 31/32, 1992, reprinted in Laura Chrisman and Patrick Williams (eds), *Colonial Discourse and Post-Colonial Theory* (Hemel Hempstead: Prentice Hall, 1993).

Narayan, R.K., *The Painter of Signs* (London: Heinemann, 1976).

Rushdie, Salman, *Midnight's Children* (New York: Alfred A. Knopf, 1981).

Shakespeare, William, *The Tempest* [1610] (London: Penguin, 1999).

Slemon, Stephen 'Modernism's Last Post', in Ian Adam and Helen Tiffin (eds), *Past the Last Post: Theorizing Post-colonialism and Post-modernism* (Hemel Hempstead: Harvester Wheatsheaf, 1991).

Thieme, John, *Postcolonial Studies: An Essential Glossary* (London: Edward Arnold, 1989).

Thieme, John, *The Arnold Anthology of Post-Colonial Literatures in English* (London: Edward Arnold, 1996).

Yeats, W.B., 'Easter 1916', in *The Collected Poems of W.B. Yeats* (Basingstoke: Macmillan, 1982).

Young, Robert, *Postcolonialism: An Historical Introduction* (Oxford: Blackwell, 2001).

Aboriginal/indigenous people

Aboriginal as a term has now been frequently replaced by 'indigenous' to connote people who are indigenous to a location, but also often the first people there. In Canada the First Nations people are identified as indigenous, in Malaysia the Orang Asli, and in Australia the Aboriginal peoples are, in fact, not one population but many 'tribes'. Indigenous peoples are defined by the *Oxford English Dictionary (OED)* as 'born in a place or region'. Ashcroft *et al.* inform us that 'The term "aboriginal" was coined as early as 1667 to describe the indigenous inhabitants of places encountered by European explorers, adventurers or seamen.' They confirm that 'The term Aboriginal or Aborigine is most commonly used as a name itself, to describe the indigenous inhabitants of Australia' (Ashcroft, Griffiths, Tiffin, 2000, p. 4), which is a much narrower usage.

Where terms such as 'First Nations' and 'Native Americans' have replaced the older settler-invader terms, this is in response to the potentially negative associations of aboriginal, defining aboriginal people not merely in terms of being first in the location but possibly with 'primitive' or 'savage' (each of these terms is riddled with colonial and imperial assumptions – of westernised cultures being more developed, progressive and valued over those found amongst the people whose lands were invaded/discovered).

Australian Aboriginal writers, whether pure blood or mixed race, include Mudrooroo Narrogin (Colin Johnson), whose *Wild Cat Falling* (1965) is arguably the first Australian Aboriginal text, and Sally Morgan, whose *My Place* (1987) was the first text by a woman which has *not* been produced in partnership with a white editor. Writing by Australian Aboriginal authors often looks at identity and the myths/beliefs about the Dreaming.

Further reading

Johnson, Colin (Mudrooroo), *Wild Cat Falling* [1965] (Sydney: HarperCollins, 2001).
Morgan, Sally, *My Place* (Fremantle: Fremantle Arts Centre Press, 1987).

Anti-colonialism

This is the political struggle of colonised peoples against the ideology and practices of colonialism. Anti-colonialism is taking place when various forms of opposition pull together as resistance to the varied operations and influences of colonialism in educational, literary, political, economic and cultural institutions. Early anti-colonialists often expressed themselves in opposition to forms of power in politics, education, law and so on, and in literary terms we might include Conrad's *Heart of Darkness* (1902) as an early anti-colonial text. It indicts the greed and pointless violence of imperial powers, although the book has been criticized by Chinua Achebe as actually perpetuating colonial misunderstandings and racist views. Much of the work of South African Nadine Gordimer continued anti-colonial expression without resorting to violent expression. Anti-colonial nationalism often began to develop within the structures of administration and education.

Some anti-colonialism is associated with an ideology of racial liberation, such as the Negritude movement, or a demand for recognition of cultural differences, such as in the work of the Indian National Congress, which worked to unite a variety of different religious and ethnic groups for national independence. Early national liberationist thinkers include C.L.R. James, Amilcar Cabral and Frantz Fanon; they and others were influenced by a radical, Marxist discourse of liberation.

A central theorist in postcolonial struggles, Cabral believed in armed struggle against inequalities and led the people of Guinea-Bissau in an independence movement against the Portuguese (1962), who were aided by NATO European powers and South America. Cabral supported indigenous cultures in the fight against imperial or colonial masters and so had a different set of beliefs from Frantz Fanon, his contemporary theorist who simply dismissed indigenous cultures. Although a less influential theorist than Fanon. It is claimed that he was murdered at the instigation of Portuguese government agents in 1973.

Further reading

Conrad, Joseph, *Heart of Darkness* [1902] (London: Penguin, 2000).
Fanon, Frantz, *Black Skin, White Masks* (London: Pluto Press, 1952).
Gordimer, Nadine, *The Conservationist* (London: Penguin, 1983).

Apartheid

Apartheid literally separated people in South Africa on the basis of their ethnic origins and skin colour. It had several phases and its implementation led to the forced movement of people, to poor living, educational and employment experiences for Black South Africans, and a great deal of violence. It also led to economic sanctions from countries outside South Africa which recognised how apartheid infringed human rights.

Apartheid is an Afrikaans term which literally means 'separation', and was used in South Africa for Nationalist Party government policy after 1948, a 'policy of separate development'. The policy has its roots in the 1913 Natives Land Act, establishing geographical separation between European and non-European farms and a limit to the land available to Black farmers. The South African Bureau for Racial Affairs (SABRA) coined the term in the 1930s and from 1948, upon the succession to power of the Afrikaners, nationality legislation was passed limiting the rights of non-European (non-white) South Africans in terms of civil liberties, jobs, education and access to the land.

When the apartheid laws were passed in 1948 and later years they included the Population Registration Act, registering people by race; the Mixed Amenities Act establishing and legalising racial segregation in public facilities; the Group Areas Act segregating suburbs; and the establishment of the Bantustans, or native homelands, to which much of the Black population was limited, the men often travelling to cities for work and the homelands remaining impoverished (the Transkei is a former Bantustan and still relatively underdeveloped).

Apartheid operated in South Africa from 1948 ('Grand Apartheid' during the sixties) until the early 1990s. It was a major example of politically legitimated racism that worked by hierarchising people because of their skin colour and segregating whites from non-whites of any description. Even as it racially configured urban and rural landscapes, so it racially configured those landscapes of the mind, people's abilities to be educated, to express themselves, to align and marry across cultures and to enjoy beaches, towns and jobs.

The Group Areas Act led to the development of racially segregated townships with low-cost housing, such as Soweto (South West Townships), south of Johannesburg. Under this Act, people of African, Cape Coloured or Indian descent were forcibly removed from their homes and urban areas. District Six in Cape Town is an example of this aspect of apartheid: it was bulldozed, and its Black inhabitants forced to move out of town to townships, while the centre is still being rebuilt, without them. The Immorality Act banned mixed race marriages. In Zoë Wicomb's *You Can't Get Lost in Cape Town* (1987), the first person narrator, Frieda, is unable to be seen in public with her white boyfriend, upon danger of imprisonment. The Pass Laws required non-whites to carry an identity pass which, unless stamped with a work permit, restricted access to white areas. In Miriam Tlali's short story 'Dimomona' in *Footprints in the Quag: Stories and Dialogues from Soweto* (1989), worker Boitumelo Kgope is arrested because he does not have his papers with him and loses his health, job and security. Non-European South Africans were effectively condemned to second-class education and prevented from accessing university and college education. Hendrik Vervoerd, architect of apartheid and Prime Minister in 1953, limited educational opportunity and opportunity for life, proclaiming that:

if the native in South Africa today, in any kind of school in existence is being taught to expect that he will live his adult life under a policy of equal rights, he is making a big mistake. There is no place for him in any European community above the level of certain forms of labour.

Vervoerd, 1953, in Pomeroy, 1971, p. 22.

The South African government continued the physical segregation and began establishing the self-governing Bantustans, which became starved of money, education and hope; they restricted the lives of Black South Africans, dividing families up as the men went away to the towns for work. There were Bantustan universities. One, the University of Fort Hare, founded in 1916, had over 600 students. Many Black students were among the 25,000 who studied through the Correspondence University.

Opposition to apartheid produced a number of violent uprisings that led to brutal reprisals. Sharpeville in 1960 is one remembered by writer Ingrid de Kok as a huge betrayal of people's faith and trust, when 69 protesters were killed by the police. The government declared a state of emergency, banned the ANC and imprisoned those who revolted against the unethical indignities and suppression of everyday life and human values, among them Nelson Mandela. He was incarcerated on Robben Island for 27 years.

Apartheid deliberately repressed hope, the quality of human life and the ability to read and express experiences of and feelings about life; it had a commensurately limiting effect on the ability of writers to express political and personal standpoints. T.T. Moyana argues that its totalitarian laws were 'legislating literature out of existence', and that 'An additional difficulty for the creative artist in South Africa, especially the Black writer, is that life itself is too fantastic to be outstripped by the creative imagination' (Moyana, 1976, p. 95).

Censorship controlled what was written, published and read. The Publications Control Board, founded in 1963, decided what was to be published and by March 1971 around 15000 books were banned. Writers such as Gcina Mhlophe explore the inhumanity of the Pass Laws, which limited the movement of non-white people and led to the imprisonment of many who had suffered night raids, stop-and-search and random arrests. Many South African writers had their books banned, non-European writing did not enter the school curriculum and several writers fled into exile. Some, such as Wally Mongane Serote, Sipho Sepamla, Nise Malange and performance poet Mzwakhe Mbuli, produced poems which were a call to action. Miriam Tlali, who remained, published *Muriel at the Metropolitan* in 1975, *Amandla, a Novel* in 1980, and *Soweto Stories* in 1989, but was prevented from entering the library which housed her books, because she was Black.

White writers remaining in South Africa found taking sides dangerous but often necessary. Nadine Gordimer continued to write essays and fiction critiquing the social and political situation, as did J.M. Coetzee.

Athol Fugard's play *Sizwe Bansi Is Dead* (1976) exposed the brutality of past legislation in action, while the popular film *Cry Freedom* (1987), concerning the death of Steve Biko, highlighted ways in which a brutal political regime can treat people as dispensable and get away with it, an offshoot of behaviours which racially hierarchise people, casting some as beneath human rights.

Black women in particular in South Africa had little education, no leisure time to write, and many suffered from economic deprivation. Those who wanted to write politically charged work against apartheid had to flee the country, for example Bessie Head, who moved to Botswana, while still others maintained an uneasy relationship with their homeland. Zoë Wicomb, author of *You Can't Get Lost in Cape Town* (1987), moved between Cape Town and Scotland, writing of her home-land's constraints and potential for enlightenment despite laws against mixed race relationships (which would have cast her and her white partner into jail). Manoko Nchwe, an unpublished woman writer, told interviewer Buttumelo:

> Women reside outside of the networks which facilitate the production of literature . . . They must be given the opportunity to express or present their works without feeling that there are few women writers around.
>
> Manoko Nchwe, with Buttumelo, 1986.

Lauretta Ngcobo left for London in 1966. Her 1981 novel, *Cross of Gold*, portrays guerrilla struggles across South Africa. Farisa Karodia, now in Canada, writes of some Canadian settings and themes, but in *Daughters of the Twilight* (1986) and *Coming Home and Other Stories* (1988) she reflects on the problems of ethnic groups in South Africa. Jayapraga Reddy produced *On the Fringe of Dream-Time and Other Stories* (1987). Sheila Fugard moved between New York and South Africa. Others remained behind but had their work curtailed.

Autobiography became one form of testimonial to survival and the establishment of identity. Ellen Kuzwayo's autobiography *Call Me Woman* (1985) is an example. Her semi-fictionalised autobiography illus-trates survival with fortitude under duress; Winnie Mandela lived under house arrest, phoning her autobiography, *Part of My Soul Went with Him*, in 1985 to her publisher abroad, and Miriam Makeba related her story to James Hall.

J. M. Coetzee, twice winner of the Booker Prize, remained and wrote cuttingly of the illegitimacy and self-destructive results of the imposition of a Western Europeanised world-view of history and culture on Africa.

He used postmodernist forms to undermine the essentialism which informs notions of race-related division (apartheid) and in so doing disrupted and exposed established constructions of subjectivity and world-views under colonial and imperial rule (*Dusklands*, 1974), moving beyond the limitations of a divided society (*Life and Times of Michael K*, 1983), offering alternative narrative versions (*Foe* 1986, which reprises a version of *Robinson Crusoe*, addressed in Ch. 2, Texts).

In recalling her education under apartheid, Betty Govinden comments that the African literary and political journal *Drum* was read at home, but never appeared in official reading. So, under colonialism, indigenous writing was unavailable and discredited for readers, as the following suggests:

> Can it be true that black women writers were writing since the turn of the century, yet they never made their way into my classrooms in this town on the north coast of KwaZulu – Natal . . . Even Olive Schreiner's *The Story of an African Farm* (1883), though presented to me as an exemplary model of 'indigenous' writing, was not depicted for its singular South African perspective, nor for its place in feminist thinking at a time when the world was moving into the second wave of feminist thinking and writing.
>
> Govinden, 1995, p. 174.

Govinden notes how reflections of her own experience were absent: 'this daily history was slighted by a politics of selection working invisibly on behalf of my colonised self' (Govinden, 1995, p. 175).

In the face of international condemnation and local pressure, both violent and legal, Apartheid was eventually crushed and dismantled in the 1980s. The Pass Laws were repealed in the 1980s. Nelson Mandela was released on 11 February 1990, to lead the African National Party (ANC). In 1991 President F.W. de Klerk repealed other key elements of apartheid and in 1994, when the ANC and its army and allies (see p. 6) won a majority, the two politicians, Mandela and de Klerk, formed an historic alliance which finally ended Apartheid in terms of legislation, and gained them the Nobel Peace Prize. Poverty and social inequalities still remain in South Africa, however, and the scourge of AIDS destroys families, as it does across the whole of Africa. Contemporary writing by Gillian Slovo, the COSAW women's collective who produced *Like a House on Fire* (1994), J. M. Coetzee and others indicates a sense of achievement but also one of disenchantment at the slow pace of change towards real equality.

See also   *Texts:* Anti-apartheid political writing, Semi-fictionalised autobiographies.

Further reading

Coetzee, J. M., *Dusklands* (Johannesburg: Ravan Press, 1974).
Coetzee, J. M., *Life and Times of Michael K* (London: Secker & Warburg, 1983).
Coetzee, J. M., *Foe* (New York: Viking, 1986).
COSAW Women's Collective, *Like a House on Fire* (Johannesburg, COSAW, 1994).
Govinden, Betty, 'Learning Myself Anew', in *Alternation, 2, 2,* 1995.
Mandela, Winnie, *Part of My Soul Went With Him* (New York: W. W. Norton, 1985).
Moyana, T.T., 'Problems of a Creative Writer in South Africa', in Christopher Heywood (ed.), *Aspects of South African Literature* (London: Heinemann, 1976).
Wicomb, Zoë, *You Can't Get Lost in Cape Town* (London: Virago, 1987).

Cannibal

The *OED* definition of 'cannibal' is 'A man (*esp.* a savage) that eats human flesh; a man-eater, an anthropophagite. Originally the proper name of the man-eating Caribs of the Antilles' (Hulme, 1986, p. 16). Hulme notes the first recording of the term 'canibales' is found in Columbus' journal. The identification of foreign Others as cannibals ushers in a mixture of terror, disgust and a sense of moral superiority on the part of the traveller and his successor, the coloniser. As Ashcroft *et al.* note, defining people as cannibals provides a moral justification for treating them as less than human. There have been cannibals, ritual flesh eaters or those who would eat flesh in extreme situations (survivors of an aeroplane crash, for example) in many historical societies, including the peasantry of Northern France. It was normal for the head hunters of Borneo or Fiji islanders, it was in fact normal. 'This term for an eater of human flesh', as Ashcroft *et al.* note, 'is of particular interest to post-colonial studies for its demonstration of the process by which an imperial Europe distinguishes itself from the subjects of its colonial expansion, while providing a moral justification for that expansion. The Other, defined as savage, can be brought to the light by the missionary zeal of the coloniser, who recognises and punishes the abject act of eating human flesh' (Ashcroft, Griffiths and Tiffin, 2000, p. 29). Cannibal as a term is aligned with a sense of moral superiority on the part of the one who labels. It becomes part of a rhetoric deployed by imperialists and colonialists to explain the need for ruling over others – in order to help those others to progress to the enlightened behaviours of Europeans and the Western world.

Further reading

Ashcroft, Bill, Gareth Griffiths and Helen Tiffin, *Post-Colonial Studies: The Key Concepts* (London: Routledge, 2000).
Hulme, K., *Te Kaihau/The Windeater* (University of Queensland Press, Brisbane, 1986), p. 16.

Caribbean

The terms 'Caribbean' and 'West Indian' are used to refer to the island nations of the Caribbean Sea and various territories on the nearby South and Central American mainland (near to Trinidad but not Jamaica, since the distance between these two ends of the Caribbean islands is extensive), that is, Guyana and Belize. 'West Indian' emerged as a term deriving from the original mistaken belief that the Indies (that is, the East Indies) could be discovered by going the other way round the world – an attempt by Columbus and others (1492) at a new trade route. The name stuck for those nations that were formerly British colonies, that is, Jamaica, Trinidad, Barbados, St Lucia, St Vincent, Antigua, Dominica, Guyana and sometimes Belize. However, for many people from the Caribbean, the term is now seen to be outdated and insulting. In Jamaica Kincaid's *Annie John* (1985), rebellious Annie John rewrites history, arguing that if Africans had met Europeans they would never have needed to enslave them, and transferring the indignity and pain suffered by her ancestors on to Columbus instead, seeing him, a figure in chains, as a slave, so that 'When I next saw the picture of Columbus sitting there all locked up in his chains, I wrote under it the words: The Great Man Can No Longer Just Get Up and Go' (Kincaid [1985] 1997, p.78). The origins of the two terms Caribbean and West Indies also differ, since Caribbean derives from a corruption of the Spanish 'caribal', derived from an Amerindian word, identifying specific South American people ('caribal' is the name of places in Mexico and El Salvador).

Further reading

Bennett, Louise *Jamaica Labrish* (Kingston: Sangsters Book Stores, 1966).
Brathwaite, Edward Kamau, *The History of the Voice* (London: New Beacon, 1984).
Kinkaid, Jamaica, *Annie John* (London: Vintage [1985] 1997)
Walcott, Derek, 'Omeros' (New York: Farrar, Straus and Giroux, 1991).

Colonialism and imperialism

Colonialism means the settlement of people and so the colonisation of lands by powers from other, usually economically richer, more powerful lands. Colonialism needs colonies, people settled in new lands. Imperialism implies control of other lands and people by a power which can be defined as having an empire which is itself a collection of lands (countries, islands), all part of a governed whole. An empire most usually will also have an emperor or empress ruling it (such as the Roman Emperor, or Queen Victoria defined as the Empress of India).

While imperialism does not necessarily settle its people in other lands, it can rule many other peoples from a distance, economically as much as politically.

Both colonialism and imperialism have long histories and involve forms of subjugation of one people by another. Edward Said offers the following distinction: '"imperialism" means the practice, the theory, and the attitudes of a dominating metropolitan centre ruling a distant territory; "colonialism", which is almost always a consequence of imperialism, is the implanting of settlements on distant territory' (Said, 1993, p. 8).

Imperialism was typically driven by ideology, belief and power, controlled from the metropolitan centre, and concerned with the assertion and expansion of state power (for example, the French invasion of Algeria can be seen as an act of imperial control by the French Empire). Imperialism operated as a policy of state and a drive for power, and also has attached to it the meaning of 'command'. The *OED* defines its use as relating to the rule of an emperor or royalty – although royalty has not always been part of the equation. Ania Loomba (1998) tells us that Vladimir Lenin saw the spread of Western capitalism as a kind of global imperialism – a capitalist economic dominance subordinating other countries' economies. Similarly, while in the contemporary world it can be argued that empires are a matter of history and there are few remaining actual colonies, lands, nations, states and islands do group together for economic and defence reasons. America is not seen as an empire, nor would it define its power probably as colonial, but it does have a strong economic control over many other poorer countries.

The Roman Empire is the empire with which we probably have most familiarity. It flourished from 30 BC to AD 476 and conquered much of Europe and the near and Middle East. The Spanish Empire took over much of the Americas, leaving a legacy of Spanish as the main language. Even now North American Spanish is a first language in many cities and areas. For the British Empire, which came to real power in the nineteenth century, Queen Victoria was a crucial element. By the time of the First World War (1914–18), Europe's empires covered 85 per cent of the globe. The sheer extent and duration of the European empires and thgeir disintegration after the Second World War have led to widespread interest in postcolonial literature and criticism.

The term colonialism defines the specific, economically based and racially entrenched cultural exploitation that developed as Europe expanded over 400 years. While it does not depend on a central imperial power, one of colonialism's main aims is to colonise, settle, take over and change forever the ways of local and indigenous people. The post-

Renaissance, European colonial expansion fuelled by eighteenth century Enlightenment thinking accompanied the development of modern capitalism. The colonies were initially established to provide raw materials for the growing economies of colonial powers. Racial difference led to hierarchies based on race and a kind of post-Enlightenment notion of progress in which the enslaved and colonised are seen as less highly developed than the colonisers (with their more developed weapons). In this relationship, colonisers typically silenced or erased and certainly undermined the cultural, religious and intellectual achievements and beliefs of the peoples in the lands they colonised.

Colonialism has operated very differently in different countries, and the spread of colonialism was vast and varied, as were the relations it inspired. The extent of this makes imperial and colonial rule difficult to theorise. Colonialism can, simply, be defined as 'the conquest and control of others' land and goods' (Loomba, 1998, p. 2), depending on a two-way flow of money and goods. As originally understood by Europeans, colonisation was initially established as a result of commercial interests, as was imperialism, and built upon histories of trade and exchange (see Seeley in *The Expansion of England* [1883]). It suggests a transfer of communities. In the early period up until the nineteenth century, colonisation was infrequently a matter of deliberate government policy. It was only in 1849 that E.G. Wakefield suggested an actual system of settlement colonisation (later employed for South Australia and New Zealand) (Wakefield, 1914).

British colonialism was historically the most widespread and various and it is largely with the effects of and reactions against British colonialism, as expressed in literature, that this book is concerned. Hodge and Mishra, considering the different experiences of colonialism, comment:

> in the Indian subcontinent the colonial experience seems to have affected the cities only; in Africa it worked hand in hand with evangelical Christianity; in Southeast Asia the use of migrant labour – notably Chinese and Indian – mediated between the British and the Malays. In the West Indies slave labour, and later Indentured Indian labour, again made the relationship less combative and more accommodating.
>
> Hodge and Mishra, in Chrisman and Williams, 1993, p. 282.

Both colonialism and imperialism, then, operated globally, albeit differently in different contexts, and are differently represented or hidden from view in literature. We find representation of the effects of colonialism and imperialism in many literary texts, although this is rarely their major focus. In Jane Austen's *Mansfield Park* (1814) Sir Thomas Bertram, travelling to visit one of his colonial plantations in Antigua, leaves the party to indulge in a minor revolt (a play) which would be an exercise of freedom unparalleled in the slave population whose labour provided the Bertrams with their wealth, as it did (off-stage) for so many landed families in the nineteenth century.

The early critic of colonialism, author Joseph Conrad, notes in his novel *Heart of Darkness* (1902) that:

> The conquest of the earth, which mostly means taking it away from those who have a different complexion or slightly flatter noses than ourselves, is not a pretty thing when you look into it too much. What redeems it is the idea only, an idea at the back of it; not a sentimental pretence but an idea; and an unselfish belief in the idea – something you can set up, and bow down before, and offer a sacrifice to.

In the novel, Marlow journeys into the Congo to find Mr Kurtz, and his journey exposes many of the problems inherent in both imperialism and colonialism. Marlow believes those serving imperial powers who established government and trading centres brought some kind of enlightenment to savages, while it is shown in the novel that European colonisers and imperialists actually invaded, fought and provoked endless small wars just for the theft of local wealth. In one instance, Marlow sees a ship firing pointlessly into the jungle, indicating the futility and destruction which characterise imperial and colonial rule. Imperial and colonial invaders were just as likely to remove precious metals and enslave the people as they were to establish an infrastructure of government, trade, hospitals and education.

Critics (notably Chinua Achebe) have criticised Conrad's dated characterisations of the indigenous peoples as primitive savages but the other side of this debate is his similar characterisation of the invading colonialists as ostensibly enlightened but in fact ruthless, blinkered, racist thieves. Kurtz, Marlow's predecessor, has not only emulated the worst ways of the local chiefs but in the context of his own education this is unforgivable; heads on sticks instead of ornaments around his compound indicate his madness. Returning to England, Marlow can only lie to Kurtz's fiancée who would never understand the darkness into which he had fallen, emblematic of the collusive darkness of the European invaders/colonisers.

Marlow, in Conrad's novel, certainly expresses unease, and this exposé of misdirected enlightenment, alongside imperial greed and cultural arrogance, was an early cultural reaction to imperialism and colonialism. Jean-Paul Sartre's Preface to Frantz Fanon's *The Wretched of the Earth* (1961) highlights the sense of unease experienced under imperial and colonial rule by noting that 'the condition of the native is a nervous condition.' These ideas have also been expressed in literary form. Using Sartre's phrase, Tsitsi Dangarembga's *Nervous Conditions* (1988) directly addresses the difficulties of living under colonial rule, from the point of view not of an enlightened colonial or imperial writer such as Conrad, but someone who has suffered such rule and can see its blight on her family and local people.

Nervous Conditions was the first novel by a Black Zimbabwean woman published in English. It won the Africa section of the Commonwealth Writers Prize in 1989 and deals with the difficulties of being female under the constrained life offered to colonised peoples. M. Keith Booker notes that '*Nervous Conditions* goes beyond Fanon, whose male-oriented analysis of the colonial condition does not explore gender issues in any substantive way' (1998, p. 191). The novel exposes ways in which African people have internalised Western values, to their own loss. The protagonist, sent from her village to be educated at her rich uncle's house, discovers that his westernised ways only enforce his rather cold and bullying manner, and that his daughter reacting against the oppression of a set of values alien to her, does so to a horrific extent, with anorexia.

Nervous Conditions pathologises the colonial inheritance, enacting the doubts, sickness, oppression and deaths which can permeate colonised others, whether they feel successful in terms of the colonial or ex-colonial power or not. In focusing on the plight of female characters, Dangarembga moves beyond enacting Fanon's theorising, intersecting with feminist postcolonial arguments about the silencing and marginalising, even physical damaging, of women under and beyond colonial rule.

While Dangarembga thus highlights the issues of colonial distress and damage to women, a sense of unease and restriction also pervades Caribbean-originated Jean Rhys' earlier work; she focuses in 'Let Them Call It Jazz', in *Tigers are Better Looking* (1968), on the difficulties of a Caribbean immigrant woman treated badly by her landlord, rejected by her neighbours, considered mad, and unable to settle into a new self in a new land, having internalised the sense of her strange, subordinate, second-rateness (what critic Gayatri Chavravorty Spivak would define as the subaltern position).

Writers such as Conrad, Forster, Rhys and later Dangarembga foreground the ways in which colonial and imperial rule silenced, oppressed and marginalised the people whose lands it affected. They showed that however well-meaning such rule might be (in some instances) it still led to the exploitation of resources, hypocrisy and – for those who internalised a sense of being second rate, *because* they had been colonised, whether educated or not – it could be seen as leading to a personally destructive unease. Jean Rhys' character has a breakdown, while Dangarembga's character develops anorexia.

See also *Texts*: Challenges to Empire, Rhys, Jean (1890–1979) *Criticism*: Fanon, Frantz (1925–61), Négritude.

Further reading

Ashcroft, Bill, Gareth Griffiths, and Helen Tiffin, *Post-Colonial Studies: The Key Concepts* (London: Routledge, 2000).

Austen, Jane, *Mansfield Park* [1814] (Harmondsworth: Penguin, 1996).

Booker, M. Keith, *The African Novel in English: An Introduction* (Portsmouth, New Hampshire: Heinemann, 1998).

Conrad, Joseph, *Heart of Darkness* [1902] (London: Penguin, 2000).

Dangarembga, Tsitsi, *Nervous Conditions* [1988] (Seattle, WA: Seal Press, 2005).

Fanon, Frantz, *The Wretched of the Earth* [1961], preface by Jean-Paul Sartre, trans. Constance Farrington (Harmondsworth: Penguin, 1990).

Fieldhouse, D.K., 'The Rise of Colonial Nationalism: Australia, New Zealand, Canada and South Africa First assert Their Nationalities', in *The Historical Journal*, June 1989, v.32, N.2 (1989).

Hodge, Bob and Vijay Mishra, in Laura Chrisman and Patrick Williams (eds), *Colonial Discourse and Post-Colonial Theory* (Hemel Hempstead: Prentice Hall, 1993).

Loomba, Ania, *Colonialism/Post Colonialism* (London: Routledge, 1998).

Rhys, Jean, 'Let Them Call It Jazz', in *Tigers are Better Looking* (London: Andre Deutsch, 1968).

Said, Edward, *Culture and Imperialism* (London: Chatto, 1993).

Seeley, John Robert, *The Expansion of England* [1883], in John Gross (ed.) (Chicago: University of Chicago Press, 1971).

Wakefield, E.G., *A View of the Art of Colonisation* (Oxford: Clarendon Press, 1914).

Commonwealth

The British Commonwealth was formerly the British Commonwealth of Nations, a political and economic community which developed after the end of the former British Empire and consisted of the United Kingdom, its dependencies and some of the former colonies, now sovereign nations. Countries still in the Commonwealth include Canada, Singapore, Jamaica, Bangladesh and Kenya, although many which have now left retain trade contacts with Britain and the other Commonwealth countries. The Commonwealth in 2006 is a voluntary association of 53 states and 1.8 billion citizens (about 30 per cent of the world's population). It has three intergovernmental organizations: the Commonwealth Secretariat, the Commonwealth Foundation and the Commonwealth of Learning. Its Harare Declaration of Principles affirms the importance of international people and order, global economic development and the rule of international law. It argues against discrimination and racial intolerance and for the importance of social and economic development, including a free flow of trade and investment in sustainable development. The Commonwealth is active in development, democracy and trade debt management and pursues these aims with a strategic and operative plan, through various programmes. Other recognisable features include sport, which is seen in the Commonwealth Games, and the Association of Commonwealth Universities, one of several bodies linking common interests and developments

Further reading

Ashcroft, Bill, Gareth Griffiths, and Helen Tiffin, *Post-Colonial Studies: The Key Concepts* (London: Routledge, 2000),

Decolonisation

Decolonisation is the process by which a colonial or imperial power reduces and then removes its rule over colonised peoples. In terms of the British Empire, decolonisation came about in response to changes in trade and as a response to the reaction against colonialism, seen through the claims for independence and own rule by those who were colonised, who asserted and sought to have recognised their rights for self government. As early as 1851 the *Edinburgh Review* published an article 'Shall We Retain Our Colonies?', questioning whether colonies should be let go. Many saw the Empire as useless and expensive, and colonial wars such as in New Zealand against the Maori (1840s–60s) as well as the costs of protecting Canada against America emphasised how expensive it was to maintain colonies. Free trade was another issue. British commerce was seen by some to be able to expand into further trade markets if the burden of colonial links was removed. Home Rule was the desire of many indigenous anti-colonial movements, the Indian Home Rule League formed by feminist Annie Besant being a case in point.

Disruption during and following the Second World War empowered independence movements and anti-colonial rebellions, leading to the granting of independence to India, Burma, Ghana, Tunisia and Libya, while in cases where demands for constitutional decolonisation were ignored, rebellions and uprisings began such as that of the Mau Mau in Kenya in the 1950s, the Vietcong in Vietnam, and the ANC and Pan Africanist Congress (PAC) in South Africa from 1964 to 1991.

Theorists and activists such as Amilcar Cabral asserted the importance of cultural autonomy as well as own rule during the decolonisation process, but they, too, had to live through the processes and experiences of turmoil, violence and some local, political oppression which often resulted as an immediate effect of the decolonisation process, in Africa in particular. Basil Davidson's *The Black Man's Burden* (1992) focuses on some of the disastrous consequences of decolonisation, while Salman Rushdie's *Midnight's Children* (1980) looks at the vast movements of people and the deaths caused by the partition of India and Pakistan when independence was granted in 1947. Anita Desai tells in *Clear Light of Day* (1980) of the night-time fleeing of the local Muslim family of Hyder Ali from Delhi at the same moment, since the decolonisation and independence process led to violence and confusion, as people travelled to whichever side of the partitioned land represented their religious beliefs – that is, Muslims to Pakistan, Hindus, Sikhs and other non-Muslims to India.

Decolonisation of countries in the British Commonwealth has in many instances produced a rich diasporan existence which has inspired many writers. Decolonisation is the process of dismantling all forms of colonial power, even those that remained after political independence. Decolonisation in many instances caused migration of those who used to be colonisers – the officials, the rulers – who left and returned to their own home countries. It also led to new opportunities for local people to develop and build their own infrastructures. However, sometimes this was problematic as the long-term experience of being ruled could have removed or prevented the redevelopment and actioning of good ideas and plans locally. Some change, therefore, was radical, and some gradual, as people began to learn or re-learn the ways of governing themselves and taking on the roles powerful in any infrastructure – of politicians, police, educators, doctors, lawyers, and so on, roles which had previously probably been played by the colonisers or those they employed.

Rules and practices which operated under colonial or imperial rule might well continue into the new postcolonial situation or be gradually or radically changed. Ashcroft *et al.* note that, ironically, much resistance and decolonisation was initially carried out using the forms and language of the coloniser, pointing out that:

Macaulay's infamous 1835 'Minute on Indian Education' had proposed the deliberate creation in India of just such a class of 'brown white men', educated to value European culture above their own. This is the *locus classicus* of this hegemonic process of control, but there are numerous other examples in the practices of other colonies.

Ashcroft, Griffiths and Tiffin, 2000, p. 63.

Caribbean poet Louise Bennett once referred to the movement of colonial and ex-colonial peoples into various other countries, which formed for those people the context of a diasporan existence, as 'colonisation in reverse' (Childs and Williams, 1997, p. 13). David Dabydeen (1991) identifies Britain as the last colony, the last outpost of colonial unsettlement and racially motivated discord. A dynamic population disturbs insularity and historically constructed notions of racial homogeneity. Susheila Nasta points out:

Many cultural critics and postcolonial scholars have already exposed the extent to which the myth of a homogenous and white British nation, an 'imagined community', was part not only of the agenda of Empire, but of an insular Eurocentric modernity which has consistently failed to acknowledge the true colours of its immigrant past. For although heterogeneity has always been the norm, an indisputable part of the crucible of cultural and racial 'mixtures' that has historically constructed British life, the nationalist myth of purity has nevertheless long endured.

Nasta, 2002, p. 2.

Focusing on a specific case of decolonisation's effects on people from India and Pakistan, but also mentioning the effects of decolonisation in the Caribbean and Africa, insofar as it led to migration and immigration, Susheila Nasta's *Home Truths* (2002) retells the history of British immigration from South East Asia and around the world. She identifies historically hidden groups of those Black and Asian British who immigrated to Britain following decolonisation and whose presence has both challenged and affected a notion of white Eurocentric homogeneity:

[a]s Jan Carew suggests in 'The Caribbean Writer and Exile', departure from the islands was not simply the other side of 'homelessness', a condition of cultural schizophrenia forever holding the artist in a passive twilight world between 'limbo and nothingness'. It enabled instead a creative space, one necessarily 'compelled by the exegesis of [the contradictions of] history', but which nevertheless bred an

inventive ethos of cultural survival, a facility for improvisation . . . It was a process which both generated innovative textual strategies whilst at the same time consuming its own 'biases', thereby effectively subverting the linear trajectories of dominant narrative forms.

Nasta, 2002, pp. 66–8.

Nasta speaks most particularly of a breed of self-confident British Asian women emerging in Britain, and thus reconfigures a positive, creative diasporan location for these women rather than some kind of limbo.

Diasporan writers

There is considerable overlap between decolonisation and diasporan writing. Diaspora comes from the Greek, meaning 'to disperse' (*OED*). Colonisation, by removing people from their homelands and forcing them to move elsewhere, sometimes through slavery, most often through economic necessity, necessarily created diasporas, as have other forms of oppression. Initially it was a term which referred to Jewish people who wandered, finding themselves at home in many places or none, always rather split. Colonialism itself led to the temporary or permanent travel and settlement of millions of Europeans over the world, and people from the colonised land then also travelled to settle elsewhere, sometimes, latterly, in England.

The practices of slavery and indenture to provide labour for a plantation and trading economy resulted in world-wide diasporas. Africans have settled in a worldwide diaspora because of slavery, while Indian and other Asian people moved to be indentured labourers following the end of slavery, and so settled in and formed minorities, sometimes even majorities, in the West Indies, Malaya, Fiji, Mauritius and colonies of Eastern and Southern Africa.

What is diasporan existence? For those who have immigrated to another country or who travel between adoptive countries and their original homeland, it could mean always feeling a little displaced, duplicitous, different, operating with a double personality and cultural identity, perhaps either managing a rich culturally diverse self, which makes the best of both worlds. It might mean that people feel they are falling between two stools, unable to find a sense of identity which can recognise and provide space for a self created and built in the new home, nurtured or problematised through time, alongside a self related to the homeland, challenged, undermined or enriched by perspectives afforded by distance.

Postcolonial people have migrated from the margins to the so-called centres; they have settled in the US and the UK and form integrated groups in those ex-imperial powers or in other ex-colonies – Canada, South Africa, Australia and Aotearoa/New Zealand. As such, they reconfigure any rather alien, wandering notion of what living in the diaspora might initially be thought to represent, and change the places in which they make their new homes:

The idea that post-colonial groups and their histories, far from being alien or Other to carefully constructed and guarded Western identities are in fact an integral part of them, derives ultimately from Said's insights on the colonial period in *Orientalism*, but it is even truer in the post-colonial period when the Other comes home.

Childs and Williams, 1997, p. 13.

For writers, finding and expressing a sense of identity, location and voice can change the dialogue with diaspora from one of loss and liminality to a new configuration of hybridity and cosmopolitanism that affects everyone. However, it is or has been by no means an easy journey. For each individual, there is the dialogue with a varied past, history, family and set of homelands that could produce a sense of dislocation and confusion rather than of celebratory hybridity and contribution to dynamic cultural change.

There is a particular responsibility for writers living in the diaspora to represent their own communities and their family's roots in their countries of origin. As Jena notes:

European countries, the Caribbean, North America and Australia all have large diasporan communities formed initially from enforced immigration through slavery, indentured labour and transportation, who then latterly escape from poverty or for work, as was the case for many Irish settlers in the nineteenth century who left Ireland to escape poverty and unemployment, and settled in Canada, Australia and New Zealand. Others left their homelands because of oppression, as was the case for Asian people who settled in Britain in the 1970s after the oppression of Idi Admin in Uganda. Britain's contemporary Black and Asian diasporic populations are very diverse and have grown gradually from imperial history dating back to the seventeenth century trading activities of the East India company. Their growing presence since the Second World War and the 1970s has challenged conceptions of 'Englishness' which have been taken for granted.

Jena, 1993, p. 3.

Britain has had a Black and Asian population for over 400 years 'It is thus worth noting that Britain was as much the *home* of the colonial encounter as were the colonies themselves, normally situated *abroad* in the so-called peripheries' (Nasta, 2002, p. 2). Different waves of immigration preceded a major movement of Anglo Caribbean immigration, the arrival of the 'SS Empire Windrush' in 1948 from the Caribbean, while a major movement of Asian immigration was the entrance of large numbers of Indian-originated people in the 1970s, following their expulsion from Kenya, then Uganda under Idi Amin.

As Caryl Phillips notes in *Extravagant Strangers: A Literature of Belonging* (1997), 'the once great colonial power that is Britain has always sought to define her people, and by extension the nation itself, by identifying those who don't belong'. Metaphors and images suggestive of these kinds of divisions abound whether in the rhetoric of politicians or in the language of cultural critics, whatever their political leanings.

As Salman Rushdie puts it, diasporan writers in the UK are 'observers with beady eyes and without Anglo Saxon attitudes' (1982, p. 8). Also, on the positive side, postcolonial migrants both unsettle and enrich what was thought of as the centre of imperial powers. Diasporan and migrant writers reflect on, record, imagine beyond and articulate newly changed, merged, differently focused perspectives on their adoptive cultures, and on their position as writers with multiple roots in the history of several cultures. In so doing, they fundamentally problematise what some consider a form of national homogeneity, and help create for everyone revitalised versions of what it means to be British, while simultaneously engaging in dialogues with varied culturally mixed origins and locations, from which are generated new hybrid identities.

Initially, many Black or Asian immigrants and their descendants in the postwar period, who did not conform to the predominant image of white cultural acceptability, felt they had no 'place' or 'space' to express their relationship to the dominant narratives of British life. Zadie Smith's streetwise teenager Millat knows he stands out as 'different':

> He knew that he, Millat, was a Paki no matter where he came from; that he smelt of curry; had no sexual identity; took other people's jobs; or had no job and bummed off the state; or gave all the jobs to his relatives; that he could be a dentist or a shop-owner or a curry-shifter, but not a footballer or a film-maker; that he should go back to his own country; or stay here and earn his bloody keep; that he worshipped elephants and wore turbans; that no one who looked like Millat, or spoke like Millat, or felt like Millat, was ever on the news unless they

had recently been murdered. In short, he knew he had no face in this country, no voice.

Smith, 2000, pp. 233–4.

Merging in entails loss, to some extent inevitable, but the same merging can be impossible in some respects if colour and custom single you out. Passing as British endows the one who performs with the privileges of the other. Erasing cultural difference helps assimilation, if that is what is wanted, but cuts off history, family and cultural elements of identity. The fate of those who inhabit a physical and an imaginary diaspora is to always be in a dialogue between the adoptive homeland and the other homeland(s), however long ago and far away and historical is that connection. But as they dialogue with the adoptive homeland, they change themselves, the new homeland, and their versions and memories of the other homelands, and as they dialogue with the other homelands they renegotiate meaning in their minds and actions. And diasporan people disturb the Britain into which they settle:

> For although the literary representations of Britain's contemporary diasporic populations attest in one sense to the rich cultural cartography of Britain's recent imperial past, at the same time, they also threaten. For in a post-imperial nation that, by the end of the twentieth century, was fast losing its grip on any sense of a coherent national identity, the presence of the *others within* exposed the underside not only of the faltering myth of Empire and its waning fantasy of an invented 'Englishness', but also complicated the apparently seamless history of Western modernity itself.
>
> Nasta, 2002, p. 3.

Critic and theorist Homi Bhabha's notion of hybridity celebrates the internalising of a self and history that not only copes with, but grows something unique and new upon, the rich ground of these tensions and dialogues.

The experiences of migrancy and living in a diaspora have formed the focus and interest of much recent postcolonial literature, criticism and theory. One indication of this is the slippages and confusions between the terms 'diaspora', 'migrant' and 'postcolonial'. Literature produced by 'diaspora writers' such as Meera Syal, Buchi Emecheta, Rohinton Mistry, Amitav Ghosh, Hanif Kureishi, Bharati Mukherjee, Caryl Phillips, Linton Kwesi Johnson and Benjamin Zephaniah is immensely popular with Western audiences and Western literary criticism, both for its new perspectives and its new versions of language and expressions. At the same time, diasporan academics such as Homi Bhabha, Avtar Brah, Susheila Nasta, Paul Gilroy and Stuart Hall focus on issues of merged histories, new perspectives, identity, language and expression, and the potential for new achievements and expression, new versions of constructing and representing knowledge, history and relationships of power, which spring from experiences of migrancy and diaspora. As John McLeod comments:

> But diaspora communities are not free from problems. Too often diaspora peoples have been ghettoised and excluded from feeling they belong to the 'new country', and suffered their cultural practices to be mocked and discriminated against. In addition, in more recent years critics such as Avtar Brah, Stuart Hall and Kobena Mercer have interrogated the shared sense of diaspora collectively as potentially marginalising certain groups inside their limits, such as lesbian and gay people.
>
> McLeod, 2000, pp. 208–9.

As a part of their living in two imaginary spaces (at least), at once holding two cultures or more in their minds, memories and histories, diasporan writers are uniquely placed to negotiate a dialogue between their countries and cultures of origin, adoption and return.

Each has their own version of this, and a mixture of responses differ according to the individual and his or her history. They might reflect anything from a consistent feeling of never being anywhere, wandering, like the original wandering diasporic peoples, the Jews, or they may wish to articulate and express in their work and their lives the ways in which they are unique fusions of cultures and histories, enriched by the different perspectives this affords them. Diasporan writers write about a whole variety of aspects of their own lives, about what it means to be human, not solely about their self-reflexive awareness of being part of a product, a contribution to the diaspora. However, many diasporan writers engage with issues to do with identity, home and memory, cultural assimilation and change, and discourse.

Like other diasporan writers, Black and Asian British writers who themselves, their parents or grandparents immigrated to Britain, engage in a dialogue with theories, histories and their felt experience of living in the diaspora. They imagine, construct, articulate and debate, modify and move on in their dialogues with themselves, with others, and with history. This modification, movement and developing expression creates a sense of shifting identity in a multi-cultural Britain, where people constantly try to find the right words to discuss the experience of living in the diaspora and the differences this makes both to those who feel they live in it, and those who find the complacencies of homeland (whether the countries of origin or Britain) challenged by diasporan visions and versions.

Some of the first moves in the dialogue take place in representations of arrivals, and in the stories we tell ourselves about arrivals and history:

> Brighteye, Brighteye,
> going crass de sea
> Brighteye, Brighteye
> Madda sen fi she
> Brighteye, Brighteye
> yuh gwine remember we?
>   Breeze, 2000, p. 54.

In her poem 'The Arrival of Brighteye', commissioned by Crucial Films and BBC TV and broadcast as part of the BBC's *Windrush* programme in 1998 to celebrate the history of the arrival of Caribbean people in 1948, the Afro-Caribbean Black British performance poet Jean Binta Breeze uses her training as an actress to dramatise a version of diasporan experience. An old woman unpacks suitcases, going through the lumber in her attic, trying on again and reactivating the self she was when she first arrived in England as a small child, characterised by her 'bright eyes'. Her mother sent for her, and she had to leave her grandmother to travel to a merely imagined country, 'an it getting cole, all de way, in a dream, to Englan' (Breeze, 2000).

Jean Breeze is a consummate performer and an enlightened insider, voicing the rich, acute sense of diasporic existence for many of those who immigrated to Britain in the middle of the twentieth century – and many who came before and after them. Brighteye remembers being excited and scared, arriving on the boat from Jamaica, wondering whether her mother was meeting her, trying to pick her out of the crowd but seeing mainly white faces and umbrellas. The gap between the ship and the land resembles gaps in her own identity: between the self she has left behind in Jamaica, the memory of the mother who travelled on ahead by so many years, the new meeting and new life she will start in Britain and, recalling these details up in the attic, the historical self, now a memory. The language is immediate in imagery and detail, compelling and personalised.

Brighteye finds herself overwhelmed with excitement and the occasion, embarrassed because she can control neither emotions nor her bladder. In the poem's present, there is new change and recognised reconfigurations of hybrid identity. After so many years, her own mother is returning to Jamaica, but Brighteye, a grandmother herself now, finds no simple version of what and where her own home is, partly defined as these are through relatives and friends, and particularly since new roots and the responsibilities of her family in England take both decisions and agency from her:

> She going home tomorrow, she say her work is over an she going home tomorrow, but ah jus want to be Brighteye again, as hard as it was it was easier dan dis burden, an wher ah going to put my head now, when all de others resting theirs on me.
>
> Breeze, 2000, p. 57.

Her dialogue with the diaspora reveals both a distant, remembered, now fictionalised 'home', where mother and grandmother are located, and her family home in Britain with her own offspring. She is the young child of her own memory, and the old woman of her present.

Meera Syal's Meena in *Anita and Me* (1997) constructs an arrival for her parents, stepping into the harsh English light from a plane, having flown for hours and hours from some dusty little Indian village (her description – replaying a stereotype) to be welcomed by a sign at Heathrow. There is no such sign at Heathrow that I have ever spotted, though I looked for it, and I see such signs worldwide – for instance in Kuala Lumpur, 'Selamat datang' (welcome), and even in San Francisco the recorded voice tracks you round the airport, 'Welcome to San Francisco'. How much more surprising must the arrival have been in the late forties and fifties and onwards for Caribbean people arriving in what they had been told in school and through history was their homeland, and for Asian people arriving often herded and bullied out of Uganda by Idi Amin in the early 1970s, not exactly meeting a land paved with gold, nor a real welcome except from family and friends. Jean Breeze, Meera Syal, Bharati Mukherjee, Debjani Chatterjee, Grace Nichols, Monica Ali, Moniza Alvi and many other Black and Asian women writers, like their male counterparts Linton Kwesi Johnson, Salman Rushdie and Hanif Kureishi, construct and represent diasporic existence in Britain that records the everyday activities of people who feel settled here but also split, their imaginative sense of being in a place in the UK and in the Caribbean or parts of South East Asia. Traditionally, the diaspora has been represented as a division, some kind of a loss, a draining, an eternal longing for what could be and was elsewhere, the home somewhere else, retained in the imagination, preserved like Arundhati Roy's famous pickling factory pickling exotic pickles (*The God of Small Things*, 1997).

East is East (1999) focuses on a family with an Asian father and

English mother and records the maintenance of dated behaviours, marriage customs, clothing and formality, unsuccessfully imposed by the fiercely nostalgic father on the diasporic, hybrid family in the North of England. A crucial moment comes when the boys are deemed ready to be married off – not to their local girlfriends or women they meet in the course of work, partying and study, but to two hideously alien sisters picked out by their father because they are the daughters of a colleague. Not surprisingly, they rebel. The sister, meanwhile, both prepares the fish and chips for the fish and chip shop and demonstrates a mix of Indian and British dance in the backyard, celebrating her own diasporic self – she is both very English, very Northern, and also aware of her Pakistani roots, and the dated version of these forced on her by her father. Such are the problems for those living in the diaspora in England. In adopting and merging with a new culture, the parents of second generation Asian and Black British people have constructed an impossible scenario for their children if they insist that somehow they must conform to the beliefs and behaviours which they themselves left behind, yet try to maintain in England.

Writers negotiate dialogues between their homes and histories and some, like Indian short-story writer and novelist Ravinder Randhawa, concentrate on issues to do with British Asian immigrants, and the social and cultural imperatives placed upon Asian women. In *A Wicked Old Woman* (1987), Randhawa explores difficulties for a second generation Indian girl, Kalwant, who is 'trying on' – literally – a series of possible identities, stereotypes and roles created by her diasporan existence. She rejects both the poor, victimised Indian of media representation and the glamorous mythical 'Indian Princess'. Kuli/Kalwant rejects her Indian upbringing, choosing education and Michael, a white boyfriend, but then, overburdened with the revolutionary act and its consequences, reverts determinedly to a stereotypical Indian role, insisting on an arranged marriage. Conflicts and contrasts of life in Britain and her own internal turmoil militate against success. Alone, old, homeless and blamed by her sons, she becomes a stereotypical victim Indian. C. L. Innes considers these issues of multiple, conflicting cultural identities:

> Ravinder Randhawa's novel does not conceal the complexities and difficulties that confront Asians who seek to be productive members of the larger community, to live in England rather than merely survive on the margins. Assimilation is shown to be neither desirable nor possible but neither is it desirable to retreat into an artificial Indianness.
>
> Innes, 1995, p. 33.

What is not sought is the safe haven of Oxfam-derived, missionary-recreated versions of home in the Asian centre:

> a simulation sub-continent patched together with a flotsam of travel posters, batik work, examples of traditional embroidery, cow bells and last but not least woven baskets that you knew were from Oxfam. It was supposed to be inviting, user friendly: a home from home for the Asian woman trapped in the isolation of her house; a helping hand for the Asian man shell-shocked from dealing with the revolving door racism and vagaries of white bureaucracy.
>
> Innes, 1995, pp. 30–1.

Nasta argues that while Randhawa transgresses boundaries of race, class and sexuality, she also 'reconfigures "home" as a site not only for nationalism, but as a space for female action, pointing the way forward for a large number of British-born Asian women writers that followed' (Nasta, 2002, p. 10).

Monica Ali's *Brick Lane* (2003) is just such an interior. Initially trapped in the East End of London high rise flats, Ali's protagonist moves out and wanders through other areas of London. Andrea Levy's characters pinpoint the conflicts and tensions of post-war London for Caribbean arrivals in *Small Island* (2004), while Zadie Smith celebrates positive hybridity in *White Teeth* (2003).

Black and Asian British writers who themselves, their parents or grandparents immigrated to Britain, offer a telling example of the diasporic condition, engaging in a dialogue with theories, histories and their felt experience of living in the diaspora. As such, they imagine, construct, articulate and debate, modify and move on in their dialogues with themselves, with others, with history. This modification, movement and developing expression creates a sense of shifting identity in a multi-cultural Britain, where people constantly try to find the right words to discuss the experience of living in the diaspora and the differences this makes both to those who feel they live in it, and those who find the complacencies of homeland (whether the countries of origin or Britain) challenged by diasporan visions and versions:

> NO DIALECTS PLEASE!
> WE'RE British!
> Huh!
> To tink how they still so dunce and so frighten o we power
> dat dey have to hide behind a language

that we could wrap roun we little finger
in addition to we own!
                    Collins, 1987, p. 119.

Caribbean Black British performance poet and academic Merle Collins'
dialogue with the diaspora expresses itself here in her use of Jamaican
English. She turns the tables on exclusive tactics, emphasising the dual (at
least) power and facility of people who have learned to speak, write and
think in a variety of manners, born of their own diasporan experiences.
The poem is empowering, challenging hypocrisy and racism in everyday
Britain and in poetry competitions which rule out 'dialects', so excluding
those who choose to express experiences in their own spoken versions.
The poem also involves the intertwined histories of Caribbean people and
Britain, one of their several homelands, as it recalls the war effort and the
transportation of slaves in ships from Liverpool. It confronts racism head
on, undercutting its premises of exclusivity of language and dramatising
the creative power of expression available to the diasporic writer.

See also   *Contexts*: Decolonisation; *Texts*: Diaspora.

Further reading

Ali, Monica, *Brick Lane* (London: Doubleday, 2003).

Breeze, Jean Binta, 'The Arrival of Brighteye' (Northumberland: Bloodaxe Books, 2000).

Childs, Peter and Patrick Williams, *An Introduction to Post-Colonial Theory* (Hemel
   Hempstead: Prentice Hall, 1997).

Collins, Merle, *Angel* (London: The Women's Press, 1987).

Innes, C.L., 'Wintering: Making Home in Britain', in A. Robert Lee (ed.), *Other Britain, Other
   British: Contemporary Multi-cultural Fiction* (London: Pluto, 1995).

Jena, Seema, 'From Victims to Survivors: The Anti-hero as a Narrative Strategy in Asian
   Immigrant Writing with Special Reference to *The Buddha of Suburbia*', *Wasafiri*, Spring
   17, 1993.

Levy, Andrea, *Small Island* (London: Hodder Headline, 2004).

Macaulay [1835] in S.I. Choudhury, 'Rethinking the Two Englishes' in F. Alam, N. Zaman
   and T. Ahmed (eds) *Revisioning English in Bangaldesh* Dkaka: The University Press Limited
   [see p. 250] (2001)

Nasta, Susheila, *Home Truths: Fictions of the South Asian Diaspora in Britain* (Hampshire:
   Palgrave, 2002).

Phillips, Caryl, *Extravagant Strangers: A Literature of Belonging* (New York: Vintage, 1997).

Randhawa, Ravinder, *A Wicked Old Woman* (London: The Women's Press, 1987).

Roy, Arundhati, *The God of Small Things* (London: Flamingo, 1997).

Rushdie, Salman, 'The Empire Writes Back with a Vengeance', *Sunday Times,* 2 July 1982.

Smith, Zadie, *White Teeth* (London: Penguin, 2000).

Syal, Meera, *Anita and Me* (London: Flamingo, 1997).

Difference and dialogue

Difference between people is an important issue for migrant and post-colonial peoples, as is a dialogue between indigenous people and immigrated settlers. The kind of postcolonial dialogue which can develop abstract or different values, culture, religion, rituals and perspectives as well as issues of assimilation, hybridity and multiculturalism is important here. Immigrated peoples might feel they fundamentally alter, settle into, are accepted by and assimilated into the land and customs to which they have moved, and/or into which they and their children have been born and in which they choose to live. One aspect of this is the enrichment and sense of dual (at least) histories and possibility of identities that accompany any kind of move from an original home to live elsewhere. Descendents of Huguenots who arrived in Britain in the Renaissance, perhaps, have little trace memory of their homelands, while French and Nordic people who settled in Britain proudly seek out or at least feel inquisitive about their European roots. However, for the more recently immigrated in the twenty and twenty-first centuries, the sense of a diasporan existence is more of an everyday reality, elaborated by having the difference of colour, that identifier of race, and differences of religion highlighted by others around them.

Some of the resultant culture mix expresses itself in discourse, the forms of language chosen by writers. Black British/Caribbean women poets use a linguistic mixture of the varieties of English spoken in the Caribbean. They entertain and explore issues of race and identity, male and female relationships, and the difficult pleasures of living in the diaspora, using irony and wit, everyday street language, puns, and well-observed colloquialisms.

Grace Nichols' collection *The Fat Black Woman's Poems* (1984) features a stereotypical/mythical island Black woman who turns into the fat black woman who cannot fully fit into the coldness and austerity of Britain. 'The fat black woman goes shopping' (1984, p. 11), a very popular poem with students and women readers, explores experiences of trying to shop for colourful and bright clothing, out of place in wintry London, where skeletal, arrogant salesgirls treat her with disdain, 'exchanging slimming glances' (1984, p. 11). The 'accommodating' clothes she searches for are as rare as acceptance and accommodation in England. With 'all this journeying and journeying', both pointless shopping and the difficulty of settling (1984, p. 11), Nichols voices the sense of everyday displacement: there is no place for the stereotypical fat black woman, her shape, taste or self, in the exchange of the marketplace, the social economy of identity in Britain. Nichols' character is a figure of fun for some who work where the valorised constructions of women are size 8 or maximum 10 (in white). Amusing and politicised in terms of race and gender, the poem shows the celebratory fat black woman refusing hostile, restrictive glances and defining herself positively. Over the series of poems she emerges as a kind of trickster figure watching from the sidelines as different values refuse and deny her. The colourfulness and generosity of the islands are replaced by the cold of England in 'Winter Thoughts':

> I've reduced the sun
> to the neat oblong of fire
> in my living room.
> Nichols, 1985, p. 122.

However, for those settled in a different culture and climate, returns are often a shock. Upon going back to Guyana, Nichols measures the differences between remembered/idealised homeland and its everyday reality. She has the diasporan writer's beady eyes, seeing through both any touristic version and her own nostalgia to see the sacrifice of youth to poverty and the hypnotic beat of music, drug culture and unemployment. She speaks to her brother in local vernacular, representing her own homecoming:

> An ah hearing dub-music blaring
> an ah seeing de many youths rocking
> hypnosis in dih street
> rocking to de riddum of dere own deaths
> locked in shop-front beat
> Nichols, 1985, p. 118.

He merely remarks that she has been away for too long (seven years), but her disillusionment is an eye opener. Through her persona, Grace Nichols highlights the benefits and limitations of both Caribbean and English lives, climates and cultures.

There is a particular burden of representation for writers living in the diaspora to relate to their own/their family's roots in their countries of origin, when there are conflicting ties and demands, confusions and distances involved. Ghettoisation, tokenism and replacing one stereotype with another must be avoided, as Yasmin Alibhai argues:

> In a society that still thrives on a colonial relationship with its own non-white populations, the dangers of black artists being flattered,

appropriated and used are great. On the other hand, when you come from a group of people denied even the basic human rights, their expectations of you are high and political.

Alibhai, 1991, pp. 17–18.

Silence continues the sense of absence, disabling attempts to join in the arena of changing discourses and representations of a multi-cultural society. Alibhai continues:

> At a conference on South East Asian writing (2001, London Museum, 'Passages') Susheila Nasta, among others, clarified the changing focus in and on reading Asian British women's writing. She asserted that we are now becoming more aware that the critical focus is 'as much about placement and settlement as about displacement and exile'. Postcolonial writers are engaged in important cross-cultural literary journeys, and reconfigure the critical geographies by which they have been defined.

One response, as Qurratulain Hyder suggests, is reinventing a version of self and the past:

> 'We have recently lost our Indian Empire and there's going to be a great demand for nostalgic novels about the Raj. You write, I'll build you up as the modern Flora Annie Steele.'
> 'Who was Flora Annie Steele?'
> 'Never mind. You begin a novel about Lucknow, right away.'

Hyder in Kumar, 2004, p. 177.

This identifies something of the contemporary popularity of writing about a lost or rediscovered people, important for many diasporan writers. Shapeshifting, a trickster activity of power, is also a metaphor used of the diasporan writer who denies endless exile and creates new versions of identity and being. Cultural difference, recuperation of the past, and rewriting histories and identities are all popular activities of diasporan writers.

Not all postcolonial and/or diasporan writers foreground cultural conflicts, however. As Atima Srivastava notes:

> I honestly believe that not all writers are caught in the kind of dilemma that certain postcolonial critics keep referring to. I admit that while I am in India I am thinking of Britain and vice versa. However, as far as I am concerned, being both there and here isn't necessarily

a contradiction, it isn't easy, and yet one can feel a certain sense of ease with it too . . . tried to fit myself into a groove for a long time and debated within that I was British-Asian then I must be either this or that . . . Now I know that I am myself, this may sound arrogant but I am unique. I am different and my connections to India are different.

Srivastava, 2001, pp. 3–5.

Her expression here reminds us of hybridity, an identity developed through a unique combination of cultural histories and individual cultural mixtures for individual people.

See also   *Text*: Diaspora.

Further reading

Alibhai, Yasmin, *New Statesman and Society,* 15 February 1991.

Hyder, Qurratulain, 'Red Indians in England', in Amitava Kumar (ed.), *Away: The Indian Writer as an Expatriate* (London: Routledge, 2004).

Nasta, Susheila, 'Passages', Conference on South East Asian writing, June 2001, London Museum.

Nichols, Grace, 'The fat black woman goes shopping', in *The Fat Black Woman's Poems* (London: Virago, 1984).

Nichols, Grace, 'Walking with mih brother in Georgetown' and 'Winter Thoughts', in *Purple and Green: Poems by Women Poets* (London: Rivelin Grapheme, 1985).

Srivastava, Atima, in interview with Mala Pandurang, 'Young Gifted and Brown', *Wasafiri*, Spring 33 (2001).

Discourse

It is argued that under colonialism and imperialism, the language of the coloniser is in control and this directs what can be spoken or written of, as well as how it can be spoken or written of. The power of the written text is just one element of control. In *Colonialism/Post Colonialism* (1998, pp. 95–6), Ania Loomba warns against the dangers of relying solely on discourse and text for interpretations of the daily realities, historical and contemporary, of colonialism and the postcolonial. There is a difference between lived experience and its representation in writing. Inscribing *postcolonial* objects in (specifically literary) discourse reduces the lived experience – blurring the relationship between material reality and ideologically charged representation in text. Reading literary versions of events could hide and distance their painfulness, and turning the colonial experience into a literary product for readers could make it popular and mostly entertaining. Elleke Boehmer similarly warns: 'discussions of text and image mask this reality of empire: the numbers who died in colonial wars and in labour gangs, or as the result of disease, transportation and starvation' (Boehmer, 1995, p. 20). Reading and viewing a sanitised entertaining version could distance readers from seeing and understanding the problems of colonial and imperial rule, so that 'in calling for the study of the aesthetics of colonialism, we might end up aestheticizing colonialism, producing a radical chic version of raj nostalgia' (Dirks, 1992, p. 5).

There is a problem where *postcolonial* studies are situated in English studies, not merely because the writings we read are limited to those in English or in translation, but also because of this kind of reduction to a textual analysis. Colonialism expressed in texts avoids the monstrosity of genocide, daily racism, disempowerment and grand theft. It can be argued, however, that a broader take on cultural studies enables a clearer picture of the lived reality to emerge. Indeed, it is important for us all as students and readers to find out as much as possible about the broader cultural and historical contexts of the texts we read.

The control of and by language, some argue, could be worse for women, who are considered 'secondary', and silenced. In the context of colonial production, which favours white over Black, male over female, 'subaltern' or secondary, women cannot speak. Critic Gayatri Chakravorty Spivak's essay 'Can the Subaltern Speak?' (1988) directly confronts the ignoring of women's different economic and social positions and lives. Spivak points out that an epistemic violence has been carried out on colonial peoples, devaluing their language, history and ways of seeing and expressing the world during the process of categorising native languages hierarchically, as of less worth (it is claimed) than the westernised, more scientific language. In this way, she offers 'an explanation of how the narrative of reality was established as a normative one' (1988, p. 76), taking for her example Hindu law and its British codification, which changes its emphases. Spivak questions how and whether, since they are doubly disempowered and secondary, women *can* speak out against such oppression.

Analysis of the language of colonialism and postcolonialism, by using the tactics of cultural studies, explores representation, that is, how images, artefacts and so on can help us to locate the text more usefully in historical and cultural contexts. It can highlight what is represented and how, and what is silenced and misinterpreted. The misrepresentation of Aboriginal, Maori and Pacific Islander women, for example, in the discourses of reports of first landings on their shores is a case in point. Through the misrepresentation of discourse we sense ways in which ideology, philosophy and world view operated to excise and subordinate peoples. Another problem of representation can be that of producing an exotic stereotype. For Pacific Islander women this has led to images of grass-skirted beauties seen as ideal partners for European men, but not seen as individuals with their own rights and views. Selina Tusitala Marsh reacts against stereotypical portrayals of Pacific women in popular song, and in novels such as those written by Somerset Maugham, where women often appeared as silent exotic beauties, part of the Pacific landscape:

> She wears red feathers and a huly huly skirt,
> she wears red feathers and a huly huly skirt,
> she lives on just coconuts and fish from the sea,
> ...with love in her heart from me.
> (Popular song of the 1940s)

This offers one popular view white:

> she wears lei
>   around Gauginesque
>   blossoming breasts
>   sweeping brown
>   round and round
>   looping above
>   firm flat belly button
>   peeking over
>   see-thru hula skirt
> (not from her island – but what does it hurt?)

> *Lovely hula hands'* (this line to be sung to the tune of the popular song which it appears in)
> *always understands*
>   *makes good island wife – for life – no strife*
> (Tusitala Marsh, 1997, p. 52)

These quotations demonstrate both popular media images and the kinds of engaged responses contemporary Pacific Rim women writers have developed to counter cultural stereotypes representing them as sexually pliable, noble savages. Maugham's versions idealise but also marginalise, using a colonial stereotype and rich language to objectify women as natural creatures or ornamental objects:

> You cannot imagine how exquisite she was. She had the passionate grace of hibiscus and the rich colour. She was rather tall, slim, with

the delicate features of her race, and large eyes like pools of still water under the palm trees; her hair, black and curling, fell down her back and she wore a wreath of scented flowers.

Maugham, 1919, p. 130.

Her enchanting natural beauty is comparable with the natural abundance of the islands' palm trees, still pools and hibiscus flowers. Like the natural blooms, it suggests, she is ready to be picked and celebrated by Westerners. She does not, of course, speak for herself. In *The Moon and Sixpence* (Maugham, 1919), Ata, an example of this stereotype, 'leaves me alone . . . she cooks my food and looks after her babies . . . She does what I tell her . . . She gives me what I want from a woman' (p. 280). Writing against this, Fijian poet Teresia Teaiwa and dramatist/critic Vilsoni Hereniko expose the construction of women as desirable colonial objects in their play *Last Virgin in Paradise* (1993/4).

Discourse can control ways in which people, places and events are seen by others at the time, subsequently and at a distance from events and experiences themselves. Colonial discourse controlled versions of public life through laws and documents, through histories and through fictional, often stereotyped, representations. For those who found themselves silenced, absent, or misrepresented in this colonial discourse, whether in the documents of state and history or the texts of popular entertainment and fictions, it has been important for them to write from their point of view in their own image, highlighting the misrepresentation and creating *new* versions. The need to create and express anew is probably of particular importance for women, who have been silenced or misrepresented by a mixture of ethnicity, control and gender.

See also   *Contexts*: Postcolonialism and feminism, Postcolonial discourse; *Texts*: Language, discourse, culture and power: reclaiming/rewriting language and power, Patriarchy and colonised women; *Criticism*: Colonial discourse.

Further reading

Dirks, Nicholas B., *Colonialism and Culture* (Ann Arbor, Michigan: University of Michigan Press, 1992).

Hereniko, Vilsoni and Teresia Teaiwa, *Last Virgin in Paradise* (Fiji: University of the South Pacific: Mana Publications, 1993/4).

Spivak, Gayatri Chakravorty, 'Can the Subaltern Speak?', in C. Nelson and L. Grossberg (eds), *Marxism and the Interpretation of Culture* (London: Macmillan, 1988).

Tusitala Marsh, Selina, 'Statued (stat you?) Traditions', in *Wasafiri*, 25 (Spring): 52, 1997.

Fanon, Frantz (1925–61)

Fanon, who was born in Martinique, was a theorist and activist who developed an ideal of Black culture which helped encourage identity awareness and cultural pride, but he has been accused of being nationalist, and thus restricted in his vision. His most famous works are *Black Skin, White Masks* (1952) and *The Wretched of the Earth* (1961). Aware of the blight of history, he refuses the idea that Negroes are a creation of a particular period of white imperialist dominance and asserts instead that there is a more generalised notion of Black culture. He emphasises the importance of national culture, and starts with that of African culture because of its importance for the emergent postcolonial nation-state, emphasising the fight for national identity and existence, moving culture onwards. In this respect, while he has been seen as arguing for national identity, he can equally be seen as emphasising Black culture, in all its variety and its roots in the African cultural past, and this led to what was called the Négritude movement in France.

Fanon's work on African identity and the importance of national cultures recognises and traces paths by which colonised intellectuals become involved in a series of responses and actions, including cultural or armed resistance, and move through three stages in their writing assimilation, uneasiness and outright rejection. In Fanon's interpretation of the effect of these stages of writing, in the first stage, works are produced which imitate European models, styles or genres; the second involves historical and cultural rediscovery, though often in a somewhat shallow way; while the third leads to the emergence of a 'literature of combat', revolutionary and national. The fact that the literature of the third stage is frequently produced by people who had previously thought themselves incapable of such creative, resistant activity exemplifies Fanon's belief in the potential of ordinary people and their ability to be active participants in their own liberation, as well as in the fundamentally transformative nature of this type of struggle. This is just one of the attitudes Fanon shares with Amilcar Cabral, another revolutionary intellectual. In reading work by a variety of writers, we might ask whether they reflect any or all of these three stages. African Chinua Achebe, for example, explores all three in his novels, as do several British Asian writers, including Hanif Kureishi, while Zadie Smith focuses on people who make one of these three choices.

See also   *Contexts:* Colonialism and imperialism; *Criticism:* Fanon, Frantz (1925–61), Négritude.

Further reading

Fanon, Frantz, *Black Skin, White Masks* (London: Pluto Press, 1952).
Fanon, Frantz, *The Wretched of the Earth* [1961], preface by Jean-Paul Sartre, trans. Constance Farrington (Harmondsworth: Penguin).

Independence

Historically, the end of colonial and imperial rule often came about after a growing movement for independence, frequently accompanied by hostility, death and imprisonment (of emerging radical leaders, such as Kwame Nkrumah and Nelson Mandela) before a more peaceful political solution was found. The First World War was launched by a rash of imperial and colonial greed on the part of the then Western powers and the imperial map changed as a result of this. It focused the energies of many colonised peoples who fought – like Yeats' Irish airman Major Robert Gregory in the First World War poem 'An Irish Airman Foresees his Death' (1919) – for a power which they themselves felt as oppressive. This questioned the relationship with the power for whom they fought and brought into focus the need for independence following the end of hostilities. For Irish Socialist and revolutionary James Connolly, architect and martyr to the Easter uprising in 1916, this violent working-class uprising was the only answer, since the desire for Home Rule had been ignored. And indeed, political agitation followed by violence, then imprisonment, and eventual granting of independence has been a pattern across the British Empire as it developed into the British Commonwealth. African reaction against colonialism is a history of political revolt and both military and guerrilla resistance, as detailed in C. L. R. James' *A History of Negro Revolt* (1937).

These African resistance movements, which contributed to recognising the imperative of independence, have their roots in earlier action. Activists in the 1920s and 1930s had a history of resistance on which to build. In Africa activists included Lamine and Leopold Senghor from Senegal, Kwame Nkrumah from the Gold Coast, and Sekou Toure from Guinea. Nkrumah, in particular, was influenced by models of the Black Atlantic, African American and African Caribbean radicalisation in the 1940s, 50s and 60s. Inspired by international socialism, Nkrumah helped and nurtured youth movements, while also in West Africa an educated literary people read and wrote various radical anti-colonial papers. Anti-colonialism evolved in Africa in two main ways, as active violent political resistance and as a kind of religious patriotism which drew from traditional values.

In South Africa, the SA Native National Congress, led by J. L. Dube (1921) evolved into the ANC. Anti-imperialist and anti-capitalist movements throughout Africa, South Africa and the Caribbean aligned themselves ideologically and philosophically with the communist movement, as did Black Radicals in Britain from 1939 onwards, noted in historian Stephen Howe's 1993 work. Even before the Second World War, Indian, African and Caribbean radicals allied with Marxism, developing their own radical movements, such as pan-African socialist nationalism, and after the war, anti-colonialists adapted Marxist Leninist thought and critical practices to challenge the dominance of those colonialist discourses and beliefs which would characterise colonial subjects as hidden or secondary.

In terms of resistance movements, Elleke Boehmer identifies 1952 as a moment when more militant resistance really established itself in Africa, with the beginnings of the Mau Mau or land and freedom, revolt in Kenya, followed by the war against French colonisation in Algeria two years later and, in South Africa anti-apartheid protests in the 1950s, as the ideology of apartheid began to be entrenched in the legal and political system.

Many former colonies and parts of the British Empire gained independence near or after the end of the Second World War. Jamaica gained self-government in 1944, Indian independence and partition took place in 1947, Britain supported the establishment of an Israeli state (1947), Burma and Ceylon (Sri Lanka) gained independence in 1948, followed by both Burma and Eire leaving the Commonwealth (1948). Ghana and Malaya gained independence in 1957, Nigeria in 1960, Tanzania in 1961. Algeria, Trinidad and Tobago, Jamaica, Uganda, Malawi and Zambia also gained full independence in 1962. During this period the United Nations first assembly was held in 1946.

Those who were not independent sometimes turned to violent response. Thus the Mau Mau resistance, begun in Kenya in 1950, intensified in 1952 and led to a state of emergency being declared. The Greek-based EOKA 'troubles' of 1950s Cyprus led to independence in 1962.

Anti-colonial nationals reacted against colonial and imperial rule physically, and gradually also through their writing. Fanon's *The Wretched of the Earth* (1961) characterises forms of resistance as uneasiness and then outright rejection (where his first term, assimilation, is not a form of resistance), which had more influence in Africa and the Caribbean than in India. It is important in the developing history of postcolonial people that modern writers, informed by armed or other struggles and earlier creative writers, recuperate some of the past, which lauded and revisited ways which had been stamped out by colonisation. Frequently and necessarily, this past work was entirely in the language of their coloniser, mostly English, so a next step for many has been to consider publication, and other forms of expression, either in their original languages or the everyday vernacular, both of which capture more of a sense of *their* experiences. Examples of this are the performance poets Jean Binta Breeze, Louise Bennett and Mikey Smith, who use the vernacular, Zadie Smith and Erna Brodber, who use complex postmodern forms and vernacular expression, and Ngugi wa Thiong'o, who writes in his own African language: Gikuyu.

Further reading

Boehmer, Elleke, *Colonial & Postcolonial Literature* (Oxford: Oxford University Press, 1995).
Howe, Stephen, *Anticolonialism in British Politics: The Left and the End of Empire, 1918–1964* (Oxford: Clarendon Press, 1993).
James, C.L.R., *A History of Negro Revolt* (London: Fact, 1937).
Yeats, W.B. 'An Irish Airman Foresees his Death' [1919], in *The Collected Poems of W.B. Yeats* (Basingstoke: Macmillan, 1982).

Independence and partition in India and Pakistan
In 1947 India won independence and the map of the Indian subcontinent was divided between India and Pakistan. Jawaharlal Nehru, Earl Mountbatten and Muhammad Ali Jinnah divided the map between them following years of unrest and then post-Second World War revolutionary reactions against imperial rule. Nehru, on the eve of independence, referred to a time 'when the soul of a nation, long suppressed, finds utterance', a demand for expression and independence which found parallels across the imperial and colonial world around and after the Second World War. This represents a major moment of decolonisation.

Historically, Indian independence is based on a long campaign. After the uprising of 1857, the Indian anti-colonial movement aligned itself with a pro-national movement similar to the later unrest in Northern Ireland. The Indian National Congress, founded in 1884–5, marked the beginning of a constitutional reform movement. The Muslim lineage in Pakistan was established in 1906, followed by a variety of other Islamic movements. India's campaign of non-violent non-cooperation, led by Mahatma Gandhi, was most effective in establishing a profound sense of the importance of the subcontinent's achieving its independence. Nehru, sympathetic to the Congress Socialist Party but not to the Communist Party, became the president of the League Against Imperialism and for Independence. Nationalist groups found a voice from the 1920s, becoming more militant across the Empire.

For people in the Indian subcontinent, the moment of freedom and independence was one also of partition, and millions died as they scrambled in coach, cart, car and on foot to be on the right religious side of the subcontinent. This is a dangerous moment, marked in Anita Desai's *Clear Light of Day* (1980) by the sudden uprooting and movement of Hyder Ali and his family in the middle of the night, leaving behind them a gramophone, old records and their dog. It is a moment where voices could jostle to be heard in Saleem Sinai's ears in Salman Rushdie's *Midnight's Children* (1981), as the protagonist has a kind of radio in his mind for picking up on the sounds and exclamations of pain following the partition. Rushdie's novel captures the mixed response: those travelling across the subcontinent were in danger of losing their lives to others who newly felt they did not belong. Muslims fled to Pakistan, Hindus to India – many died. Independence and partition in India were a result of a long campaign but the actual partition and subsequent violence was an example of the difficulties of unpicking a long history of imperial control.

Further reading

Desai, Anita, *Clear Light of Day* (London: Vintage, 1980).
Rushdie, Salman, *Midnight's Children* (New York: Alfred A. Knopf, 1981).

Land rights

Historically, land has always been an essential ingredient in the determination of identity. Location, geography and land ownership contribute fundamentally to people's sense of belonging, and in many cultures, such as the Australian Aboriginal, they provide a fundamental sense of the wholeness of existence, of which all creatures and people belong, the mythical element known as 'The Dreaming'. Imperial and colonial travellers seeking new trade routes and new discoveries, finding lands new to them, historically conceived of the place where they landed very often as *terra nullius*, white spaces without inhabitants, open for development/exploitation. So Columbus, following others, 'discovered' the Americas, including some of the Caribbean islands, and famously misnamed the Caribbean the West Indies (thinking he had found India or the East Indies by travelling round the world the other way to the well-trodden routes). He named the native inhabitants of the Americas Indians. So, also, the first fleets entering Botany Bay in 1788 perceived a potentially huge land whose peoples were clearly primitive because of their lack of formal ways, dress and Western manners, and ready to be governed or destroyed in the establishment of control and the settling of a new land.

Colonising spaces and places, making them part of vast empires, seems to have been a human enterprise at least as far back as recorded history, with the Roman Empire standing out as the largest and best known. This was followed by the huge imperial and colonial expansion and control which was the Western and European enterprise of the nineteenth century. It has been a deeply and permanently destructive experience for all people whose lands have been invaded, appropriated, cut up, relabelled and owned by others. Also destructive has been the negation of their own perceptions about land and human interaction and their relationship to the land and their own use of it, whether hunter gathering, workshopping, farming or whatever, and the reappropriation by an invading other who redescribes your land and removes your land rights. Vociferous amongst those people who have declaimed against such thefts or retribution are the Maori, themselves settlers of New Zealand, of Melanesian descent. Their land rights were to some extent respected in the Treaty of Waitangi (1840), although these types of claim still continue to be politically charged today. Aboriginal Australians were hunted to extinction for their own lands, the Tasmanian Aboriginals being entirely wiped out (some trace elements remain in Aboriginals of the mainland).

A different kind of land rights invasion is taking place in the tropical rainforests of Latin America, where deforestation feeds the needs of multinationals for everything from fuel to furniture. In his book *Postcolonialism* (2001), Robert Young spends some time discussing the tree huggers of India, who refused to let their trees, in particular, their ash trees, be cut down, though 300 had been sold. They literally formed a human bond round the trees to protect them. For some, the land with its trees, leaves and vegetation is part of their identity, for others it has a mystic significance which explains identity – as it does for the Aboriginal Australians. The disputes over borders between modern-day Israel and Palestine are raging still as this book is being written, although the bitter clearance from the Gaza strip of Israeli settlers is now enforced by the same government which paid them to settle there in the first place. Modern Israel, an historically and geographically recognisable place, was itself constituted by the drawing of lines on a map by the Allied powers following the Second World War. However the lines, as with the line in the partitions between India and Pakistan, has caused misery, dispossession and disenfranchisement for many, and loss of life for others.

Further reading

Young, Robert, *Postcolonialism: An Historical Introduction* (Oxford: Blackwell, 2001).

Nation and nationalism

The idea and reality of a nation grows out of social communities and is 'an imagined political community', as Benedict Anderson suggests in his book *Imagined Communities: Reflections on the Origins and Spread of Nationalism* (1983, p. 6). Nations are held together through rituals, beliefs, traditions, and a sense of belonging, though not necessarily of identicality, since multiculturalism and many faiths are present in many nations. Historian Eric Hobsbawm noted the development of flags, stereotypes and traditions as characterising the public face of nations. Other indicators are retelling and reconstructing versions of history, and in many cases a single dominant language. Historian and critic Paul Gilroy notes that nations are founded 'through elaborate cultural, ideo-logical and political processes' (1994, p. 49) which lead to a sense of unity and identity which overcome, for example, the divisions of class, religion and race.

Those who have struggled to assert their identity as community and group with shared versions of history, against the imposition of colonial and imperial rule, have over the last 200 years, and most forcibly in the middle of the twentieth century, worked to form national liberation movements leading to independence and the establishment of 'nations'. Significant in the movement against colonialism and for nations were both Amilcar Cabral and Frantz Fanon.

There are some fundamental difficulties in defining and developing nations and national identities. One of these is the history of forced migration under slavery, which dispersed African-originated people around the globe, and the migrancy of Asian indentured labourers led to a similar dispersal. How are versions of national identity developed and maintained in the face of such dispersals? Another issue is that as new nation states began to self-identify, the maps they were working with were those of the colonisers and sometimes these allocated very diverse people to a single location or cut relatively homogeneous groups up with a line on a map.

Both the construction of modern Israel in 1948 and the line drawn dividing Pakistan and India in 1947 are cases in point of colonisers granting independence to new nations but inflicting cultural problems on those emerging nations by apparently arbitrary lines drawn on maps. Millions died as they travelled to settle in India or Pakistan depending on this division – Muslims died leaving India, Hindus and Sikhs leaving Pakistan. In Israel, the settlement of Jewish peoples with Arab members of the new Israel used and appropriated land hitherto known as Palestine. This problematic geographical creation of the nation state of Israel has had endless trouble with all of its defended borders as a result.

Israel 'settled' the West Bank and Gaza Strip but in 2005–6 moved those settlers out and away from the Palestinian border, after a great deal of death and terror suffered on both sides.

The force of nationalism historically fuelled colonialism. European and latterly American national identities were historically established through their seeking and gaining markets abroad and in their self-definition against the identities and rights of other peoples. Homi Bhabha comments (1990, p. 59) that 'European Nationalism was motivated by what Europe was doing in its far-flung dominions. The "national idea" is, in other words, flaunted in the soil of foreign conquest.'

How, then, do the anti-colonial movements which led to the nationalist movements and establishment of nation states differ from this earlier national development? Nationalist groups formed in the wake of colonialism and asserted their rights to identity and land. A key issue remaining is whether nations enforce unity and exclusivism, or have a broader conception which enables the inclusion of ethnic, religious, linguistic and racial diversity.

National liberation movements were led by Marxist-oriented intellectuals such as Fidel Castro in Cuba, Kwame Nkrumah and Sekou Toure in Africa and Ho Chi Minh in Vietnam. Intellectual theorists and activists included Frantz Fanon and Amilcar Cabral. As explained in the discussion on independence, nationalist movements often led to revolutionary acts, imprisonments, then recognition of the previously imprisoned leaders who formed new nation states and settled in them.

Frantz Fanon's crucial contribution to the theorising of national culture and nationalist representations moves from the original concept of Négritude, which is based on a recognition of a valuing of the similarities shared by African-originated people, through to his arguments about national culture being dynamic and changing in response to changes in tradition, while the cultural inheritance of people enables them to establish and maintain a national identity the nation itself is as a living being, changing over time. Fanon was particularly concerned about the destructive activities of what he called an educated national middle class, a bourgeoisie whose interest in self and economic success prevented them from alignment with the masses. Fanon warned that even when a nation was established and nationalism flourishing it must ensure it was founded and maintained in the interests of the people who define their identities by it and treasure their shared cultural heritage.

C. L. Innes in *New National and Post Colonial Literatures: An Introduction* (1996, pp. 120–39) looked at nationalist writers such as W. B. Yeats (Ireland) and Chinua Achebe and Wole Soyinka (West Africa), noting that nationalist literary writers assert the existence of a national culture against that of the colonisers, often by reversing derogatory terms and characteristics; they emphasised the relationship between the people and the land, often gendering representations of colonial domination (masculine, patriarchal) and nationalist resistance (feminine). Tensions at the heart of nationalism emerge alongside the need for a national identity, which could exclude diversity and prove as oppressive as its precursor. Colonialism and nationalist movements sometimes lead to brutal uprisings against those who previously claimed the land, such as in the case in Mugabe's Zimbabwe, where white farmers have been brutally attacked and their land reclaimed, but where nationalism has not been a truly uniting and harmonious factor under the desperate rule of one who crushes difference and development as easily as he crushes the remnants of colonialism. Another problem is the language, laws, values, behaviours and culture available to new nations, since quite often the colonisers leave infrastructure, language and world-views (and neo-colonial trade controls) which are at odds with a new relation to the land and an economically sound development of a new nation.

Key literary texts which explore nationalism and the struggle for independence and identity include Ngugi Wa Thiong'o's *A Grain of Wheat* (1967), set in the period of Kenyan Mau Mau resistance, Mazisi Kunene's *Emperor Shaka the Great* (1979), which celebrates the great Zulu king, and C.L.R. James's *The Black Jacobins* (1938).

See also *Contexts:* Fanon, Frantz (1925–61); *Criticism:* Fanon, Frantz (1925–61).

Further reading

Bhabha, Homi, *Nation and Narration* (London: Routledge, 1990).
Gilroy, Paul, *Small Acts* (London: Serpent's Tail Publishing, 1994).
Gilroy, Paul, *The Black Atlantic* (Cambridge, MA: Harvard University Press, 2005).
Hobsbawm, Eric, *Nations and Nationalism since 1780: Programme, Myth, Reality* (Cambridge: Cambridge University Press, 1990).

Neocolonialism

The term 'neocolonialism' emerged in 1961, and was clarified in theoretical terms by Kwame Nkrumah, the Ghanaian leader, in *Neo-Colonialism: The Last Stage of Imperialism* (1965). It suggests that although independence has been achieved, education, economics and power systems have not moved on, in effect the land is still colonised and old values and rules still operate, even if only in the vestiges of colonial laws and in the mindsets of people who find it difficult to shake off colonial views and behaviours so soon. Nkrumah argued that 'The essence of neo-colonialism is that the State which is subject to it is, in theory, independent and has all the outward trappings of international sovereignty. In reality its economic system and thus political policy is directed from outside' (Nkrumah, 1965, p. ix). There is considerable critical debate as to whether a state can indeed escape colonialism and how best it can do so.

Further reading

Nkrumah, Kwame, *Neo-Colonialism: The Last Stage of Imperialism* (London: Heinemann, 1965, 1966).

Pan-Africanism

First conceived in Africa by Tiyo Soga in the 1860s, the concept of Pan-Africanism is a uniting belief and movement which recognises and emphasises the shared African heritage of peoples across the world, and by so highlighting helps to encourage an embracing and enacting of African political, cultural, religious and social beliefs and behaviours. As such, it developed in popularity during the Harlem Renaissance in America in the 1960s and has affinities with the Négritude movement (1920s and 1930s). Robert Young tells us that 'by the 1940s Pan-Africanism had come to embrace a broadly socialist economic policy of industrialisation and co-operative forms of agricultural production for independent Africa'. Its exponents developed arguments for colonial reform prior to the Second World War, while the political activism of Kwame Nkrumah and his followers asserted a commitment to self-determination and socialism.

Young in his discussion brings together both the African-originated and worldwide strands of Pan-Africanism in the definitions of W.E.B Du Bois and George Padmore. Neither, strikingly, was actually born in Africa: 'the idea of one Africa uniting the thoughts and ideals of all native peoples of the dark continent', Du Bois observed, '. . . stems naturally from the West Indies and the United States' (Kedourie, 1971, p. 372). Ideologically, both men travelled different paths but met somewhere in the centre (Young, 2001, p. 236, Hooker, 1967, p. 40). In 1934, inviting Du Bois to the Paris Negro World Unity conference organized by French Africans (led by Garan Kouyaté), Padmore wrote: 'Will you help us in trying to create a basis for unity among Negroes of Africa, America, the West Indies and other lands?' In fact, there were several movements of different political textures, each striving for a unifying vision and practice for African people worldwide. Using L. M. Thompson, Young differentiates the following strands in Pan-Africanism:

(1) the 'Africa for the Africans' mass movement of Garvey; (2) Du Bois' more moderate, middle-class Pan-African Congress movement; (3) the intellectual and political activities of the communist-dominated West African Students Union, and Padmore's International African Service Bureau in London; (4) the activities of the National Congress of British West Africa and related organizations, as well as that of the African National Congress in South Africa; (5) and the activists in Paris and Francophone Africa of whom the best known was Léopold Senghor.

(Thompson, 1969, p. 54).

By 1945, the Pan-African Congress fully reflected these mixed currents in its own agenda and distinctive political blend (Young, 2001, p. 237).

By the time the sixth Pan-African Congress was held, for the first time on African soil, in Dar es Salaam in 1974, discussion of African national liberation was dominated by either violent struggles or decisions to withdraw, which were taking place in Angola, Guinea-Bissau and Cape Verde Islands, Mozambique, Namibia, Somalia, South Africa, Spanish Sahara and Zimbabwe. Non-violent resistance was now inappropriate, and Pan-Africanism was renamed Revolutionary Pan-Africanism.

Further reading

Esedebe, P. Olisanwuche, *Pan Africanism: The Idea and Movement 1976–1963* (Washington DC: Howard University Press, 1994).

Hooker, J. R., *Black Revolutionary: Padmore's Path from Communism to Pan-Africanism* (London: Pall Mall Press, 1967).

Kedourie, Elic (ed.) *Nationalism in Asia and Africa* (London: Weidenfeld & Nicolson, 1971).

Soga, Rev. Tiyo, *The Journal and Selected Writings of the Rev. Tiyo Soga* (Cape Town: AA Balkema, 1983).

Thompson, L. M., *African Societies in Southern Africa: Historical Studies* (London: Heinemann, 1969).

Young, Robert, *Postcolonialism: An Historical Introduction* (Oxford: Blackwell, 2001).

Postcolonial discourse

Language is a form of power and so the analysis of discourse is a key area in scrutinising postcolonial writing and its context. Discourse analysis indicates analysis of verbal structures functioning within texts – the language, expression and arguments of texts that convey representations conditioned by culture and enabled by linguistic structures. The term postcolonial discourse, however, often groups together ex-colonial peoples and the texts they have produced as if there was everything in common in their experience and situation, which itself accords immense significance and importance to the colonial influence when, as Elleke Boehmer points out, 'indigenous religious, moral, and intellectual traditions in colonized countries were never as fully pervaded by colonialism as the authorities might have desired' (Boehmer, 1995, p. 245). Analysing the discourse of postcolonial writers should take account of the different histories of their homelands, the different versions of rule. It should also recognise how some have been less silenced, perhaps, or less translated by colonial values and discourse than others.

Forms of resistance as literary expression tend to take several shapes: recuperation of history from the point of view of the ignored, silenced Other; forms of expression based on or deriving from traditional indigenous forms which have also been silenced or marginalised; a focus on subject matter which has been absent; and writing from the perspective of and in the words of people whose lives have been erased, ignored and hidden from history. In many ways, postcolonial resistance writing and writing or expression which moves beyond focusing on resistance alone has a great deal in common with the writing of pre-feminists such as Virginia Woolf, who argued in A Room of One's Own (1929) that women wrote differently from men, and about different subjects with different perspectives, and even used different forms of writing.

Latterly, feminists in second wave feminism, such as Hélène Cixous and author Angela Carter among others, have further embodied this argument in their work, and some of the expressive creative work of feminist writers – life writing and oral literature, because it has expressed the experience of the silenced other, in this case woman – often resembles that of indigenous or silenced Others, that is, people in a postcolonial context. There could be a parallel between writers from different contexts in their desire to write about their own lives, first hand. We find life writing, appearing in the work of Bessie Head among many others in South Africa, and Aboriginal women writers Sally Morgan, Ruby Langford and Glenyse Ward. We also find more radical women's writing challenging conventional forms and discourse, from writers such as Margaret Atwood in Canada and Teresia Teaiwa in Fiji/New Zealand, to name but two.

Literary movements such as that of performance poetry and drama have revived traditional expression, writing and performing against the versions perpetrated by writers or artists from the days of the empire, with writers expressing their experience and worldviews anew and recuperating a history which denied them. In 'Unity and Struggle' (1980), Amilcar Cabral identifies this as a return to history. He notes that 'The actual liberation of a people is the regaining of the historical personality of that people, and it is their return to history.' This identifies something achieved through writing against imposed terms.

While passive resistance might have been a characteristic of earlier texts such as Raja Rao's *Kanthapura* (1938), works which re-write colonial history from the viewpoint of the colonised include Achebe's *Things Fall Apart* (1958) and *Arrow of God* (1964), which recuperate a version of Nigerian Igbo history just before the advent of the colonisers' rule, and Ayi Kwei Armah's *The Healers* (1978). Armed struggles emerged as a theme as early as Ngugi Wa Thiong'o's *A Grain of Wheat* (1967), which features a hero who dies during the Kenyan anti-colonial struggle and is remembered as inspirational. And later, the reconnection with communal memory and history, the ancestral, features in Caribbean poet Derek Walcott's 'Omeros' (1991), as it does in Grace Nichols' *I Is a Long-Memoried Woman* (1983), which partially relives the Middle Passage or slave crossing from Africa, through the words of a slave woman, then speaks about the presence and power of the sugar cane, the economy of which dominated plantations in the Caribbean and the lives of those transported there against their will.

Discourse is a key issue in the construction, limitation, expression and representation of experience. As Declan Kiberd notes:

> The struggle for the power to name oneself and one's state is enacted fundamentally within words, most especially in colonial situations. So a concern for language, far from indicating a retreat, may be an investigation into the depths of the political unconscious.
>
> Kiberd, 1995, p. 615.

Those who hold language hold the power, as Michel Foucault (1978) would argue. Throughout colonial histories, the language of British-ruled colonies has been English, which relies upon certain ways of constructing knowledge of the world, and upon certain underpinning beliefs. Language not only constructs and colours our experiences of the world, it can also be used to marginalise, to constrain, or to enable. It is mainly for this reason that the opportunity to speak and write out, to publish and to express in creative writing is so powerfully important, particularly so for those whose colonised experience has rendered them absent, silenced, marginalised, and for whom the discourse of imperial and colonial rule has been one of relegating their own experience to a subordinate position or entirely erasing its expression. Those in power ensure that language controls others, enabling or preventing, translating where necessary, and maintaining certain hierarchies. It is with this in mind that looking at historical and contemporary discourse is so important.

The English departing India, for example, left it the English language but, more importantly, the values, bureaucracies, world-view and hierarchies which that language maintained. In so doing, they first empowered colonised peoples to become involved in the English-speaking world, but also disempowered national identity and expression. Asserting nationhood and difference is one element in independence, but it is not the only element. Stressing national difference for its own sake is often a first step, followed by moving on towards recognition of differences between all peoples, and equalling a common humanity – what theorists and critics Homi Bhabha and Martha Nussbaum would begin to think of variously as cosmopolitanism.

See also *Contexts*: Discourse; *Texts*: Language, discourse, culture and power: reclaiming/rewriting language and power, Patriarchy and colonised women, *Criticism:* Colonial discourse.

Further reading

Achebe, Chinua, *Things Fall Apart* (London: Heinemann, 1958).
Achebe, Chinua, *Arrow of God* (London: Heinemann, 1964).
Armah, Ayi Kwei, *The Healers* (London: Heinemann, 1978).
Boehmer, Elleke, *Colonial & Postcolonial Literature* (Oxford: Oxford University Press, 1995).
Cabral, Amilcar, *Unity and Struggle* (London: Heinemann, 1980).
Foucault, Michel, *The History of Sexuality, Volume 1, An Introduction* (London: Penguin Books, 1978).
Kiberd, Declan, *Inventing Ireland* (London: Jonathan Cape, 1995).
Nichols, Grace, *I Is a Long-Memoried Woman* (London: Karnak House, 1983).
Raja Rao, *Kanthapura* [1938] (New York: New Directions, 1967).
Thiong'o, Ngugi Wa, *A Grain of Wheat* (London: Heinemann, 1967).
Walcott, Derek, *Omeros* (New York: Farrar, Straus and Giroux, 1991).
Woolf, Virginia, *A Room of One's Own* (London: Harcourt Brace Jovanovich, 1929).

Postcolonialism and feminism

Many Black, Asian and postcolonial women have argued that feminism is a largely white, Westernised construct which ignores the daily experience of race and economic hardship (see Talpade Mohanty in *Feminist Review*, 1988), and which also makes certain assumptions about motherhood, sexual and gendered relationships, and women's ability or desire to use irony or speak out critically. For many postcolonial women who are not European and not white, their postcolonial position is affected by economic problems too. Some Black and Asian women writers argue that feminism, as a largely white construct, ignores economic differences. African American Alice Walker, among others, has been criticised for asserting women's rights rather than subsuming these beneath an overall insistence on racial equality (which would yet again marginalise the issue of challenging women's subordinated position). There are several strands to this argument.

Susheila Nasta comments on the development of Black and Asian women's 'feminism' in the context of more general struggles for racial equality:

> In countries with a history of colonialism, women's quest for emancipation, self-identity and fulfilment can be seen to represent a traitorous act, a betrayal not simply of traditional codes of practice and belief but of the wider struggle for liberation and nationalism. Does to be 'feminist' therefore involve a further displacement or reflect an implicit adherence to another form of cultural imperialism?
>
> Nasta, 1991, p. xv.

Debates can be represented in several ways. On the one hand, Trinh Minh-Ha in *Woman, Native, Other* (1989) questions where women of colour recognise their loyalties, to race or to gender, as if there were a hierarchy. On the other hand, Sara Suleri insists that a concern for colour above that of gender produces a constrained sense of identity, a feminism merely 'skin deep in that the pigment of its imagination cannot break out of a strictly biological reading of race' (1992, in Chrisman and Williams, 1993, p. 251). Trinh Minh-Ha considers the importance accorded the voice of some kind of rather heterogeneous postcolonial woman.

There is a problem with feminist critics in postcolonial writing, connected with individual subjectivity and speaking out. Under the influence of post-structuralism, feminist critics argue about the relationships of identity and subjectivity, essentialism and constructivism. On the one hand, there is an argument that all women are basically the same, essential 'Woman', a biological argument, *but* on the other hand, we are differently constructed in our lived roles, products of different cultural situations. Feminist critics have tended more recently (end of twentieth century, early twenty-first) to argue that people are affected and produced by their cultural contexts. In this respect, it is important to avoid putting all postcolonial women together as if they have the same experience, which clearly they don't. A Black African woman trying to write in modern Zimbabwe would be doing so against economic hardship, lack of education and physical danger, while a white European-descended postcolonial woman in, for example, Canada, shares the relative economic comfort even of the local empire (America) which might be seen as trying to take over the cultural differences of Canada. Tsitsi Dangarembga and her women writer colleagues (whoever they might be – largely silenced) in Zimbabwe have a very different cultural experience from that of Margaret Atwood, Aritha Van Herk or Alice Munro in Canada. Each might choose to write of colonial oppression and to assert both their cultural context and their own individual experience through that of their characters, narrators, images, language and themes, but context, education and economics, as well as colour, make their lives very different.

A privileging of the term 'postcolonial woman', as if everyone was the same, iconic, idealised, always good, is also just another simplifying gesture which ends up absurdly homogenising, idealising and marginalising women of different backgrounds and cultures:

> The coupling of *post colonial* with *woman*, however, must inevitably lead to the simplicities that underlie unthinking celebrations of oppression, elevating the racially female voice into a metaphor for 'the good'. Such metaphoricity cannot exactly be called essentialist but it certainly functions as an impediment to a reading that attempts to look beyond obvious questions of good and evil.
>
> Suleri, 1992, in Chrisman and Williams, 1993, p. 457.

An alternative problem to homogenising postcolonial women, however, and recognising that cultural contextual difference, is that perhaps no one can ever be able to speak about anyone else without inside experience of their subject position. This is a doubly disempowering argument and results in lack of comment, appreciation or discussion. So critic Sara Suleri says we should read and comment on postcolonial writers, but not *for* them:

> The claim to authenticity – only a Black can speak of a Black; only a post-colonial subcontinental feminist can adequately represent the lived experience of that culture – points to the great difficulty posited by the 'authenticity' of female racial voices in the great game that claims to be the first narrative of what the ethnically constructed woman is deemed to want.
>
> Suleri, 1992, in Chrisman and Williams, 1993, p. 247.

See also *Contexts*: Discourse; *Texts*: Language, discourse, culture and power: reclaiming/rewriting language and power, Patriarchy and colonised women; *Criticism*: Colonial discourse.

Further reading

Minh-Ha, Trinh, *Woman, Native, Other: Writing Postcoloniality and Feminism* (Bloomington, Ind.: Indiana University Press, 1989).

Nasta, Susheila (ed.), 'Introduction.', in *Motherlands: Black Women's Writing from Africa, the Caribbean and South Asia* (London: The Women's Press, 1991).

Suleri, Sara (1992), in Chrisman and Williams (eds), *Colonial Discourse and Post-Colonial Theory* (Hemel Hempstead: Prentice-Hall, 1993).

Talpade Mohanty, Chandra, 'Under Western Eyes: Feminist Scholarship and Colonial Discourse', in *Feminist Review*, 30 (Autumn) (1988).

Resistance

Resistance against colonialism and imperialism has taken many forms. The First Fleet (1788) arriving in Australia found a friendly welcome and then resistance when it was realised that they intended to take over, reconceptualise the systems and settle the land. It could be argued that any imperial or colonial rule necessarily breeds resistance because, unless people are totally disempowered, some at least are likely to question the imposition of others' ways upon their own. Some resistance emerges from those traditionalists who refuse change and interpret any imposition of the ideas and practices of another power as necessarily destructive and evil, while historically some of this imposition was initially well meaning. Missionaries to Africa brought education as well as religion, and imperial administrators in India brought education and an administrative infrastructure. Other resistance, such as the alliances with communist groups in the early part of the twentieth century, is more easily explicable as reactions against the exploitation of a set of rules and discourses which would marginalise and disempower the indigenous peoples or those who settled the land first. In short, resistance from colonised peoples rejects the new intrusive power and recognises ways in which both discursively (in documents, rules, education and language) and practically (in laws applied, in violence and the movement of people bodily into settlements, territories, reservations, etc), these colonial or imperial powers, which now see their rule as normal and natural have in fact Otherised the inhabitants of the country.

Resistance can take both a violent form, as in the Indian Mutiny or First War of Independence (1857) and the Mau Mau rebellion in Kenya (1950s), and a more political form. In many cases, resistance takes both violent and political forms, with captured and imprisoned leaders (African Kwame Nkrumah, Archbishop Makarios in Cyprus) finally being released and leading a newly independent nation state or republic. Once an imposed rule is removed, rules, values, language and culture can be re-established. These may be traditionally based, or perhaps adaptive. There are great thinkers, some of whom also called others to action, whose views about hierarchical difference, traditional rights and discourse have influenced the establishment of postcolonial powers and lives since the publication of their work. Frantz Fanon, Amilcar Cabral, Marcus Garvey, Kwame Nkrumah, Mahatma Gandhi, Jawaharlal Nehru, Nelson Mandela, Edward Said, Gayatri Chakravorty Spivak and Sara Suleri, leaders and/or theorisers, all speak about the importance of rights linked to resistance.

See also   *Contexts:* Postcolonial Discourse.

Further reading

Fanon, Frantz, *The Wretched of the Earth* [1961], preface by Jean-Paul Sartre, trans. Constance Farrington (Harmondsworth: Penguin, 1990).
Suleri, Sara (1992), in Chrisman and Williams (eds) *Colonial Discourse and Post-Colonial Theory* (Hemel Hempstead: Prentice-Hall, 1993).

Rewriting history

As the epigraph at the beginning of this section suggests, history seems to be that of the coloniser, the successful in any exchange. It is not surprising, then, that postcolonial people would wish to rewrite a history which excluded or misrepresented them and, in fact, to point out that history itself, the named dates, the events and the priorities, are a construct put together and given emphasis by those in power, the imperial, anticolonial mainstream, the postcolonial nations and great powers whose commercial and business enterprises rule the twenty-first century world. In this respect, Jean Rhys' *Wide Sargasso Sea* (1966) was an early novel dealing with recognising versions of the past. It grew from her own origins in the Caribbean as a white Creole, and her questioning of her favourite reading, recognising the biased versions in this reading in terms both of ethnicity and gender. Rhys' novel rewrites Charlotte Brontë's *Jane Eyre* (1846), giving voice to the heiress Bertha, left stranded in cold, dark England, destitute and going mad, trapped in the attic, the hysterical suppressed emotional side of the empire's hidden secrets, female and of mixed race. Rhys notes:

> I was curious about black people. They stimulated me and I felt akin to them. It added to my sadness that I couldn't help but realise they

didn't really like or trust white people – white cockroaches they called us.

Plasa, 2000, p. 82, Rhys, in Howell, 1991, p. 21.

Wide Sargasso Sea is a striking postcolonial expression of questioning metanarratives or grand narratives which represent versions of history and values to people. Such questioning is a sure sign, according to philosopher Jean-François Lyotard, of the postmodern condition:

> Bertha is consistently represented in terms of three of the commonest stereotypes through which blackness, in the nineteenth century, is fetishistically constructed: sexual licence, madness and drunkenness. Yet as a subject of action, punctuating 'the deadest hours of night' with 'fire and . . . blood' by turns, she functions as a figure of colonial revolt, linked specially, to cite Meyer again, with the black Jamaican antislavery rebels, the maroons.

Lyotard, 1984, p. xxiv.

Wide Sargasso Sea provides an argument against canonical texts and colonial versions of history. Bertha speaks as Creole heiress Antoinette, and Rochester also speaks, but as the impoverished second son who must marry a rich colonial in order to survive and who has to hide this guilt – which represents colonial guilt at taking over others' lands and wealth, slavery, and exporting excess sexual energies – by defining its 'cause' (Bertha) as mad and shutting her up in his attic/out of his consciousness. The novel is a powerful indictment of the evils of colonial history, especially in the treatment of women.

Margaret Atwood's *Alias Grace* (1996) also rewrites history, in this case that of the impoverished, mainly Irish, classes who arrive to work in Canada, as in other colonies of the British empire, their histories misrepresented or hidden, their truths untold. Grace Marks, a notorious murderer or murder suspect, was imprisoned for joining her lover in the killing of her master and the housekeeper, it seems at the incitement of this lover, who was hanged for the crime. Because of her gender and evidence of gentility, Grace Marks was spared and first stayed in prison then was excused by the warden's wife and brought home to sew, becoming something of a spectacle. At the warden's home she was psychoanalysed by Freudian-influenced Simon Jordan, who transferred   on to his relations with Grace his repressed sexual longing for the servant class, a version of the colonial export of sex. Doubting and being unable to discriminate between Grace's stories, we are left wondering also about the validity of reported recorded histories of the censored and the colonised.

Further reading

Atwood, Margaret, *Alias Grace* (London: QPD, 1996).

Brontë, Charlotte, *Jane Eyre* [1847] ed. and intro. Margaret Smith (Oxford and New York: Oxford University Press, 1998).

Lyotard, Jean-François, *The Postmodern Condition: A Report on Knowledge*, trans. Geoff Bennington and Brian Massumi (Manchester: Manchester University Press, 1984).

Plasa, Carl, *Textual Politics from Slavery to Postcolonialism: Race and Identification* (Basingstoke: Macmillan, 2000).

Rhys, Jean, *The Wide Sargasso Sea* (Harmondsworth: Penguin, 1966).

Rhys, Jean, *The Black Exercise Book*, cited in Coral Ann Howell, *Jean Rhys* (Hemel Hempstead: Harvester, 1991).

Settler societies

Settler societies literally settled and lived in their new homelands, rarely intermixing with local people. Such settler societies include Australia, New Zealand and Canada and Southern Africa. As Hodge and Mishra (1991) have noted, there is a lot of difference between the settler societies in these countries and their indigenous peoples, even though the settlers might wish to be called postcolonial too, since 'the experience of colonisation was more similar across all the white settler colonies than in the non-settler colonies' (Hodge and Mishra, 1991, p. 282). Settlers, although living under colonial rule, have different experiences from colonised indigenous peoples and they also often feel somewhat different and at a distance from the versions of culture which remain in their original homelands. These tend to be transferred or preserved almost as historical artefacts in their consciousnesses, so that sometimes the behaviours in the settler society have become rather out-of-date versions of what is happening in the original homeland. They differ from other colonised people because initially they were the colonisers, though latterly as they develop independently to settle, they were subject to colonial rule:

> white settlers were historically the agents of colonial rule, and their own subsequent development – cultural as well as economic – does not simply align them with other colonised peoples . . . white populations here were not subject to the genocide, economic exploitation, cultural decimation and political exclusion felt by indigenous peoples.
>
> Loomba, 1998, p. 9.

In the former settler colonies, the period of decolonisation represented a time of growing cultural self-assertion and national self-consciousness, what George Woodcock, founding editor of *Canadian Literature* (1959), called 'the rising up of national pride' ('Possessing the Land', 1977). Only Ireland and the eighteenth-century United States had a violent revolt as political resistance. Historically, any anti-colonial struggle and demand for independence has appeared very late, and even the argument for leaving the British Commonwealth was rejected in the late twentieth century by Australians.

The relationship of these countries to the mother country can be seen as one of margin to centre. Their versions of colonialism and postcolonialism range from mimicry to rejection. Australian, New Zealand and Canadian settler writers have asserted their right to question and reject colonial dependency and, like Margaret Atwood in *Alias Grace* (1996), recuperate a history of immigration and alternative versions of historical events otherwise captured by those 'back home'. They write about the alien landscape, hardships and poverty. 'Though *never* as severely marginalised, settler writers experienced in their own way anxieties about the cultural mimicry produced by metropolitan domination. And they too began to seek an identity distinct from Britain' (Boehmer, 1995, p. 215). Atwood's Grace Marks tells her own dubious history of impoverished Irish settlers, the duplicity of her tale matched by the official stories of journalism and diary, ballad and note-taking during analysis – none of which really captures the real experience which is hidden from history.

One task of the settler writer is to replace the hidden history, talk of the struggles, centralise the marginal; another is to bring this new landscape and its ways into people's minds through writing of it. Katherine Mansfield does this in writing of her 'undiscovered country' in her collection of short stories, *Prelude* (1917), in the early part of the twentieth century. The old colonial heritage and new settler reality also get mixed up, as shown by Caribbean British writer David Dabydeen, on reading of daffodils, or by Ruby Langford, Aboriginal novelist, mixing up Australian and English writing and imposing it on her landscape, so that Wordsworth and Tennyson vie in her mind's eye with Clancy, local ballad character, as she stares out the school window (see *Don't Take Your Love to Town*, 1988).

If the position of settler societies is different from the colonised, so, too, is their literature, which sits uneasily in either the categories of First or Third World writing; as Slemon (1990) argues, it cannot be ascribed unproblematically to the category of the literature of empire (the First World), precisely because its position is ambivalent, these people, once settled, being neither fully coloniser nor colonised. Much settler writing, also known as Second World writing, actually develops into resistance writing, so it can be seen in terms of postcolonial resistance debates:

Slemon maintains that the settler communities have been excised from many analyses of resistance strategies and yet their writings articulate the dominant concerns of postcolonial theory: an ambivalent position between oppressor and oppressed plus a complicity with colonialism's territorial appropriations in the process of forging a resistance to its foreign rule – such that resistance has never been directed against a wholly external force.
Chrisman and Williams, 1993, p. 81.

An interesting example of exactly this issue in practice is Australian Thea Astley's *It's Raining in Mango* (1987), which explores an Australian settler family's response over time to the horrors of Aboriginal genocide. The novel follows the family as the land is cut, shaped and settled. The reader feels the shock of entering a land without roads or infrastructure, and the contradictions of settling such a land. As one group of people feel they tame, improve, settle and develop, another sees their history of life destroyed. Astley captures clashes of world-view and values and shows us the ambivalence of some of the settlers. We read of the intrusion of the very diggers whose long-term work re-shaped Australia, and from which the more contemporary land-owning branch of the novel's family benefits. The family in contemporary times remains concerned, seeing the everyday remnants of racism against Aboriginals in Queensland society. Peter Carey's novels, particularly *Oscar and Lucinda* (1988), *Jack Maggs* (1997) and *True History of the Kelly Gang* (2001), recuperate particular moments of settler history in Australia, revisiting outlaws, real (Ned Kelly) and fictional (Maggs is a character based on Dickens' Magwitch in *Great Expectations* [1861]).

See also   *Texts*: Aboriginal literature, Aboriginal writing: Tale-telling and women's experience

Further Reading

Astley, Thea, *It's Raining in Mango* (Sydney: Penguin, 1987).
Atwood, Margaret, *Alias Grace* (London: QPD: 1996).
Carey, Peter, *Oscar and Lucinda* (London: Faber & Faber, 1988).
Carey, Peter, *Jack Maggs* (London: Faber & Faber, 1997).
Carey, Peter, *True History of the Kelly Gang* (London: Faber & Faber, 2001).
Hodge, Bob and Vijay Mishra, *Dark Side of the Dream: Australian Literature and the Postcolonial Mind* (North Sydney, NSW: Allen & Unwin, 1991).
Mansfield, Katherine, *Prelude* (London: Hogarth Press, 1917).
Slemon, Stephen, 'Unsettling the Empire Resistance Theory', in *World Literature Written in English*, 30, 2 (1990).

Woodcock, George, 'Possessing the Land', in David Staines (ed.), *The Canadian Imagination: Dimensions of a Literary Culture* Cambridge, MA: Harvard University Press (1977).

SS Empire Windrush

The SS Empire Windrush was the first ship that brought significant numbers of Caribbean British immigrants to the UK in 1948, following the Second World War and a crisis in the British economy. Those travelling the distance from the Caribbean to Britain came feeling they were, in a sense, coming home, since Britain was their motherland in terms of education, language and history, the land whose peoples had originally taken their forebears hundreds of years ago across the seas from Africa to the Caribbean to be slaves in the open-market economy. Many found friendship and jobs, many met racism and hostility, all discovered the weather was appalling and the streets were not paved with gold, and that while rates of pay were higher than back home, so, too, was the cost of living higher in a post-war world which was still rationed, and where the colour of someone's skin was the most significant thing anyone noticed about you. Open University commentator Darcus Howe notes: 'Fifty years after SS Windrush docked, we should remember that we came, not simply as black immigrants, but as members of the working class' (Howe, 1996, 1998). Howe identifies those who came from the Caribbean in 1948 as working class, a hard-working class paid much less than their services were worth and who survived in white society without losing their sense of class:

> Those who had nothing to sell but their labour power had arrived in this country and contributed way beyond their numbers to the reconstruction of the productive and service industries after the Second World War.
>
> They transcended the enormous hurdles placed in their way, worked from sun-up to sun-down for meagre wages and spawned a new generation of lively and creative offspring. Cause for celebration, I insisted.
>
> Howe, 1996, p. 30.

The celebrations of 1998, marked 50 years since SS Windrush arrived in Britain, recognised the arrival of Caribbean Black British Creole and recognised the major contribution they made to the labour market. The hardships had been great, many had returned home, and others sent money back. Darcus Howe notes that 'the meagre collection of educated middle classes spawned by the Caribbean migrant workers celebrate their parents' achievements. So they should', but that their achievements were partly enabled by their working-class solidarity with other workers who were white.

Jean Breeze's poem 'Brighteye', written and acted as part of the 'Windrush' celebrations, dramatises the thoughts and plans of a middle-aged woman whose old mother is returning home to the Caribbean and leaving her behind, now with her own children and grandchildren. In this poignant poem, Breeze characterises the sense of history and diasporan existence, torn between the place of origin, the Caribbean, and the place of settlement, England. In her recent prize-winning novel, *Small Island* (2004), Andrea Levy follows the fortunes of, among others, a Jamaican couple who settle in London in 1948. Hortense, arriving at the tall terraced house, expecting more space when joining her new husband, Gilbert, is horrified at the cold and poverty of the promised land of England; the memories of others, such as Bernard, encompass army slaughter in Calcutta in the attempts to get the British out of India, and Queenie knows the damning everyday racism on England's streets which make her give up to the young Black couple her own mixed-race baby boy, because he would never fit in or be accepted in a white family at that time.

In *Windrush: The Irresistible Rise of Multi-Racial Britain* (1998), Mike and Trevor Phillips talk of the terror of the unknown faced by those first travellers who crossed the world from the Caribbean to London in 1948. They note:

> When our parents and their fellow immigrants arrived during the post-Second World War years, they felt themselves to be confronted by an exclusive and impenetrable image of British society, backed up by the ideology of race and racial superiority, which had for so long been an essential pillar of imperial power. This was a moral environment which steadfastly refused to acknowledge change, or the possibility of change, in the nation's self image.
>
> Phillips and Phillips, 1998, p. 4.

They are surprised at the extent of which those who fought in World War II were somehow obliterated from public memory, but did not actually identify any response of racial discrimination or hostility as rejection. Their argument points to the awareness, since the arrival of the SS Empire Windrush in 1948, that that generation, and those since, have so fundamentally altered British society that words such as rejection or acceptance are irrelevant. They note:

In the last fifty years the minority to which we belonged had become an authentic strand of British society. If we were engaged in a struggle, it wasn't about our 'acceptance' as individuals. Instead, it was about our status as citizens, and it seemed obvious that if our citizenship was to mean more than the paper on which it was written, it would be necessary for the whole country to reassess not only its own identity, and its history, but also what it meant to be British.

Phillips and Phillips, 1998, p. 5.

Phillips and Phillips' book is moving, significant and valuable; those they interviewed and quote range over forty years and comment on lack of jobs, difficulties of housing and finding identities in a changing multiracial Britain. Some very moving incidents include the interview with a woman (p. 332) who cared for one of the 13 teenagers burnt to death in a fire at a birthday party in New Cross, south London, in January 1981, following a decade of 'demonstrations by the National Front, street fighting and letterbox bombings' (p. 324). The popular history of this event emphasises that the crime was hardly reported beyond south London, and insufficiently investigated. The popular belief is that racism lay behind the crime, and the silence.

Some of the key figures of the Windrush generation who have made a distinct impression on British society are lauded in Phillips and Phillips' book and include one of the leading Black academics and critics, Paul Gilroy (Guyana) who, with a group of young Black British academics, wrote *The Empire Strikes Back* (1982), the first work exploring Black British experience from the inside. Gilroy's *The Black Atlantic* (2005) has also made a key contribution to understanding the legacy of the slave trade on people of African descent. Stuart Hall (Jamaica), a Rhodes scholar at Oxford, arrived in 1951 and became a leading figure among radical sociologists, founding *The New Left Review* and becoming a professor at the Open University, thereby influencing writing which reflects and highlights Black British culture.

Professor Rex Nettleford, new pro vice chancellor of the University of the West Indies, came to Britain as a Rhodes scholar and is acknowledged as a leading scholar, cultural critic and creative artist. Influential Trinidadian Darcus Howe arrived in 1961, became editor of *Race Today* and was outspoken on the TV talk show which he hosted: *Devil's Advocate.* He is an independent TV producer. Influential independent book publisher Jessica Huntley (Guyana), who arrived in 1950, is a political activist and founder of the bookshop and publishing press Bogle L'Ouverture, bringing to a wider readership such writers of the Windrush generation as Linton Kwesi Johnson, Andrew Salkey, and Walter

Rodney. Other key figures include politicians Paul Boateng and Diane Abbott, comedian Lenny Henry, footballer Wayne Haynes and Trinidadian, Calypsonian, Aldwyn 'Lord Kitchener', Roberts.

One of the more positive products of the changing times has been the focus on redressing racial injustice in terms of education, employment and living standards, led by the Commission for Racial Equality. Celebratory evidence of Black British culture can be seen in the yearly Notting Hill carnival.

Further reading

Breeze, Jean Binta, *The Arrival of Brighteye* (Northumberland: Bloodaxe Books, 2000).
Howe, Darcus, *New Statesman* (1996), June 12, 1998, v. 127, n.4389.
Levy, Andrea, *Small Island* (London: Hodder Headline, 2004).

Terra Nullius

Those arriving at lands they believe they have discovered, wishing to take the lands and settle them for themselves, were prone to describe these lands as empty (*terra nullius*), so ignoring and dispossessing the indigenous peoples, and in many cases proceeding to commit mass genocide to ensure that the lands were indeed bereft of people. Such is the history of the landings in North America, Australia and New Zealand, to different extents. This doctrine was introduced by the British colonisers of Australia, who dispossessed Aboriginal peoples of the continent on which they already lived, arguing the land belonged to no one and the inhabitants lacked social organisation or 'civilisation'. In the 1980s, the Mabo Case successfully established Aboriginal rights to land ownership.

Further reading

Young, Robert, *Postcolonialism: An Historical Introduction* (Oxford: Blackwell, 2001).

Tricontinentalism

Tricontinentalism suggests the linking together of three continents, and it is a politicised phrase which aligns the continents of the southern hemisphere, a kind of recognition of and speaking beyond the term 'Third World', which always suggests hierarchy and poverty.

The coining of the term 'Third World' emerged from the identification of a Third Estate in the French revolution, to define those who 'have not', that is, the underdogs, sometimes the working class, often the classless. It also indicates those states and countries which defined themselves as non-aligned, following the Bandung conference of 1955, when 29 often newly independent countries from Asia and Africa, but also including Indonesia and Egypt, Ghana and India, so defined themselves, recognising that their political interest and perspectives might be very different from the imperial and colonial powers who made up the First World. Tricontinentalism is another term which has developed to incorporate the recognition of anticolonialism. Anticolonialism in itself was always more than an idea, or a theoretical position. Instead, it recognised social, cultural and material infrastructures, balances of power and economic regulations governing life.

In Havana in 1966 the three continents of the Southern hemisphere – Asia, Latin America including the Caribbean, and Africa – came together and the term tricontinentalism took a firm hold. The conference founded a journal called *Tricontinental*, which published Frantz Fanon, Ho Chi Minh, Jean-Paul Sartre, Amilcar Cabral and Che Guevara, featuring the letters 'Message to the Tricontinental' in its first issue on 16 April 1967. Here, Guevara makes a revolutionary empowered statement about the role of the 'Third World', the disempowered, the hidden from history, and states:

> The contribution that falls to us, the exploited and backward of the world, is to eliminate the foundations sustaining imperialism: our oppressed nations, from which capital raw materials and cheap labour (both workers and technicians) are extricated and to which new capital (tools of domination), arms and all kinds of goods are exported, sinking us into absolute dependence. The fundamental element of that strategic objective, then, will be the real liberation of the peoples.
>
> Guevara, 1967.

Tricontinentalism, like postcolonialism, grew from a political commitment and a desire for a practical application. Young says of those committed to tricontinentalism that 'They were organic intellectuals who lived and fought for the political issues around which they organized their lives and with which they were involved at a practical level on a daily basis' (Young, 2001, p. 427). Young identifies it as the precursor to informed postcolonialism, wrought from the daily realities of poverty and rejection of imperialism and colonial rule: 'Tricontinentalism operates out of a knowledge that was formed through the realities of such conditions: its politics of power-knowledge asserts the will to change them' (Young, 2001, p. 428). As the term 'tricontinentalism' implies, this also involves changing the language used in the political sphere.

Further reading

Guevara, Che, 'Message to the Tricontinental', *Tricontinental 1,* 16 April 1967.
Young, Robert, *Postcolonialism: An Historical Introduction* (Oxford: Blackwell, 2001).

2 Texts: Themes, Issues, Concepts

Introduction

This section sets out to explore and engage with the reading of post-colonial literatures in English, most of which have been written by writers from ex-British colonies or from lands under imperial British rule, although mention is made of other writing or oral literature from postcolonial contexts historically influenced by American and European rule. A book with a much broader focus might consider Latin American writing more extensively in relation to its postcolonial relationship to the USA, while other books might critically engage with histories from the former Soviet Republic, for example, or works written under or against the rule of China.

In reading postcolonial literature we consider themes and issues and also we recognise concerns about language. The latter include whether to write in the language of the indigenous people, 'nation language', or the language of the coloniser, and we consider if there seems to be any aspect of language *not* affected by colonial influence. Issues such as identity, hybridity, location and role are all considered as they appear in postcolonial literature, while we also look at forms of writing such as semi-fictionalised autobiography and oral literature, rather than scribal or written literature, and even the existence or accessibility of literature. The issues, themes, authors and texts considered here are ones you will find widely studied and read, but mention is also made of some of the less well-known or less well-studied authors. Some others are included because their work is not yet widely if at all available outside the circles in which they write or, in the case of those who try to write under oppressive regimes, it is suppressed and hidden. Discovery and sharing of new postcolonial literature and writers continues to refresh and revitalise the field. This section considers some of the themes and treatment of forms and influences of postcolonial literature, while the previous section on context dealt with historical, ideological and pivotal moments which affected such literature, and the section on criticism will consider critical ways into reading. The approaches, critics and writers mentioned deliberately overlap and converse between the book's three main sections.

Some postcolonial literature is very radical in form and expression, drawing from literatures of precolonial times or producing new, merged and developed forms. Some writers deliberately engage with forms more commonly found in colonial and canonical texts, while others use canonical literary forms and cast them into a new light. We can expect, perhaps, in former colonies and lands which have experienced imperial rule, to find a merging of influences – the classical myths and parables of Christianity, legacies of English literature which were transmuted and then augmented by the mythological folk tales and teachings of other origins and cultures. Chinua Achebe's *Things Fall Apart* (1958) is a good example here, as it is based on the tale of a waning or dying King – such as Christ, the Fisher King, John Barleycorn, Osiris – and uses myths drawn from classical and Western and near Eastern origins explored in the tale of Okonkwo, at the turn of the twentieth century. Celebrated and powerful, he is linked to African mythology. He has strength, warlike effort and tenacity, but like those other king figures, he is sacrificed to usher in the new ways. In the text, oral forms are used amidst narrative forms and references from English literature. The phrase 'things fall apart' itself derives from English (or rather Irish) literary roots in W.B. Yeats' poem 'The Second Coming' (1921), which foretells a new brutalism replacing Christianity. Similarly, Okonkwo's ways and those of his culture are seen as overtaken by the spread of Western ways, laws, railways, technology and values. But there is no simplistic sense either of progress with the coming of the coloniser's 'enlightened' views, nor of a nostalgia for the old ways, since tribal slavery, brutal murders and wife beating, norms in Okonkwo's village, are increasingly questioned and problematised within the narrative.

Achebe reveals an alternative history to that of the textbooks celebrating colonialism, imperialism and the Commonwealth, but he avoids glorifying the past. Although Okonkwo is celebrated as typical chief and leader, his ways and days are seen as outdated. Things should change perhaps, Achebe's text seems to suggest, rather than falling apart under the destructive, blind ignorance of a kind of cultural steamrollering away of all established ways. The clash of the two versions of existence, history and representation erase Okonkwo and his village's ways and history, giving way to Western versions and control. As David Punter has noted (*Postcolonial Imaginings,* 2000), even Okonkwo's personal story, his narrative (not his narrative voice), is replaced by a different authorial voice which takes over after his suicide. This second voice is clearly associated with the spread of British colonial rule, and the memorable conclusion to the novel effects a brilliant apparent replacement of one narrative by another (see Weinstock and Ramadan, 1978; Innes, 1995, pp. 21–41; Gikandi, 1991, pp. 24–50). However, while Okonkwo's point of view and narrative seem to be erased, replaced by, in book form, *The Pacification of the Primitive Tribes of the Lower Niger*, to be written by the Imperialist white District Commissioner, the original actually survives, in the novel Achebe has written.

Things Fall Apart captures and dramatises a crucial historical, psychological and philosophically charged moment, recreating and examining both Western colonialism and the end of African traditional ways. As such, the novel sets a pattern for a range of postcolonial texts which scrutinise versions of history and the destructive imposition of colonialism, imperial rule and their legacies, while in each case refusing to offer instead a nostalgic version of a perfect, lost past. Writing your own version of history and dialoguing between different interpretations of that history is an act of empowerment for postcolonial writers.

For readers and students alike, from whatever cultural context, some understanding of the history and the cultural context of postcolonial texts is a crucial element in our reading practice, because otherwise we might query wrongly, misinterpret or transpose some of our own familiar constructs of contexts on to these various texts. Informed by contextual, conceptual and critical approaches, readers can then better appreciate, for instance, how, why and to what effects Caribbean performance poets use oral or vernacular language and forms in their live performances and on the page, involving an audience or readership, and expressing the histories and voices of people of whom we and the audience might otherwise never hear because history and politics have silenced them. So, in the work of, for example, Linton Kwesi Johnson, a Caribbean Black British oral performance poet (and sociology graduate), we hear about racism and violence in the very abrasive and powerful, engaged poem 'Five Nights of Bleeding', a response to the marginalisation and unemployment of Black youth in the 1980s in Britain. In an Open University film (Lit A 306, *Literature in the Modern World*, 1991), Johnson's poetry is set against footage of the riots in Brixton, South London, in the 1980s, where Black youths, angered by unemployment, marginalisation and the recent ignoring of the burning to death of a group of Afro-Caribbean Black British teenagers at a party, rioted and warred with white police. These versions had never made their way into the headline news but figure in alternative records and local papers. Johnson uses repetition, everyday street language, historical and political detail, and rhythms which derive from Reggae and Dub in order to give an authentic voice to an expression of rage at and social criticism of covert and overt racism.

In the entries that follow, many of the issues touched upon in this Introduction are explored further in comment on the varieties of culture, language, forms, issues and concerns in the writing of postcolonial people, such as Black British culture. Many historical moments are explored which may have influenced literature, such as the arrival of the 'SS Empire Windrush' in 1948. We also consider unemployment, racist behaviour, exploration of oral and performance poetry, immigration, assimilation, multiculturalism and hybridity. The rest of this section also explores key figures and ideas that connect postcolonial literature with culture, context and postcolonial criticism. It looks at challenges to Empire, forms such as oral literature, performance poetry, indigenous writing, and themes such as motherhood, identity and the double subordination of postcolonial women writers.

See also   *Contexts:* Discourse, Postcolonialism and Feminism; *Texts:* Postcolonial settler writing, New literatures in English; *Criticism:* Commonwealth literature.

Further reading

Achebe, Chinua, *Things Fall Apart* (London: Heinemann, 1958).

Brathwaite, Edward Kamau, *The History of the Voice* (London: New Beacon, 1984).

Gikandi, Simon, *Reading Chinua Achebe: Language and Ideology in Fiction* (*Studies in African Literature*, new series) (London & Portsmouth, N.H.: James Currey; Heinemann, 1991).

Innes, C.L., 'Wintering: Making Home in Britain', in A. Robert Lee (ed.), *Other Britain, Other British: Contemporary Multi-cultural Fiction* (London: Pluto, 1995).

Johnson, Linton Kwesi, 'Five Nights of Bleeding', *Dread, Beat an' Blood* (London: Bogle-L'Ouverture, 1975).

Punter, David, *Postcolonial Imaginings* (Edinburgh: Edinburgh University Press, 2000).

Walcott, Derek, 'The Schooner Flight' in *Collected Poems* 1948–1984 (New York: Farrar, Straus and Giroux, 1987).

Weinstock, Donald, and Cathy Ramadan, in C.L. Innes and Bernth Lindfors, (eds) *Critical Perspectives on Chinua Achebe* (Washington D.C.: Three Continents Press, 1978).

Aboriginal literature

Some of the postcolonial writers whose work has gained critical acclaim include indigenous writers such as Canadian First Nations and Australian Aboriginal writers. Growing out of the oral tradition, many of the works of Australian Aboriginal writers which we might discover are life stories, some co-authored, some semi-fictionalised. The first published work by an Aboriginal woman was Ursula McConnel's *Myths of the Munkan* (1957). Autobiographies include tennis-player Evonne Goolagong's *Evonne! On the Move* (1973) and work by Margaret Tucker, Theresa Clemens and Shirley C. Smith who, with the assistance of Bobbi

Sykes, wrote *Mumshirl: An Autobiography* (1981). Marnie Kennedy, *Born a Half Caste* (1985) and Sally Morgan's *My Place* (1987), Glenyse Ward's *Wandering Girl* (1988) and Ruby Langford's *Don't Take Your Love to Town* (1989) followed. The very first novels, which have a great deal of auto-biographical content, are Faith Bandler's *Wacvie* (1977) and Monica Clare's *Karobran* (1978). (Fuller lists are available in Claire Buck [ed.], *Bloomsbury Guide to Women's Literature* [1992] and Davis *et al.* [eds], *Paperbark, an Anthology of Black Australian Writing* [1990].)

Autobiographical and semi-autobiographical works are in a long tradition of Aboriginal creative response:

> The widespread use of biography and autobiography by Aboriginal writers can be linked to a cultural tradition in which verse or song would detail the lives of dreaming ancestors . . . It remains to be seen if this tradition was used to detail the lives of ordinary people . . . It may have been so.
>
> Narrogin, 1985, p. 2.

But the scripting of oral histories might mean it is difficult to retain and build upon the traditional cadences and spiralling forms. What can be lost in the written recording of oral history or oral literature is a 'different voice', 'its rhythms, its spiral not linear chronology, its moods of non-verbal communication, its humour, and its withholding of information. Many of these things will be untranslatable to the printed page' (Ferrier, 1985, p. 135). In Aboriginal cultures, women were oral story-tellers like the griottes of Africa, the repositories of ritual and ceremony, and custodians of the stories of the Dreamtime which involves creation myths and also suggests a constantly present depth of being in connection with all life, including animals and the land. The Dreaming is the imaginative order in which the essential beliefs of the Aboriginal peoples reside and of which they tell in creative work and ritual:

> Hence the Dreaming, the legendary cycles, the sacredness of land, the magical songs, the mesmeric rhythms of music and chant and dance, and the primacy of religion as the core and defining characteristic of that society.
>
> Evans, 1982, p. 8.

The intention of involvement in and creative expression of the Dreaming is 'to be saturated with the primordial Power of Nature which seemed to pulsate through all creation' (Martin, 1979, p. 155).

White male anthropologists misunderstood the roles of women, believing them to be as subordinate to the hunting roles of their menfolk. Women held the secrets of ceremonies of rites of passage, which have important social and psychological functions – one example of a colonial mistranslation of another culture. Ruby Langford and others have reasserted the importance of storytelling, emphasising the ways in which Aboriginal writing functions:

> Our ancient tribal people sat down and sang the spirits into this land giving it its physical form. Whiteman called our Dreamtime a myth. Our people know it is a fact, it was before creation time! they sang the trees, they sang the mountains, they sang the valleys, they sang the rivers and streams, all round, all round . . . They sang life in its vastness, into this brown land; and the spirit lives still, never has it been silenced, by white man or his restrictive ways, and the song had a beginning, and there will never be an ending until justice is returned to the singers of songs, our ancient tribal people!
>
> Langford, 1991, p. 36.

Some Aboriginal writers do not seek publication, but prefer to create within their own communities. To achieve recognition, others have had to work initially with white co-authors, who have necessarily become something like cultural translators, altering the (predominantly) women's work and somewhat misunderstanding the circling, repetitive patterning of the established forms of storytelling. This was the case in the work of Labumore (Elsie Roughsey). Although they altered the forms, the two male, non-Aboriginal white editors, Memnott and Horsman, compromised on retaining some of the original form and expression yet managing other elements of Labumore (Elsie Roughsey)'s work for a wider audience. They said at the time of *An Aboriginal Mother* (1984):

> it became apparent that some editing would be required in order for it to be acceptable for commercial publication and accessible to the average white Australian reader . . . Despite the changes to the text, we feel that we have preserved the flavour and flow of Elsie's work. It remains comprehensible to her fellow Mornington Islanders, and will be of interest, no doubt, to many Aboriginal readers, as well as to the white audience.
>
> Memnott and Horsman, Preface to *An Aboriginal Mother*, 1984.

Margaret Somerville, who worked with Patsy Cohen on *Ingelba and the Five Black Matriarchs* (1990), recalls Patsy's resistance to scripting the oral literature form. She wished to retain her 'wandering around and around' (1991):

If this story about my life is jumping from one thing and place to another, that is because that's how memories are. It is as if life is a big puzzle and we live through bits of it, and then later, from another spot in our years, we look back and that piece fits in. But while we are living it, can't really answer all the whys and wherefores of it.

Somerville, 1991, p. 95.

Latterly, work has been written without co-authors and most recently in quite different forms, from life writing or semi-fictionalised autobiography. Sally Morgan's *My Place* (1987) is a record of the lives of her family and her people, as is Glenyse Ward's *Wandering Girl* (1988), which uses a realistic, wryly humorous style and testifies to the ability of this self-aware, outspoken woman to survive bigotry and racism when, brought up on a Mission away from her family and employed for basic wages in domestic labour, she is treated as though non-human, is silenced and is nameless.

Carole Ferrier (1992) notes the differences in Aboriginal forms of writing which enable cultural resistance; she highlights the use of wry humour and irony, an Aboriginal form of resistance through withholding information, or of deliberately telling, and use of a spiral, non-linear narrative form. So, in Sally Morgan's *My Place* (1987), we are aware of a layering and repetition, build-up and patterning, as family members Nan and Uncle Arthur Corunna retell stories and recall and alter the versions of incidents as if using an oral form. One key feature of Sally Morgan's tale is that of the discovery and re-evaluation of her origins, which have been hidden by her mother, since to be Aboriginal is something of a disgrace socially and liable to attract criticism at school. Sally's artwork, intelligence and social position are similarly threatened:

The kids at school had also begun asking us what country we came from. This puzzled me because, up until then I'd thought we were the same as them. If we insisted that we came from Australia, they'd reply, 'Yeah, but what about ya parents, bet they didn't come from Australia'.
One day I tackled mum about it as she washed the dishes.
'What do you mean, where do we come from?'
'I mean, what country, the kids at school want to know what country we come from. They reckon we're not Aussies. Are we Aussies, Mum?'

Morgan, 1987, p. 38.

Beginning to acknowledge her Aboriginality, Sally is confused by stereotyping and racial prejudices:

'Don't Abos feel close to the earth and all that stuff?'
'God, I don't know. All I know is none of my friends like them.'
Morgan, 1987, p. 98.

Poignant and powerful, the relationship between Sally and her family, particularly her grandmother, develops as she grows to realise that her Nan is Black and to glean from her her story and that of her brother. Layering, patterning and use of certain repeated items and oppositions provide an underlying abstract text, a symbolic or a formal comment alongside the tale-telling and testimony, as Hodge and Mishra note: 'Aboriginal realist texts are always structured by an underlying abstract text which is a primary means of encoding Aboriginal meanings and the metameaning of Aboriginality itself' (Hodge and Mishra, 1991). There is a 'dialectic between speech and silence in working simultaneously with and against history' (Ferrier, 1985, p. 215).

Glenyse Ward and Ruby Langford also circle round events, repeat and recall different elements, withhold or reveal information with a witty naiveté. Incidents recalled are likely to be typical, not necessarily individual. Ward's *Wandering Girl* (1988) and *Unna You Fullas* (1991) deliberately set out to speak for Aboriginal women in the community. This is an important political statement, as Bruce McGuiness comments, emphasising the importance of authenticity: 'If it's going to be legitimate Aboriginal literature, then it must come from Aboriginal people and their communities without any restrictions placed upon them' (McGuiness in Davis and Hodge, 1985, p. 49).

Ruby Langford's *Don't Take Your Love to Town* (1988) tells her battling tale of bringing up children, working and living in the bush, erecting fence posts then, latterly, living in the town, campaigning for decent living standards and gradually becoming a political activist for Aboriginal people. Langford's writing testifies to the difficulties and pleasures of transposing literary reading from Britain into the Australian landscape, a difficulty familiar to Caribbean writers. Reading a poem about a dingo and looking out of the window, the children intermix local poets (Banjo Patterson) and British Victorians:

and when we looked out the windows we saw Clancy with her thumbnail dipped in tar, and Andy crossing for the cattle and the Man from Snowy River galloping up the rise. Through the same windows we saw the Lady of Shalott, we saw the solitary reaper, the deserted villages, the swains and bowers and the golden sheaves and behind that the boys' toilets and the woodwork room.
Langford, 1988, p. 30.

Langford's is a cleverly recalled, circling, oral-literature-based narrative. She foretells incidents of the future, later in the narrative, and recalls parallels and hints from the past, proceeding through events in time and then returning to remind us, to repeat, fill in gaps, reinterpret. The dispossession of Aboriginal families and communities is a key issue for her:

> I felt like I was living tribal but with no tribe around me, no close-knit family. The food-gathering, the laws and songs were broken up, and my generation at this time wandered around as if we were tribal but in fact living worse than the poorest of poor whites and in the case of women living hard because it seemed like the men loved you for a while, and then more kids came along and the men drank and gambled and just disappeared. One day they'd had enough and they just didn't come back.
>
> Langford, 1988, p. 96.

She does not seem resentful and depressed at this; it causes her to develop more strength and to concentrate on her kids, one of whom is imprisoned several times and destroyed by this incarceration, a pattern for many young Aboriginal men. Through her life we see the everyday hardships and valiant spirit of a tough Black woman, an individual community representative, speaking for the lives of others and herself through telling her own tale, and through political activism.

Aboriginal writing: testimony, tale-telling and women's experience

> I just don't think white people have come to terms with themselves, and their history here in this land yet. And so it's very difficult for them to come to terms with Aboriginal people, and it's very difficult for them then to try and pass onto their children, or teach them anything about Aboriginal culture, or Aboriginal history. And so, they choose not to do it. Or, they'll present only the traditional culture.
>
> Walker, in conversation with Levy, 1991, p. 189.

Writers highlight the ignorance there is about Aboriginal people, even amongst liberal Australians. Lisa Bellear (Noonuccal) echoes *Feminist Review* (1984) arguments that white feminists cannot understand the complexities of oppression and the contexts of Black and Asian feminists. She adopts the voice of a white Australian feminist, fairly well-meaning but misguided, and selfish in her assumptions of homogeneity and shared struggle:

I don't even know if I'm capable
of understanding
Aborigines, in Victoria?
Aboriginal women here, I've never seen one,
and if I did, what would I say,
damned me if I'm going to feel guilty
             ('Women's Liberation', Lisa Bellear (Noonuccal), 1991)

Sharing a feminist position is not enough when reading the work of women from different cultural contexts. Middle-class white feminism has had a rather poor history in its ability to recognise the difference that race and class adds to a Black or Asian woman's experiences of sexism and abuse.

See also   *Contexts:* Postcolonial discourse; *Texts:* Semi-fictionalised autobiography.

Further reading

Bandler, Faith, *Wacvie* (Adelaide: Rigby, 1977).
Bellear, Lisa (Noonuccal) 'Women's Liberation', in *Hecate*, 17, 1/2 (1991).
Cohen, Patsy, and Margaret Somerville, *Ingelba and the Five Black Matriarchs* (Sydney: Allen and Unwin, 1990).
Ferrier, Carole (ed.), 'Aboriginal Women's Narratives', in *Gender, Politics and Fiction* (Brisbane: University of Queensland Press, 1985).
Goolagong, Evonne, *Evonne! On the Move* (Sydney: Dutton, 1973).
Govinden, Betty, 'Learning Myself Anew', in *Alternation, 2,* 2 (1995).
Hodge, Bob and Vijay Mishra, *Dark Side of the Dream: Australian Literature and the Postcolonial Mind* (North Sydney, NSW: Allen & Unwin, 1991).
Kennedy, Marnie, *Born a Half Caste* (Canberra: AIS, 1985).
Labumore (Elsie Roughsey), *An Aboriginal Mother* (Ringwood: Penguin, 1984).
Langford, Ruby, *Don't Take Your Love to Town* (Ringwood, Penguin, 1988).
Langford, Ruby, 'Singing the Land', *Hecate,* 17, 2 (1991).
Narrogin, Mudrooroo, in J. Davis and Bob Hodge (eds), *Aboriginal Writing Today* (Canberra, AIAS, 1985).
Somerville, Margaret, 'Life(H)istory Writing: The Relationship between Talk and Text', *Women/Australia/Theory,* Special Issue of *Hecate,* 17, 1 (1991).
Walker, Maureen, in conversation with Bronwen Levy, *Hecate,* 17, 2 (1991).

Anti-apartheid political writing

Apartheid in South Africa literally separated people and hierarchised them because of differences of colour and ethnicity. As is explored in the entries on Apartheid in *Contexts,* many writers fled South Africa during the apartheid years as their works were banned and burned, while others were imprisoned along with intellectuals, academics and a wide range of people who found such divisions abhorrent and intolerable. Some writers left for other lands (Bessie Head went to Botswana, Zoë Wicomb to Scotland, while others remained and spoke out against the regime, its origins, the inhumanity of everyday racism, and the disgrace to humanity of the problems and behaviours apartheid produced and tolerated.

J.M. Coetzee is probably the most famous contemporary anti-apartheid writer whose work moves beyond an indictment of the regime to recuperate and rewrite history, retell colonial tales (for example, in *Foe*, 1986), and focus on the pains of people's lives under racist, hierarchical forms of power. Born in Cape Town (1940), Coetzee studied at the Universities of Cape Town and Austin in Texas. Twice winner of the Nobel Prize for Literature, his work is always engaged with issues of Otherness, ethnicity, hierarchy, politics and the position of the artist. He is also an experimental postmodernist writer. While much postcolonial writing is seen to reject as apolitical the strategies of postmodernism, Coetzee's work is notable for using postmodern techniques to rewrite history, incorporating multiple perspectives and consciousnesses, in order to explore and express ways of undermining and exposing the essentialism which underpins both apartheid and its legacy. Colonial and neo-colonial oppression are the subject of his first novel *Dusklands* (1974), which uses two seemingly separate narratives, while *In the Heart of the Country* (1977) looks at the fate of an isolated South African woman. *Waiting for the Barbarians* (1980) is a postcolonial allegory in a distant outpost, and *Life and Times of Michael K* (1981) considers escape from a divided society. *Foe* (1986) responds to Defoe's *Robinson Crusoe* by rewriting the tale from the perspective of the African family, a woman and her son who sail away from the tropical world to London. *Boyhood* (1997) and *Youth* (2002) deal with autobiographical material and the legacy of shame and destruction following apartheid, focusing on ethnic hatred.

Ingrid de Kok is another white writer who spoke out against apartheid. An Afrikaner poet, Ingrid de Kok trawls and questions the racist deceptions of her own upbringing, explores childbirth and loss as it crosses cultures and race, and uses imagery of children, closed rooms and brutality to characterise the monstrous everyday destructiveness of life under apartheid. Recording police brutality in Victoria West, she focuses on children's suffering, a common theme in her work. The violence done to children is indicative of an end to innocence. But what she does hope for is the return of that innocence to the family house, and the 'house' or home which could be a new South Africa:

They took all that was child
and in the dark closed room
visions of a ripe split melon
were at the tip of the knife
they held to the child's dry tongue.
And this torn light,
this long torn light
will repair itself
out of the filaments of children.
and all that is child will return to the house,
will return to the house.
(de Kok, 'All Wat Kind Is', 1997)

Finally she expresses a glimmer of hope for change and return.

Ingrid de Kok also writes of mothering and motherhood under apartheid, and in 'Small Passing' recognises the pain of loss of a stillborn child, whose white mother is brutally told to stop mourning 'for the trials and horror suffered daily by black women in this country are more significant than the loss of one white child'. Mothers losing children, white or Black, would understand her pain and sympathise. The poet negotiates difficulties which transcend racism. However privileged or otherwise exploited a mother may be, the loss of her child, beyond race and social politics, is devastating. The racism of apartheid was explicit, and as a politically focused period on the world stage, it can provide insights into the hostility, hatred and violence within racism, the latter both a producer and product of some elements of imperialism and colonialism. Under apartheid, children are mourned, lost, removed, their families split up and unable to support them – all this a result of racism and economic pressure which removes hope as well as living standards from mothers trying to bring up their families. The results are isolated children, and a threat to the future:

See
The newspaper boy in the rain
will sleep tonight in a doorway.
The woman in the bus line
may next month be on a train
to a place not her own.
The baby in the backyard now
will be sent to a tired aunt,
grow chubby, then lean,
return a stranger
(de Kok, 'Small Passing', 1997)

Stoical African women resist and survive. De Kok's poetry transcends racial difference with an empathy born of gender alignment. A South African writer now living in Britain, Lauretta Ngcobo, comments that writers and artists value the importance of sharing their experiences, with others. As a large-scale example of the silencing of those who wish to write of their experiences whether political or personal or both, apartheid and its end are crucial to an understanding of the need for writing, expression, reading, publishing and sharing:

> What validates the experience of an artist is knowing that somewhere out there someone will acknowledge and share your deepest thoughts, your joys, your pain, your muses. Yet in South Africa we have lived for a very long time in the stifling isolation of our separate worlds both as individuals and as groups. Only now do we, as South African writers and artists, self-consciously grope and reach out to find fellow South African kindred spirits.
>
> Ngcobo, 1994, p. 1.

See also   *Contexts:* Apartheid, Postcolonialism and feminism.

Further reading

Coetzee, J.M., *Dusklands* (Johannesburg: Ravan Press, 1974).
Coetzee, J.M., *In the Heart of the Country* (London: Secker & Warburg, 1977).
Coetzee, J.M., *Waiting for the Barbarians* (London: Secker & Warburg, 1980).
Kok, Ingrid de, 'All Wat Kind Is', pp. 184–5, 'Small Passing', p. 195, in Denis Hirson (ed.), *The Lava of This Land: South African Poetry, 1960–96* (Evanston, Ill.: Triquarterly Press, 1997).
Ngcobo, Lauretta, 'Introduction', *Like a House on Fire: Contemporary Women's Writing, Art and Photography from South Africa* (Johannesburg: COSAW Publishing, 1994).

Head, Bessie (1937–86)
Bessie Head's work is political and personal: 'In her concern for women and madness, Bessie Head has almost single-handedly brought about the inward turning of the African novel' (Larson, 1973). A South African writer, Head uses experimental forms and life writing intermixed with the more conventional novel and short story form to explore issues and feelings of ethnic and gendered identity, and in so doing brings to the African novel a focus on the inner experience of individuals set in the context of a variety of community and other voices.

Born in Pietermaritzburg in 1937 in a mental hospital, Bessie Head was of mixed race in a time when to be so was itself both a crime and some kind of indication of madness. She had a wealthy white mother with a dead child and a failed marriage behind her, who was committed to a mental hospital because of her breakdown but really because of her relationship with a Zulu stable boy. Her mother died six years after Bessie's birth, her family having rejected the child, and Bessie was visited just once by her grandmother in one of the foster homes where she grew up (the first of which rejected her when it was clear she was not white).

Apartheid operated a strict social hierarchy based upon colour, in many ways not unlike that practised in the USA and the Caribbean where, for example, the 'high coloured' or light skinned were/are seen as preferable to those with darker skins. This hierarchy of colour leads those of mixed race descent who have light or white skins to have more opportunity to gain the same kind of status as whites in terms of professional standing, social acceptance among the broad social spectrum, even – as is the case with Clare in Harlem Renaissance writer Nella Larson's *Passing* (1929) 'passing for white' and so gaining the privileges that accorded in a racially hierarchised society. Such an internationally adopted and fundamentally internalised colour hierarchy is a clear legacy of the post-Enlightenment racism which cast white as progressive and Black as primitive, leading to the kind of potentially fatal self-disgust and self-loathing we find in Toni Morrison's abused child, Pecola Breedlove, in *The Bluest Eye* (1969).

Under apartheid in South Africa, the colour hierarchy was imposed by law. Here, it was thought to be socially superior to be 'coloured', that is, of mixed race, rather than to be of Black African, that is, of Xhosa, Hausa or Zulu descent. Colour has been an issue for Bessie Head, Zoë Wicomb and other South African writers who explore their acceptability and that of their characters (or otherwise), often based on such colour hierarchy. Growing up in an orphanage until she was 18, Bessie Head then became a teacher and journalist, marrying fellow reporter Harold Head in 1962 and having a son, Howard, in 1963.

Deeply uncomfortable in a divided South Africa, Bessie Head left with Howard (and without a passport – which was refused) in 1964 to live in Botswana, a more 'authentic' African culture removed from apartheid, saying 'I desire above all else to be ordinary'. She lived in the bleak, arid Serowe for years, writing of her rootlessness, 'restless in a distant land'. Her work tackles the divisiveness of racism, agrarian life, identity and the roles of women, using the established South African form of life writing, transmuted and intermixed with modernist and postmodernist forms of self-referential writing which, particularly in *A Question of Power* (1974), enables her to engage with breakdown through the confronting of a variety of personal nightmares about sexuality and identity, and to move towards a more contained and self-aware persona.

Bessie Head's work is filled with imaginative power and moral engagement. Her first novel, *When Rain Clouds Gather* (1969), based on her time at the Bamangwato Development Farm, shows some of the problems of development in a Third World agrarian society. The descriptions of the area's dryness and the sense of death and suffering are very fine and detailed. The novel deals with an experiment to found an ideal 'new world' at Golema, a utopia in which sexual equality is intended and much practised. Although this provides a cutting comment on the non-utopian world outside the community, male leadership still operates in the cooperative. Head's idealism, a response to the harsh realities around her, fuels the moral promise in *When Rain Clouds Gather* (1969) that if people work hard and invest in their future, they will reap rewards.

Head is practical and interested in both communal development and the inner self. Her work is very thoughtful and self-conscious, much of it containing traces of autobiography. *A Question of Power* (1974) fictionalises her own breakdown and mental illness. She says she chose the novel form because it was 'like a large bag into which one (could) stuff anything – all one's philosophical, social and romantic speculations' (Barnett, 1984, p. 198, ref. to Head, p. 13). Although some critics have commented on her sense of bleakness and disdain (Brown, 1981, p. 159), Bessie Head herself asserts the importance of recognising humanity and, indeed, positive relationships emerge from her novels. She says: 'I believe in the contents of the human heart, especially when that heart was a silent and secret conspiracy against all the insanity and hatred in mankind' (Head, in Donga, 1977, p. 6).

A Question of Power is highly subjective, its narrative filtered through the perception of Elizabeth, the protagonist, who is working in Motabeng, Botswana, as a teacher. The dominant reality of the novel is Elizabeth's consciousness, which is filled with self-doubts, always partially in breakdown, processing the events of her social environment. Elizabeth's hallucinations revolve around Sello and Dan, two male figures who nightly operate a power game through her semi-waking dreams. Sello is the symbol of love and compassion, Dan of male destructive egotism and power. Although resembling men she knows, they are actually imaginative constructs embodying her divided self. They war, reflecting ways in which she perceives oppressions of misplaced power, especially as enacted through male behaviour. Dan is erotic and seductive, disgusting and powerful; Sello seems Dan's opposite – standing for love as a religious principle and harmony. However,

Sello has developed this play between the two of them in order to test Elizabeth, so he turns out to be yet another manipulative male. Her dichotomous view of the world dominates her hallucinations, showing moral idealism versus power and evil, but Elizabeth gradually recognises these two images as ways of helping her deal with her own conflicts, with an analysis of the insidiousness of power (racial and sexual) which she has experienced. Hospitalised, she moves out of breakdown into self-awareness and a sense of possibility for change. Like the work of Doris Lessing, Head's investigations into breakdown as a form of break-through were highly topical for women writers at that time.

In *When Rain Clouds Gather* and *Serowe, Village of the Rain Wind*, Head concentrates on celebrating the stoicism, the working realism of the women who throw themselves into agricultural work and child rearing, recognising that romance is an irrelevant westernised pastime and not a foundation for marriage (Ola, 1994, p.71). Seeing 'Private growth as a prerequisite for social change' (Ravenscroft, 1976, p. 180) suggests that Head's work offers more than mere protest but indicates suggestions for development and change. Head finds hierarchical separation of people an intolerable evil, so in *Maru* (1971) she confronts the horrors of racism directly, concentrating on the life of missionary-educated teacher Margaret Cadmore, a Bushman (or San, considered the lowest form of humanity by Africans). Margaret experiences discrimination and abuse in her first job but, loved by Maru, who is set to be chief, befriended by the powerful Dikeledi and talented in her teaching and artwork, she rises against this destructive version of herself and achieves a sense of self-worth. Discrimination based on race and colour is challenged by this novel, with its careful insights:

> If the white man thought that Asians were a low, filthy nation, Asians could still smile with relief – at least they were not Africans. And if the white man thought Africans were a low filthy nation, Africans in Southern Africa could still smile – at least they were not Bushmen. They all have their monsters.
>
> Head, *Maru*, 1971, p. 11.

Alice Walker recognised Bessie Head as one of her favourite uncele-brated foreign writers. Gillian Stead Eilersen's edition of some of Head's short narratives in *Tales of Tenderness and Power* (1989) and Craig MacKenzie's *Bessie Head: A Woman Alone – Autobiographical Writing* (1990) provide chronological samplings of her prose and a large number of her works. She combines an exposure of alienation and a very posi-tive sense of community and commitment (Ogungbesan, 1979, p. 207).

Cherry Clayton, writing of Head in *A Bewitched Crossroad* (1984), considers Head's liberation from constricting protest paradigms, creating an 'artistic matrix, an imaginative equivalent of her moral and social ideal for Southern Africa' (p. 55). Historian and artist, Head focuses less on the daily problems of Apartheid and more on underlying cultural beliefs and formations, emphasising the need for social and political recognition of equality. She does not merely protest, but through exploring community relationships and how individuals, including the semi-fictionalised autobiographical Elizabeth in *A Question of Power*, find identity, starts to suggest social and moral ideals for South Africa based on self-worth and racial harmony.

See also *Contexts:* Apartheid.

Further reading

Barnett, Ursula, *A Vision of Order: A Study of Black South African Literature in English* (London: Sinclair Browne, 1984).

Clayton, Cherry, *A Bewitched Crossroad* (Oxford: Heinemann, 1984).

Head, Bessie, *When Rain Clouds Gather* (Oxford: Heinemann, 1969).

Head, Bessie, *Maru* (London: Gollancz, 1971).

Head, Bessie, *Serowe, Village of the Rain Wind* (Oxford: Heinemann, 1981).

MacKenzie, Craig, *Bessie Head: A Woman Alone – Autobiographical Writing* (1990).

Ola, Virginia Ozoma, *The Life and Works of Bessie Head* (Dyfed, Wales: Edwin Mellen Press, 1994).

Ravenscroft, R., *A Rich Estate* (London: Hale, 1976).

Challenges to empire

Early challenges to imperialism and colonialism emerged from within the British middle and upper classes in the work of E.M. Forster, Naomi Mitchison and several women writers of the 1920s, 30s and 40s, including Virginia Woolf. Forster's *A Passage to India* (1924) provides an enlightened criticism of British imperial rule in India from the viewpoint of several of those integral to the imperial endeavour. In this novel, both Adela Quested and Mrs Moore journey to India to find new life and vision but find instead a version of Englishness which is imposed, stagnant, blinkered, rigid; it is also ruling through trying to homogenise the vast range of cultural and religious differences of India into a solely English-defined and so subordinate Other, while the vital difference and refusal of India to conform to any limited perspective or definition is seen by those in power as merely confusing. This confusion is reflected in the experience of Adela in the Marabar caves, where she is faced with her self and her own thwarted hopes of finding identity and a voice through a relationship with Mrs Moore, who is so unlike Mrs Moore's own son, the dreadful, boorish, priggish ex-public school Ronny Heaslop.

Forster hated the British public school system as insensitive and boring, archaic, didactic and individualistic, serving significantly fatuous rules, and replicated in the insensitivity to cultural difference shown by its products, military or bureaucratic rulers of Imperial India. Forster's depiction of cultural snobbery is broad. He shows that Indians such as Dr Aziz, a key figure in the novel, are not allowed near the Club, their wives are only spoken to if they are royalty, since royalty are considered by British rulers to be their equals – before the British retired, Forster points out, to little cramped bungalows in the south of England. His evocation of spiritual and cultural variety, incomprehensible to many Western eyes and minds, gives us both an indictment of blinkered, ignorant racist attitudes, and a glimpse at the diverse otherness of different cultures whose worldviews are not reducible to a translation, by imperial and colonial masters, into something less than British.

Chinua Achebe has criticised another great modernist, Joseph Conrad, for his depiction of African people as savage natives in *Heart of Darkness* (1902). One of Conrad's central arguments in the novel, however, is that an initially well-meaning missionary zeal, 'bringing light' to the darkness of the dark continent, Africa, too soon accelerated into the imperial race for power found all over Europe and the lands it colonised or ruled over at the height of imperialism. This was close to the time of the First World War, itself set off by imperialist greed and jostling for power. Conrad's Marlow, sent up the Congo to find the initially potentially positive British envoy figure, Mr Kurtz, dislikes the dehumanisation of native peoples, whom he sees chained together, dying from a lack of care and of any coherent plan, just as the boat of imperial endeavours lies idle for lack of rivets. Kurtz, who has gone mad, is more culpably and excessively brutal than the local chiefs, whose habit of sticking the heads of enemies on poles he has copied. His aim of enlightened improvement has dissolved. Virginia Woolf's *Mrs Dalloway* (1925) exposes the impulse to force conversion and compliance, indicting the forces of a patriarchy which incarcerates the shell shocked, sees sensitivity, pregnancy and creativity as weakness, and forces compliance on colonial others. 'Conversion, fastidious goddess' is indicted in this novel as feasting on the souls of those who cannot fight back.

Several other modernist writers, such as W.B. Yeats and Charlotte Mew, expose the destructive blunders of imperialism and colonialism, while early critics of empire such as Hobson theorise a similar position.

None of these is strictly postcolonial, but each articulates similar sentiments, exposes contradictions, even in some senses constructs versions and expressions of their views (Forster's Professor Godbole, his Hindu man of religion, and Muslim Dr Aziz). At the close of *A Passage to India* Dr Aziz and Mr Fielding feel their nations can never be together, but Forster is less certain.

See also   *Contexts:* Postcolonial Discourse.

Further reading

Conrad, J., *Heart of Darkness* [1902] (London: Penguin, 2000).
Forster, E.M., *A Passage to India* [1924] (Harmondsworth: Penguin Books, 1998).
Woolf, Virginia, *Mrs Dalloway* (New York: Modern Library, 1925).

Colonial status and cultural inequalities

Several early texts engage with issues of colonial power, savagery and political inequalities due to cultural and racial difference. Some of these have become classics which later critics and authors have re-written to re-explore their views of the world and sometimes overturn any implicit or explicit racism. While it is important to identify and question racism in colonial texts, it is also important to recognise that, given the times and context in which they were written, they might well just be echoing popular views and there were few or no other choices of perspective or view open to them. However, the issues they raise about power, perspective, language, identity, position and so on continue to be topical and so discussion and reinterpretation of these texts enables readers to engage in longstanding debate.

Shakespeare's *The Tempest* (1611), Joseph Conrad's *Heart of Darkness* (1902) and Daniel Defoe's *Robinson Crusoe* (1719) are three canonical texts which overtly engage with particular phases of English colonialism. In *The Tempest,* the figure of Caliban has been seen as one who is enslaved by another's rules, those of the deposed Duke Prospero who has been exiled. Caliban, depicted as a primitive savage and forced to speak the coloniser's language, is an archetype of a colonised person, only able to really use the colonisers' language for cursing his own lot while the imperial colonial master, Prospero, rules and debases him. Of course, Caliban sides with unruly sailors and like many other colonised people rises up and is crushed. His case as such (he feels he has the rights to the island as a first arrival with his mother, the witch Sycorax) and that of the unfairly deposed Prospero, lead audiences to speculate upon power, rule, mutiny and enlightened alternative rule.

Daniel Defoe's Man Friday and Robinson Crusoe in *Robinson Crusoe* (1719) have also frequently been seen by postcolonial critics as archetypes of the coloniser and colonised. *Robinson Crusoe,* a product of the Enlightenment, the eighteenth century with its set of beliefs that the world was progressing towards reason and order, replays its values, and is concerned with late seventeenth- and early-eighteenth-century's expansionist mercantilist culture. Political economists such as Karl Marx identify Crusoe as *homo economicus* (economic man), who is concerned with calculating, charting and depicting everything (in terms of double-entry book-keeping) so as to order and control it. Man Friday is rescued by Robinson Crusoe from the clutches of a group of cannibals who have enslaved him and then tried to kill and eat him. Crusoe is positioned, then, as heroic and enlightened and, as Friday's rescuer, Crusoe is always his master on the island, which he has measured, planted and tries to control.

Not surprisingly, there has been a wealth of postcolonial responses to Defoe's novel and its depiction of the white man and Black servant relationship, including a revisionist comic treatment of the Friday–Crusoe relationship in Sam Selvon's *Moses Ascending* (1975) and Derek Walcott's play, *Pantomime* (1980), which is set in a Tobago hotel. Both re-work amusing variants of the roles of Friday and Crusoe, renegotiating and destabilising the colonised/coloniser relationship.

Several of South African writer J.M. Coetzee's novels also react to *Robinson Crusoe* and other work by Defoe, most specifically *Foe* (1986), in which Cruso (omitting the final 'e') dies early on and a tongueless (silenced Other) Friday with a woman castaway, Susan Barton, come to London, where most of the action is set. By focusing both on the colonised Other and a woman, the novel destabilises race and gender norms, but more radically, challenges that other oppressor, the form of the canonical novel, through Coetzee's postmodernist writing.

The Tempest, Robinson Crusoe and *Heart of Darkness* all portray indigenous people as savages: barbaric and simple but potentially evil. Contemporary writing often refers to these key texts in order to challenge and rewrite their positions and let Caliban, Friday, or African peoples speak. Similarly/in a parallel way, *Jane Eyre* is rewritten by Jean Rhys to present things from the perspective of the culturally oppressed.

See also *Contexts:* Apartheid.

Further reading

Coetzee, J.M., *Foe* (New York: Viking, 1986).
Conrad, Joseph, *Heart of Darkness* [1902] (London: Penguin, 2000).

Defoe, Daniel, *Robinson Crusoe* [1719] (New York: Signet Classics, 1998).

Selvon, Sam, *Moses Ascending* (London: Davis Poynter, 1975).

Shakespeare, William, *The Tempest* [1611] (London: Penguin, 1999).

Walcott, Derek, *Pantomime* (New York: Farrar Straus & Giroux, 1980).

Cultural change

Cultural change, through interaction with those from other cultures, as well as cultural stagnation are important themes in the work of many postcolonial writers who seek to engage with history and change, with the diversity of world-views offered and the diverse cultures with which we now interact as global citizens. Homi Bhabha's notion of cosmopolitanism indicates the positive hybridity of people who are formed by and recognise the influences of culturally diverse others and behaviours. For many postcolonial writers the opportunity for interaction, change or refusal are important themes. Arundhati Roy, Salman Rushdie and Michael Ondaatje each deal with myths, histories and the effects of cultural interactions on history, on individuality and on physical change.

Arundhati Roy is a Kerlan journalist and author whose defence of her principles and of the underprivileged and the endangered in her homeland has led to outspoken comments, court and prison. She has campaigned against the flooding of lands to build a dam and the testing of nuclear weapons. Her *The God of Small Things* (1996, Booker Prize 1997) is semi-autobiographical and mixes her childhood experiences in Aymanam with a postcolonial scrutiny of history and relationships.

The Indian family in her great novel suffers from a preservation of the ills of the old ways, paralleled/embodied in the Pickle Factory which they run. The twins and their mother suffer a devastating summer in which a cousin drowns and the mother's 'untouchable' boatman lover is blamed (wrongly) and tortured to death. The island on which Velutha, the boatman, lives is a haven for the twins, but the love between him and Amma has no place in a caste-ridden (pickled, preserved) society. It's a tragic tale told using circular, oral storytelling forms. The English Indian cousin cannot survive the cultural difference into which she is thrown, but neither can the family cope with change in terms of the questioning of gendered roles, and of caste.

Sri Lankan/Canadian Michael Ondaatje deals with moments of change or stagnation. Ondaatje is the author of numerous novels, poems, plays and an assortment of pieces of literary criticism. His 1992 novel *The English Patient* received worldwide acclaim, leading to its 1996 film adaptation. *The English Patient* is set during the later stages of World War II in a damaged villa north of Florence. The story revolves around the four occupants of the villa: Hanna, the fatigued and dispassionate

20–year-old nurse who is unable to accept the death of her father; Carvaggio, the former spy/thief who was caught by the enemy and physically maimed; Kip, a young Sikh Indian 'sapper' who was instructed in bomb disposal techniques in England before applying his talents in Italy; and the English patient, an initially nameless man who is severely burned in the war and who turns out to be the Hungarian Count Laszlo de Almàsy. Much of the novel attempts to reconstruct Almasy's mysterious past. Ondaatje argues that we are all creatures of the past. By incorporating a variety of nationalities into the novel while depicting the last stages of the war in Italy, Ondaatje interrogates the notion of 'home', through the endless movement of the characters and the parallel dangers of war, Almásy's sufferings and Kip's act of bomb disposal.

The English Patient uses World War II to raise questions about the dispersion and subjection of people in general, indicting the nationalism and militarism of European powers. Critics have noted that it both refuses and confuses naming in a period of nationalism, which insisted on ownership, labels, land and identity control. All four occupants of the villa retell and reconstruct their stories. Ondaatje suggests through this that we are all affected by our past and it affects who we are and will become. In his earlier Coming Through Slaughter (1976) – which is inspired by pictures, jazz and historical fragments as well as oral legends, many of which are included in the final published works – he shows how all stories and knowledge of people are reconstructions. Oral history, fragments, pictures and music inform his work, which questions origins, identity and creativity.

See also Contexts: Diasporan writers; Criticism: Global citizenship and Cosmopolitanism, hybridity.

Further reading

Ondaatje, Michael, The English Patient (Toronto: McClelland & Stewart, 1992).
Roy, Arundhati, The God of Small Things (London: Flamingo, 1997).

Diaspora

The word diaspora suggests a line or space between two places – somehow a permanent displacement, always travelling and never fully feeling as though you have arrived. It seems to suggest that people are living somehow out of place in a new culture and yet making their own versions of it, their own version of self, while still retaining versions of the home culture. This version of the home culture is probably out of date and will never fully feel comfortable because of the experiences and perceptions enabled (for good or ill) by the self constructed in the new or Other, different culture. In this definition, Afro Caribbean, African and Asian, as well as Greek, Polish, Turkish and the wealth of writers whose origins are other than the land in which they live might be felt to be permanently suppressed, wandering and troubled. They could be seen to reinvent out-of-date versions of the homeland and long for, recreate or reimagine its delights as well as its constraints. They feel they don't 'fit in', and find it difficult to manage a balanced self in a country which ignores, silences or abjects them.

For many Caribbean Black British writers, the diasporan existence expresses itself in terms of constructing a dialogue between Caribbean and British identities and locations. Remembering and reimagining the original home, a kind of historical, mythic Africa, and thinking back to the Middle Passage, the crossing between Africa and the Americas, is also a popular subject, appearing in work by Grace Nichols, Toni Morrison and Alice Walker. Merle Collins' 'Chant Me a Tune' takes us with her on the crossing, urging support and strength:

> move with me across the weeping Atlantic
> through the blood tears death pain and hurt
> . . .
> i need you
> to remind me
> that i am
> the oceanic roar of angry strength
> that never dies
> that never dies
> that will never die
>   ('Chant me a tune', Collins, 1985)

Like the historical Caribbean-originated nurse, Mary Seacole, women's strength is hidden behind white stories (in Mary's case that of Florence Nightingale). Merle Collins' poetry is also concerned with giving a voice, recognition and identity to marginalised Black women in general, and specifically in London. In 'She was so quiet' Mary, a Nigerian cleaner, dies, but her memory is assured in the poem's naming, so she is no longer

> just another faceless person
> unseeing and unseen
> on the streets of London
>   ('She was so quiet', Collins, 1985)

Other poems recall her father's history, as he vainly sought his ancestral footprints in Britain, and advice in 'Butterfly' that she should bloom, 'be a butterfly' and express herself rather than remain as a kind of caterpillar, hidden. Merle Collins' riveting performances involve audiences directly in her exploration of Black history and issues of identity.

Salman Rushdie points out in his phrase 'observers with beady eyes and without Anglo Saxon attitudes' (1982) that diasporic writers can be aware of culturally inflected attitudes, but by not being part of them can reproduce new perspectives on the culture and country in which they now live, as well as the one to which they return from time to time. However, diasporan writers could be treated as 'tokens'. Being expected to be a spokesperson for your own cultural community or, as sometimes happens when the foreign Other is taken to somehow represent all foreign Others, any other community which is not indigenous, can be very demanding. As Debjani Chatterjee has pointed out, this role of spokesperson can be heightened to ridiculous proportions. In *Animal Regalia* (1989), she finds she is expected to be able to speak for a whole variety of different cultures. Her critique highlights the cultural insularity of those who, perhaps well meaning, so position her. However, living and writing about diaspora is not necessarily a regional experience. Writers might well offer greatly informed insights into their adopted home (and their parents'/grandparents' adopted home) unavailable to people whose ancestors have always lived there. Similarly, they can then offer different perspectives on the life of both and can write from multiple stances.

Diasporan writer Anita Desai in *Clear Light of Day* (1980) positions Bakul, the ambassadorial husband of Tara, one of the women central to the novel, as an inappropriate spokesperson for his country. He has a diasporan existence in the US, which has warped his version of home so he only has notions of stagnation or tourist attractions. Bakul's pomposity and sense of what is expected by tourists and foreign dignitaries lead him always to represent India in a stereotypical light. Instead of identifying change and diversity, he ignores rural poverty and represents India as that icon of romance and the exotic, the Taj Mahal. Although Bim, Tara's sister, has remained behind in what seems to be an out of date India, the decadent part of old Delhi, her historical perspective and reflective mode enable her to locate herself and her society in the bigger picture, avoiding the merely stereotypical. In this instance, staying at home leads to enlightenment. Desai enables the reader to see that a balanced perspective is preferable to stagnation on the one hand, and a merely cosmetic or touristic version of foreign travel on the other.

Born in 1937, Anita Desai is a culturally diasporic writer with a German mother and an Indian father. Married with four children, she lives in India, the US and the UK. Her novels include: *Cry, the Peacock* (1963), *Voices in the City* (1965), *Bye, Bye Blackbird* (1971), *Where Shall We Go This Summer?* (1975*), Fire on the Mountain* (1977), *Clear Light of Day* (1980) – short listed for the Booker prize – *In Custody* (1984), *Journey to Ithaca* (1995), *Baumgartner's Bombay* (1988) and *Fasting Feasting* (2000). They use a richly mixed mode, making something new of the several cultures from and about which she writes, mixing oral story-telling, circularity and repetition, motifs, revelation of origins and versions of events with postmodernist intertextuality, which in its turn utilises Victorian and twentieth-century European and US-originated work (Tennyson, T.S. Eliot) as frequently as the many voices and writing of India and Pakistan (Iqbal, Tagore). She mixes realistic detail with the symbolic and the historically documented (Partition of India 1947, wife burning) with stream of consciousness (Miramasi, inebriated and delusional, in *Clear Light of Day*).

Desai deals with East–West relations, understandings and misunderstandings, with the insights of one who has left but returns, who can negotiate these different versions with a very wide readership. Varied perspectives (the characters', the writer's, the readers'), travel, fixedness, return and reflective review are central to her work. *Cry, the Peacock* (1963) and *Voices in the City* (1965) use stream of consciousness. *Bye, Bye Blackbird* (1971) focuses on London, nostalgia and alienation. *Baumgartner's Bombay* (1988) re-creates the fascination, complexity and teeming life of India: 'India was two worlds, or ten. She stood before him, hands on her hips, laughing that blood-stained laugh: Choose! Choose!' (Desai, 1988, pp. 85–6). In this novel, the natural generosity of Indian people and the social rectitude of a Jewish holocaust survivor are each trampled, deceived and destroyed by a representative of the new imperial and colonial intrusion, selfish wealthy European (and elsewhere American) hippies.

Desai's vision is one which negotiates paradoxes and differences, the real and the imaginary, providing no simplistic cultural critiques or solutions. It is in line with Wole Soyinka's and David Punter's advocating a literature that can 'look squarely at its own paradoxes, that would be able to own to prior damage while at the same time insisting that such damage is, in a sense "common property"' (Punter, 2000, p. 188), without losing the specificity of each embodiment of damage and paradox. Desai shows us that fictions of escape into an idealised, liberated, postcolonial condition 'elsewhere' are themselves only a transfer: imaginative escape fantasies. Those who move to live in the West in

Desai are often harried by excess consumption (Arun in *Fasting Feasting*) and the dominance of the diary controlling a fairly vacuous existence (Tara in *Clear Light of Day*).

One critic sees Desai's work as focusing on spaces, locations and travelling: 'All her novels reflect a concern with spatial metaphors and her imagery is built upon cities and open spaces, islands and mountains which affect her characters who are uprooted or alienated figures, nomads or refugees' (Sage, 1999). Indeed, this could perhaps be seen as the necessary condition and subject matter of the diasporic writer, but it misses out ways in which spaces and locations also construct and constrict people, particularly women, whose social, cultural, religious, educational, economic and psychological conditioning might well prevent them from seeing beyond and certainly from being able to escape the confines of the home, family, kitchen and back room. In this respect, the travelling Tara (*Clear Light of Day*) is actually more constrained than Bim, who remains with the family home, but flourishes as a teacher. The two aunts Miramasi, one in each novel, provide interesting contrasts with each other. One is entirely constructed and constrained by the kitchen and its domestic servitude, a second-class citizen who nonetheless livens up the imaginative and emotional lives of the children with and for whom she lives, and the other is an eternal wanderer and adventurer, taking in ashrams and religious treks and taking Uma and her imagination at least temporarily with her, out of the home.

In *Clear Light of Day*, Miramasi's young husband travels to the UK to study, contracts a cold and dies. In *Fasting Feasting,* Arun, the intellectual son, becomes culturally displaced when studying in the US, faced with intensive food-oriented materialism in the form of 'shop till you drop' supermarket expeditions:

'Excuse me,' said a voice, and a woman leant over to pick her own cantaloupe: she wore a T-shirt that declared *Shop Till You Drop*.
This unnerved Arun but Mrs Patton did not seem to see.
Her joy lay in carrying home this hoard she had won from the maze of the supermarket, storing it away in her kitchen cupboards, her refrigerator and freezer. Arun, handing her the packages one by one – butter, yoghurt, milk to go in here, jam and cookies and cereal there – worried that they would never make their way through so much food but this did not seem to be the object of her purchases. Once it was all stored away in the gleaming white caves where ice secretly whispered to itself, she was content. She did not appear to think there was another stage beyond this final, satisfying one.

Desai, Fasting Feasting, 2000, p. 184.

Arun watches in horror as Mr Patton relentlessly and endlessly grills meat. Travel, then, does not *necessarily* bring enlightenment. It can bring loss, or the furious guarding and maintenance of the (often outdated) ways of home, but it *can* also offer new perspectives. And by the same token, staying put does not necessarily lead to ossification and small-mindedness. It really depends on the ability to maintain an imaginative, ironic worldview which can celebrate difference and paradox rather than forcing either the accepted, old, traditional ways or the ostensibly progressive Western ways.

Aunt Miramasi was married at 12, widowed at 15, prematurely aged in domestic work, and sidelined by her relatives, a telling example of women's subordinate position. Her circumstances are also set against the romantic love tale which swept her sister Tara (named after the house in that grand romantic fiction *Gone With the Wind*) away to the US with her domineering ambassadorial husband, Bakul, whose paternalistic behaviour regulates her entire life and thought processes. In *Fasting Feasting* (2000), Desai tackles the even more sensitive issues of arranged marriages and bride burning, when Anamika, talented, beautiful cousin, is sold off to her new husband's grasping family only to be sacrificed to their mercenary selfishness. Meanwhile, Uma's own near misses with marriage are treated with a mixture of the comic and the tragic.

Diasporan writers aim on the one hand to represent and recognise their differences, their experiences and those of others in all/both of these spaces/places. On the other hand, they also try bridging these differences, recognising similarities and the coalescence of these in themselves as writers. This is a necessary step to understanding one's identity as a migrated subject, or as any subject. In many ways, the diaspora is effectively a double dispossession for women, involving colonial oppression as well as dispossession and subjugation of women by men. A third, economic divisiveness also operates in the UK. Second and third generation women of Afro Caribbean, African and Asian descent are often high achievers in both the educational and professional systems, but their mothers are more commonly less well economically positioned, often ghettoised by their hesitancy with the English language. Both wider cultural isolation and community-based cultural identity result from living in specific ethnic communities.

Some second generation writers are discovering roots, imagining homelands and visiting these lands for the first time. The 'New Generation' poet Moniza Alvi writes of an imagined Pakistan, of an idealised wedding in the hills, imagining the everyday lives of her aunts in Pakistan, who sent her brightly coloured saris. Considering her family's entrance into the UK, she retraces the arrival of her father,

Tariq, into a cold Britain of washing lines and brown houses. Others, like Debjani Chatterjee, commute between family in India, England and the USA. Theirs are complex lives, split between different cultures.

Diaspora suggests a space between two places, emphasising belonging to two cultures, feeling some gap in between, a gap into which you might fall culturally. Possibly, a diasporan writer might find it difficult to shake off the colonial legacy and a sense of marginalisation. Alternatively, writers can claim the diaspora as a location in its own right, a basis for the celebratory recognition of cultural 'hybridity', a term reclaimed by Susheila Nasta and Homi Bhabha. However,

> although the literary representations of Britain's contemporary diasporic populations attest in one sense to the rich cultural cartography of Britain's recent imperial past, at the same time, they also threaten. For in a post-imperial nation that, by the end of the twentieth century, was fast losing its grip on any sense of a coherent national identity, the presence of the *others within* exposed the underside not only of the faltering myth of Empire and its waning fantasy of an invented 'Englishness', but also complicated the apparently seamless history of Western modernity itself.
>
> Phillips, 1997. p. ?.

British Asian and Black women writers often wish to represent and recognise their differences, their experiences and those of others in all/both of these spaces/places, while many of them also seek to establish something new, a hybrid voice. These are necessary steps to understanding one's identity as a migrated subject. Many women writers evidence ways in which the diaspora is effectively a multiple dispossession of colonial oppression because of racial difference, the subjugation of women by men and economic subordination. For these first generation women, cultural isolation results from living in specific ethnic communities, but the firm establishment of an often rather imported (outdated, locally affected) community-based cultural identity also results and, as Amitava Kumar notes, a creation and adherence to a version of Indianness could result: 'diasporic writers have crafted for themselves a script which allows them to be seen as more Indian than the Indians they have left behind' (Kumar, 2004, p. xvi).

Conflicting ties and demands, confusions and distances are involved in diasporan identity, including the danger, for writers and readers alike, of merely replacing one stereotype with another, a course deftly negotiated by writers such as Meera Syal. Syal's satiric and comic voice steers a course between gentle mockery and farce, undercutting the Othering and ignorance which stereotyping feeds by dramatising examples of Asian culture, and enabling people from all cultures to be amused at the comic take on stereotypes common within Asian communities, originating from themselves.

Immigrated people translate and transform rigid, oppositional racial and natural categories through their writing, metamorphosing perceptions and developing hybrid identities. In this interaction, the diasporan experience can be seen as active, progressive, producing its own literary response, what British Asian critic Susheila Nasta calls 'a poetics of migrancy':

> The experience was one both of migration and immigration. The crossing of the waters and subsequent passage across the threshold of Britain enacted a symbiotic movement both linking island and metropolis as well as suggesting an intervention into what has recently been called 'the double time of national identity'. This voyage across both enabled what Claire Alexander has called the 'transgression of absolute and historical boundaries, in which the migrants are placed outside and in opposition to the wider imagined nation', and also set in motion a discourse for diaspora in which the experience of im/migration could be seen as an active process, marking a stage on a continuum which was to develop into a poetics of migrancy within subsequent writings in the 1980s and 1990s.
>
> Nasta, 2002, p. 69.

See also   *Contexts:* Diasporan writers, *Criticism:* Global citizenship and Cosmopolitanism, hybridity.

Further reading

Alibhai, Yasmin, *New Statesman and Society,* 15 February 1991.

Collins, Merle, 'Chant Me a Tune', 'She was so quiet' and 'Butterfly' in *Because the Dawn Breaks: Poems Dedicated to the Grenadian People* (London: Women's Press, 1985).

Desai, Anita, *Clear Light of Day* (London: Vintage, 1980).

Desai, Anita, *Fasting Feasting* (London: Vintage, 2000).

Nichols, Grace, 'The fat black woman goes shopping', in *The Fat Black Woman's Poems* (London: Virago, 1984).

Punter, David, *Postcolonial Imaginings: Fictions of a New World Order* (Edinburgh: Edinburgh University Press, 2000).

Sage, Lorna (ed.), *Cambridge Guide to Women's Writing* (Cambridge: Cambridge University Press, 1999).

Forms of writing – identity and subjectivity

In the early days of postmodernist writing there was a direct link between postmodernism's radical world-view and its experimental, fragmented focus, its questioning of all roles as performances and refusal of the 'subject', which produced its assertion that there was indeed no real individualised subject or self and that we are comprised of many experiences, the words of others, fragmented and varied (depending on how positive the writer is feeling). This assertion of the lack of self and the decentering of the 'subject' was at odds with the needs of those from ex-colonies, those who had been silenced, to develop and express a sense of national identity and individual self, set against the erasure of those identities under colonial and/or imperial rule. For them, life writing, the assertion of individual identity and the forms that took were impartial testimonies to ways of establishing both a voice and a history.

The forms in which postcolonial people, and in particular Black women, write have been debated by many critics, some of whom take an ideologically related position. bell hooks in *Talking Back: Thinking Feminist, Thinking Black* (1989) argues that personal narrative, also called testimony, is the only form possible, while Sara Suleri questions the authentic record of lived experience as the only valid writing format. When you allow the 'native' to speak and use his or her subjectivity as a basis for information, Suleri argues, you are left with the problem of how subjectivity can provide truth. Lived experience uses realism, does not have to be first person, but shows experience in action. This debate continues with any critical reading of the work of many writers, particularly indigenous writers. Interestingly, many Black and Asian writers choose realism and testimony, but still others choose to write complex symbolic poetic works. Whichever form is chosen, testifying to life experiences and establishing history, subjectivity and the voice are popular among postcolonial writers.

It can be argued that expecting postcolonial writers to always write using testimonial realism is an arrogant, culturally imperialist act, but so, too, is insisting that using symbolism and the poetic is an indication of (preferable, advanced) sophisticated writing. Different writers use different forms of expression. Is J.M. Coetzee siding with the cultural and other imperialists in using forms of postmodernism? Is Erna Brodber fusing both oral storytelling with postmodernist forms, as does African American Toni Morrison? Are Ruby Langford and others who testify reinforcing versions of indigenous writers as being unable to write in conventional forms? These questions inform both testimony and life writing.

See also *Criticism:* Cosmopolitanism, Essentialism, Fanon, Frantz (1925–61), Negritude, Global citizenship and cosmopolitanism, Hybridity, Mimicry.

Further reading

hooks, bell, *Talking Back: Thinking Feminist, Thinking Black* (Boston, MA: South End Press, 1989).

Gender and convention: African women's novels

Many women writers challenge conventional representations of women as subservient, silenced, the 'subaltern'. Several African women writers have engaged with the dominant image of woman as mother, with Africa as mother, 'mother Africa', as with women's roles as entirely dependent upon and defined by their ability to bear and rear children – in short, motherhood. Both diasporan writers Buchi Emecheta and Flora Nwapa, along with Ama Aita Aidoo and several others, challenge this representation of woman as only valued and worthy of a place in society if she is a mother. In most instances, however, the challenge takes place without being able actually to imagine the deconstructing of this role or identity, or finding success in alternative ways.

The first Black African woman novelist to be published, Flora Nwapa, has written poetry and prose fiction: *Efuru* (1966), *Idu* (1970), *Never Again* (1975), *One Is Enough* (1981), *Women Are Different* (1986), and short stories: *This Is Lagos and Other Stories* (1971) and *Wives at War and Other Stories* (1980). Her best known novel is *Efuru,* which focuses on 'the women's world', depicting women's lives from a fresh perspective and valuing women's expression and rights in a society close to pre-colonial roots. Nwapa challenges versions of the representation of women as silenced and secondary, using oral literary techniques to consider women in community life, getting particularly close to seeing through their eyes and using their voices, showing them as powerful, economically secure and socially important, but also limited in their choices in a restrictive culture. Using oral literary techniques, Nwapa evokes indigenous traditions and society. Her style is understated, deceptively realistic and everyday.

Discourse and its power over people is one of Nwapa's themes, as she dramatises how people are inducted into certain behaviours because of the pronouncements of the elders, who argue using phrases such as 'our fathers say' and 'people say' to back up traditional activities such as female circumcision. Their masculine dialogue, full of anecdote and proverb, convinces and insists. Their talk is considered important. However, Nwapa's novel is a deliberate challenge to this 'important' model of discourse because she bases it in oral literature, and utilises women's everyday talk and mythology as an alternative form of knowing and engaging. This has caused critics to underestimate the originality of her work, which they say is 'full of small talk' (Jones and Palmer, 1967 pp. 127–31), whereas one of its greatest contributions is giving voice to the silenced and to the expression of women's ways of seeing and communicating about the world.

Efuru is set from 1900 to 1930, during a period which raised questions about the power relations of the coloniser and colonised, male power-lessness under colonial rule being compared to that of barren women. Since *Efuru* is so spirited and alternative, the novel can be seen as using women's challenge to traditional power relations in the rural village as a model for challenge to the coloniser. Efuru's own choices cast a new perspective on the 'natural' power relations between men and women in the traditional village contexts. The novel rewrites elements of a popular folk tale which focuses on a remarkable woman who marries two worthless men, has no children and worships a strong female deity, Umahiri, a water goddess who does *not* represent fertility, that token of women's position in African society. Umahiri's influence empowers Efuru as a woman in tension with traditional values of stability, fertility, child bearing and obedience. Efuru seeks her own new identity, and in so doing provides a cultural challenge to established forms of power in terms both of gender and colonialism. Through the folk tale, Nwapa questions the community beliefs and values of motherhood and fertility.

Efuru focuses on the issues and practices of women's lives, parallel-ing their collusion with that of all involved under colonialism. Nwapa challenges established beliefs that educated women are lazy, collusive with white women's values, and not as industrious as their more conformist counterparts, and shows the building skills of those who worship the water deity, Umahiri. Moreover, Nwapa repositions women's value as more than mothers alone, so that infertility is actually put forward as a feminist strategy (Stratton, 1994, p. 97).

Nwapa's short stories continue the dialogue on the competing values of the modern and traditional, the rural and urban; in 'This is Lagos' a village girl, Soha, who stays with her aunt Mameze, takes up with and marries a Lagos man. The couple's reluctance to share the event with the family until it is too late isolates them and represents a sense of slip-page of the old values, a loss of family ties – a fairly conventional reading which again sets up a dialogue with the reader, who might well feel that Soha is just moving into the twentieth century and city ways.

There are losses and gains with change, and some of the changes are an interpretation of values and behaviours imposed by Western colonisers, rather than enlightened development. Sometimes, as Nwapa illustrates, repositioning in terms of re-entering and reviving myths, and from women's points of view, can empower women, an alternative route to adopting Western ways wholesale. In *One is Enough* (1981), Amaka divorces her husband and sets up business in the city, but does so through using her power over men, defined as 'bottom power', so questioning whether she is challenging conventional moral values and launching out economically for her own success, or reaffirming subordination by using her body. *Women Are Different* (1986) indicts Western ideologies of women's roles and the perpetuation of gender inequalities through the false dreams perpetuated by reading 'true romances' such as those of Marie Corelli, which sold well in the 1940s and 50s.

Emecheta, Buchi (1944 –)
Nigerian born, UK resident Buchi Emecheta has – up to 2006 – written 13 novels, an autobiography, short stories, children's stories and television plays. She has supported herself by her writing since the late 1970s and embraces a feminist perspective, stating: 'If I am now a feminist then I am an African feminist' ('Feminism' p.175). Her work interrogates issues of identity, women's roles and economic status, and in *Destination Biafra* (1982) she wrote the only woman's novel of the male-dominated Biafran war, giving the perspective of Debbie, a strong woman, and focusing on rape, brutality and the search for an identity amid the difficulties of women's secondary social positions and their vulnerability.

Buchi Emecheta's work constantly shows how her protagonists' lives and successes, or otherwise, are related to their economic, historical and social contexts, not merely their gendered ones. She challenges sometimes portrays her characters succeeding over women's subordinated status, asserting the power and stoicism of African women from different social contexts, their many abilities and skills and, in the earlier novels, their rejection of male violence. She questions traditionalism in *The Joys of Motherhood* (1980), her most famous novel, taken from the last words of Nwapa's *Efuru* (1966). She uses intertextuality to identify with a female literary tradition beginning with Nwapa and questions the erasure of identity and of oppressive traditions associated with women's fertility and the role of mother. In each of her novels she explores different women's roles in Africa or Britain, asking:

God, when will you create a woman who will be fulfilled in herself, a full human being, not anybody's appendage? . . . What have I gained for all this? Yes I have my children, but what do I have to feed them on? On my life . . . who made the law that we should not hope in our daughters? We women subscribe to that law more than anyone. Until we change all this, it is still a man's world, which women will always help to build.

Emecheta, 1980, pp. 196–7.

The Joys of Motherhood ironically explores externally enforced, internalised social and cultural pressures. Nnu Ego, love-child of her father and his concubine, overcomes her socially denigrated and subordinate position as a childless wife, even in a society which believes 'when a woman is virtuous, it is easy for her to conceive' (p. 52). Her second marriage leads to the death of her child and the maintenance of some kind of stand-off from hostilities with her lazy, brutal husband Naife. In *The Joys of Motherhood* Emecheta wryly explores how spiteful and hierarchical marriages can be which involve several wives. Thus, upon the death of Naife's brother and Naife's necessary marriage with his brother's wives, what emerges rather than sisterhood is jealousy and jostling for power, in which Nnu Ego is sidelined, her independence and earning power removed. Initially, this looks like an economic problem but emerges as a personal one: '"Oh Naife, how are you going to cope? All those children, and all those wives." Here she stopped, and the truth hit her like a heavy blow' (p. 54). A battle of dominance and ownership ensues between the new wife, Adaku, and Nnu Ego.

Umahiri the river deity also appears in this novel, in a deliberate reference to Flora Nwapa's earlier novel, *Efuru* (1966) see F140. Nnu Ego's mother was buried with a live slave woman, who became Nnu Ego's 'chi', or spirit, and taunts her, holding first a beautiful then a dirty baby before her and promising her several dirty babies. It is a sad tale because, while Nnu Ego overcomes the social forces working against her, eventually, mother of seven children, she dies by a roadside. Nnu Ego's life is thus conditioned by her poverty, her traditional need for children, and obedience to men. When her sons grow up they reject the values she has tried to instil in them, instead gaining university education and adopting the Westernised city values of Lagos. The second wife, Adaku, refuses to conform but retains ties with Nnu Ego when she leaves.

Buchi Emecheta shows that there is little opportunity for many African women from different social contexts to change their lives. Tradition insists that there are no options, no professional opportunities, only motherhood and work. Lone women are totally displaced, a theme she returns to much later in *Kehinde* (1994), which is set largely in London and looks at the ways in which an African family is rent apart by the father's return to African traditional ways when called back to Nigeria.

When Kehinde, the mother, tries maintaining the relative equality they developed in their London home she is ridiculed and sidelined in Africa, expected to play the role of the chief wife while her husband fathers children with a new woman (soon followed by several others). Kehinde, who had a good job in London but left to rejoin her husband in Nigeria, rejects this traditional role, seeing it as disempowering, and returns to London, falling further down the economic ladder because she has no husband and her skills are unrecognised. As a cleaner, she reaches the lowest ebb before establishing a new relationship with her Caribbean lodger. This tale is one of several of Emecheta's in which traditional ways vie with modern demands in urban and rural Africa and England, and in which it is women who both suffer and change, moving into new ways of being as a result.

Emecheta's *Destination Biafra* (1982) is a feminist intervention in the masculine tradition of records of the Nigerian civil war (1967–70). She concentrates on rescuing and recording the harrowing tales of women's war experiences: of treks through the bush, rape, murder and the death of small children. The protagonist Debbie Ogedemgbe, who journeys across the warring country following the death of her (corrupt) wealthy father, comes to represent stoicism and a determination to survive. Escaping the war with her mother and servant, dressed in army uniform, Debbie and her party are attacked by soldiers, and in a terrible moment the young soldiers turn from joking to torture, gang rape and murder, for which others excuse them because it is war, where anything goes and women can be easily sacrificed:

'Madam, the dead woman was an Ibo, you said so yourself.'
'What of my daughter?'
'Give her hot water to wash herself. Hundreds of women have been raped – so what? It's war, She's lucky to be even alive. She'll be all right.'

Emecheta, 1982, p. 135.

Ethnic conflict is assumed as a perfectly legitimate excuse for dehumanising brutality. Debbie transfers her rejection of this brutality on to a similar rejection of the relationship she is offered, which in the light of her experiences seems based in colonial oppression. The personal is political; here gender, power and ethnicity are intertwined: 'I am a daughter of Nigeria and if she is in shame, I shall stay and mourn with her in shame. No, I am not ready yet to become the wife of an exploiter of my nation' (Emecheta, 1982, p. 258). Alan Grey's 'thoughtful' internal response springs from the coloniser's superiority: ' "That was the trouble with these blacks. Give them some education and they quoted it all back at you, as if the education was made for them in the first place"' (Emecheta, 1982, p. 259). Emecheta explores complex relationships between gender, power and race throughout her work, whether set in Nigeria or London (*Kehinde*, 1994, *Gwendolen*, 1989). Her novels offer a dialogue between women's search for self-identity and self-affirmation against colonialism and racism, and a variety of possible relations with men, between traditional and modern ways, African and Western feminism.

Like Nwapa, Buchi Emecheta's men are shadowy or stereotypical, and she often uses paired women, socially, culturally, economically and historically contextualised, who offer what look like different choices, conformity or change. Similarly, Nwapa's novels debate women's ability to refuse beliefs and behaviours embedded in patriarchal society and to achieve an alternative for themselves, rather than forcing a complete change of direction. In so doing she empowers women to define themselves rather than being defined by patriarchy or colonialism.

Emecheta's *The Joys of Motherhood* (1979) grows from Nwapa's *Efuru* and both contribute to debates about women's roles, Mother Africa, the subordination of women to their reproductive worth, and the ways in which oral-literature-based works which revive and replay folk tales and give a voice to the views of the people can, through their forms, challenge the imposition of colonial-originated forms of writing, and set up debates about the new value systems brought by the colonisers, which are a mixture of gain and loss.

In reading Nwapa, Emecheta, Ama Ata Aidoo and other West African women writers, readers need to consider the debate between Western values and traditional ways and between the country and the city, oral forms and the questioning of myths and parables as always the right way to guide peoples, especially women's lives. Readers also consider ways in which African women writers both reinforce the joy of being a mother *but* severely question the limitations of only being valued as an essentialised 'Mother Africa' figure – the novels present such debates.

See also   *Contexts*: Apartheid.

Further reading

Emecheta, Buchi, *The Joys of Motherhood* (London: Heinemann, 1980).

Emecheta, Buchi, *Destination Biafra* (London: Heinemann, 1982).

Emecheta, Buchi, *Kehinde* (London, Heinemann, 1994).

Frank, 'The Death of the Slave Girl: African Womanhood in the Novels of Buchi Emecheta', *World Literature Written in English*, 21, 3, (1982).

Nwapa, Flora, *Efuru* (London: Heinemann, 1966).

Nwapa, Flora, *One is Enough* (London: Heinemann, 1981).

Stratton, Florence, *Contemporary African Literature and the Politics of* Gender (London: Routledge, 1994).

Language, discourse, culture and power: reclaiming/rewriting language and power

It is commonly accepted that language and discourse create and maintain relationships of power; much of the work of critic Michel Foucault (1977) concerns this. It is not surprising, then, that using discourse to rewrite and reverse relations of power and biased histories, particularly changing expressions which could oppress or silence, has been a challenge for postcolonial writers. History and perspectives are reclaimed, resurrected and retold by postcolonial writers, and for many this involves a modernist-derived use of intertextuality, referencing and replaying while subtly refocusing some original texts so they no longer reproduce the views of the coloniser or imperial controller. Some other writers choose to be more radical by also recuperating forms of expression which have hitherto been seen as secondary, not high art, as incapable of complex expression, of the people, and so as secondary to the narrative and poetic forms found in the canonical texts of the literary establishment.

Those who recuperate oral literatures are among the creative and engaged 'writers' whose work challenges what is effectively a cultural hierarchy of expression, both at the level of focus and form. Still others might not be solely writing to assert the politically charged power of hidden cultural forms such as oral literature and performance poetry, but, in writing or performing and using language and myths deriving from their own cultural backgrounds, they find a sensitised critical perspective which expresses histories, identity and experience of their own background and culture. It is possible this cultural grounding could seem a little exclusive, but for many writers it is important that their work can be read or appreciated not only by their own cultural groups, who might well find the opportunity for such expression a liberating experience, but can also bring hidden lives and ways of expression to light for an international audience, especially where culturally aware peoples embrace their work.

Declan Kiberd, discussing the possibilities or impossibilities of writing using the colonisers' language in Ireland, notes how imposed forms prevent the speaker or writer from articulating their own lives in their own way. In many senses, this is a tongue-tied experience resembling that of women starting to write, as explored in Virginia Woolf's *A Room of One's Own* (1929). As in the case in Woolf's perception about women, for colonial people, there is literally no form for them to use, or language in which to express themselves, which does not originate from that of the coloniser – and thus carries with it the remnants at least of a hierarchy which denied and disempowered the colonial Other. In this way, any writer or speaker feels very uneasy using the language of the coloniser. Several postcolonial critics take up this argument, and relate language and expression to identity. So, African American Barbara Smith and Mae Gwendolen Henderson, another critic, propose that perspectives of race and gender intermix in Black women's writing, seeming to suggest that postcolonial writers could well be exploring *versions* of self and history and finding new and newly developed modes of expression to do so. Smith and Henderson argue that Black women's writing is dialogic in character – always, that is, in a dialogue with the Other outside the self, and with several selves.

Smith and Henderson's work largely focuses on African American women's writing, but for readers it provides a model. The notion of several selves and dialogue is one which can help us read much postcolonial writing. Postcolonial selves, Black and white, male and female – white Canadian Margaret Atwood as well as Nigerian British Buchi Emecheta, white South African J.M. Coetzee as well as Sri Lankan-Canadian Michael Ondaatje – are just as likely to be split, to be developing new versions of self, history and language, even though they are responding differently in relation to race, gender, history and location, some by living in and recognising divided identities within the diaspora, some by developing individualised identities influenced by race and gender, and by a dialogue with a colonial and imperial past.

Traces of the past and past selves, past language, myths of the times before colonialism and the times during colonialism necessarily linger on in versions of identity, history and language, but it is possible to be in dialogue with these and move on, developing new versions of those selves, myths and language. In looking at the work of performance poets Grace Nichols, Jean Binta Breeze and Merle Collins, for example, it is possible to see how this rewriting of a slave crossing history (Nichols' *I is a Long Memoried Woman*, 1983), or the settling of Caribbean Black British people in Britain in the 1950s, need to be considered anew and expressed using perspectives and language of these postcolonial people, rather than that of the coloniser. Some of this is achieved through using oral vernacular forms.

More unusually, some postcolonial writers choose to write in their own language rather than any version of their coloniser's. In line with his decolonising aim, Ngugi Wa Thiong'o has campaigned for African writers

to write in their native languages. He writes in Gikuyu. While this effectively removes a wide, English-speaking readership from his work, it
would, he argues, enable African languages to gain recognition alongside
other literary languages and, importantly, would make contemporary
cultural production accessible and relevant to the writers' own people.

Ngugi's reclamation of African languages is an important element in
the urge for postcolonial writers to claim power and identity through
recuperating expression and forms and so represent and dramatise
different mindsets and perspectives.

See also   *Contexts:* Discourse, Postcolonialism and feminism; *Criticism:* Hybridity, Nation
language.

Further reading

Smith, Barbara, *Towards a Black Feminist Criticism* (New York: Out & Out Books, 1997).
Woolf, Virginia, *A Room of One's Own* (London: Harcourt Brace Jovanovich, 1929).

Literature and politics

It can be argued that all postcolonial literature is in some ways engaged
with politics, or the political as broadly conceived – in other words, not
with party politics as such, necessarily, but with the ideologically
nuanced, politically engaged issues of ethnicity, power, gender,
economics, education, equality and history, and the relationship of the
individual to the community.

Postcolonial literature writes out of and against the kinds of political
constraints which historically marginalised and silenced people and
which attempt to do so in contemporary times. In so doing, postcolonial
literature grows from the politicised work of, for example, Edward Said,
whose *Orientalism* (1978) offers a critique of the way in which some
Western people Otherise, or position as radically different, people from
the East – how they legitimise both an idealising and a demonising,
oppressing fantasy which leads to subordinating the people they have
constructed as Other because Oriental. So, too, postcolonial literature is
political in the ways in which it is informed by the social and psychological politics of Paulo Freire, whose *Pedagogy of the Oppressed* (1972)
articulates an argument against the ways in which forms of power,
including education and language, can oppress people (most often those
Oriental Others, but also anyone who is not Western and white, and for
the most part male) and keep them oppressed, since they internalise the
destructive self-doubts and hierarchical inferiority which such values,
practices and discourse suggest. Much postcolonial literature also

engages with Michel Foucault's explanation of ways in which language, discourse, power, sexuality and difference operate to maintain control over the subordinate, colonised Other.

The politics of postcolonial literature in action, in text and expression, whether written or oral, exposes, explores and offers alternative versions of worldviews in which hierarchies of power, values and ways of living in privilege under colonial and imperial rule can be fundamentally undercut, through discourse and expression. Postcolonial literatures offer criticism and exposure of the colonist's language which enables or prevents the development of arguments, creation and expression, and the articulation of national and individual identity, and they expose, write against and write in alternative, constrictive, enlightening ways of different views of identity, education, history and power, views which reinstate the once (or, in many ways, still) colonised Other to centre stage. So, Marlene Nourbese Phillip's 'Discourse on the Logic of Language' (*She Tries Her Tongue Her Silence Softly Breaks*, 1989) exposes ways in which use of an imposed language prevents articulation of indigenous or colonised peoples' thought processes in their own ways. Politicised uses of language in postcolonial literature also helps develop nation language (see the work of Edward Kamau Brathwaite and Louise Bennett). In this respect, it provides a structure and forms of developed expression for oppressed peoples to explore their histories and present alternative histories. So, Chinua Achebe in *Things Fall Apart* (1958) uses the myths and expression of Nigerian people to tell the tale of colonisation and disempowerment under colonial rule, and Ngugi Thiong'o offers alternative insider versions of reasons for and experiences of political uprisings against such rule, in the Mau Mau-oriented novel *A Grain of Wheat* (1967). So, too, Buchi Emecheta deals with daily sexual politics as well as the politics of economic difference and ethnic hierarchy in most of her work and has written the only woman's novel dealing with the civil war in Biafra in her *Destination Biafra* (1982), a highly politicised work which explores the brutalities of war and the perpetuation of inequalities during and after war.

Many write of colonial oppression as a gendered issue. In the poem 'Skin Teeth' (1983), Grace Nichols writes as a slave-woman who must collude with the oppressive advances of her master on the plantation, but offers him only a false smile, 'skin teeth', not a real response of love or agreement with the relationship into which she has been forced. In Singaporean Catherine Lim's novel, *The Bondmaid* (1998), the young bondmaiden acts politically to maintain her own self-worth in her ongoing relationship with the young master of her house. While she remains a servant, she nonetheless holds power in this relationship, seen after her death, when a shrine is dedicated to her memory. Brutally political, too, is the radical mythic response to colonial and gendered oppression in Beth Yahp's *The Crocodile Fury* (1992), in which reactions to colonial oppression up in the Malaysian hills, in the convent and around it, are expressed in the bandit form of an invading crocodile, who is also an alternative self for those who wish to reject the constraints of power. Politics is important for Tash Aw's *The Harmony Silk Factory* (2005), which rewrites the largely hidden history of the time just preceding and partly during the Second World War, as British colonialists worked with Malay and Chinese in Malaya to maintain plantations and ensure trade and economic buoyancy, while the Japanese invasion grew closer. In this novel, the protagonist tells of his father, Johnny Lim, whose political dealings on a personal level led to the deaths of the managers and shop owners who held him back, and of tangled relationships with colonialists (Peter) and the vanguard of the Japanese invasion, the intellectual, aesthetically sophisticated Japanese Colonel.

Much postcolonial writing is not merely political in terms of its focus and content, but actually written to make a direct political statement. The work of Wole Soyinka and J.M. Coetzee, as that of Linton Kwesi Johnson, can be seen in this light. Dramatist and political figure Wole Soyinka was born in Western Nigeria in 1934. Soyinka studied at Government College in Ibadan, then at the University of Leeds, where he later took his doctorate (1973). During six years in England he was a dramaturgist at the Royal Court Theatre in London (1958–9). In 1960, awarded a Rockefeller Bursary, he returned to Nigeria in order to study African drama. He taught drama in various universities, becoming a professor of comparative literature in 1975, and founded the theatre groups 'The 1960 Masks' in 1960 and 'The Orisun Theatre Company' in 1964, in which he has produced his own plays and acted. Soyinka is also a political figure, and spent 22 months in jail between 1967 and 1969 for appealing for a cease-fire during the civil war in Nigeria.

Wole Soyinka has published drama, novels and poetry. His drama is based on the mythology of the Yoruba, fearing Ogun, the God of Iron and War, at the centre, incorporating both European influences and traditional African theatre. His first plays, written in London and performed in Ibadan in 1958 and 1959, were *The Swamp Dwellers* and *The Lion and the Jewel*. Later, he wrote satirical comedies, a rewriting of the Bacchae for the African stage, *The Bacchae of Euripides* (1973), and in *Opera Wonyosi* (performed 1977, published 1981) a reworking of Gay's *Beggar's Opera* and Brecht's *The Threepenny Opera*. Soyinka's two novels, *The Interpreters* (1965) and *Season of Anomy* (1973), focus on Nigerian intellectuals and writers.

Directly political, also, is Linton Kwesi Johnson's indictment of insti-tutionalised racism and economic deprivation in Britain, suffered by Black youth in the 1980s, when in 'Five Nights of Bleeding' he takes his audience into the dynamics of race riots in South London. Elsewhere, Benjamin Zephaniah explores the tragic, brutal, racially motivated death of Black teenager Stephen Lawrence in London, his murder at the hands of white thugs being a message that racism is still politically active on a daily basis in some places.

See also   *Contexts:* Diasporan writers; *Criticism:* Global citizenship and cosmopolitanism, Hybridity.

Further reading

Aw, Tash, *The Harmony Silk Factory* (London: Fourth Estate, 2005).

Freire, Paulo, *Pedagogy of the Oppressed* (New York: Herder & Herder, 1972).

Lim, Catherine, *The Bondmaid* (New York: Warner Books, 1998).

Nichols, Grace, 'Skin Teeth', in *I Is a Long Memoried Woman* (London: Karnak House, 1983).

Nourbese Philips, Marlene, 'Discourse on the Logic of Language', in *She Tries Her Tongue Her Silence Softly Breaks* (London: The Women's Press, 1989).

Said, Edward, *Orientalism: Western Conceptions of the Orient* (London: Penguin, 1978).

Soyinka, Wole, *The Swamp Dwellers* (Ibadan, Nigeria: Mbari Publications, 1958).

Soyinka, Wole, *The Lion and the Jewel,* (Oxford: Oxford University Press, 1963).

Soyinka, Wole, *The Bacchae of Euripides* [1973] (New York: W.W. Norton, 2004).

Mother Africa, Mother India, motherhood, mothering

Mother Africa is a term used both of Africa as the first mother or origin of humankind, and a label for African women. The idea of Mother Africa tends to indicate a close connection between women and the land and women and the maintenance of certain social behaviours, which is, however, an identification which limits women's own development. Much writing by male authors in particular depicts Africa as a woman, Mother Africa in a celebratory, essentialist, mythic way. But so too, colonisers, Europeans in the nineteenth century in particular, also saw Africa as a woman, the Other – deceptive, fertile, to be owned and taken, as, for example, in Rider Haggard's novel *She* (1887) among other colo-nial, imperial works. African lands appear as a female body and a source of wealth. As such, both the land and women are made exotic, exciting, sensual, rich, to be feared as Other, to be owned, altered and ravished. It is necessary but difficult for women to write against the myth of Mother Africa, particularly because the myth is aligned with recognising national Black identity, so that rejecting this myth which idolises woman's earthiness and fecundity (and then subordinates her), might be seen as rejecting motherhood or national identity itself. The 'trope' or regular features and formulae of Mother Africa as used by male writers positions woman as subordinate:

> She is pure physicality, always beautiful and often naked. He is constructed as a writing subject, a producer of art and of socio-political visions; her status is that of an aesthetic/sexual object. She takes the form either of a young girl, nubile and erotic, or as a fecund, nurturing mother. The poetry celebrates his intellect at the same time as it pays tribute to her body which is frequently associated with the African landscape that is his to explore and discover. As embodying mother she gives the trope a name: the Mother Africa trope.
>
> Stratton, 1994, p. 41.

Mariama Ba, speaking out against such cultural and literary wrongs, provides contemporary African women writers with a manifesto:

> The woman writer in Africa has a special task. She has to present the position of women in Africa in all its aspects. There is still so much injustice . . . In the family, in the institutions, in society, in the street, in political organisations, discrimination reigns supreme . . . As women, we must work for our own future, we must overthrow the status quo which harms us and we must no longer submit to it. Like men, we must use literature as a non-violent but effective weapon. We no longer accept the nostalgic praise to the African Mother, who, in his anxiety, man confuses with Mother Africa. Within African literature, room must be made for women . . . room we will fight for with all our might.
>
> cited in Schipper, 1984, pp. 46–7.

Tackling the myth, women also write about mothering and motherhood. Motherhood is central to the lives of many women, and to their position and self-image within the community. As such, then, it is not surprising that the issues of mothering and motherhood are pivotal in much writing, particularly by African women writers. While some Western feminists might view the role of mother as problematic, preventing economic freedom and self-realisation, many African women writers both celebrate mothering and criticise a society which denigrates childless women. They refuse the representation of women as merely child rearers. Buchi Emecheta writes of enjoying the sound of children's voices while writing.

Taiwo (1984) identifies the role of women and women writers as 'custodians of traditions'. Communities of women in traditional African villages share the upbringing of children, and this network of sisterhood can be seen in the work of contemporary African women writers as both positive and constraining. Under slavery, the role of women as elders and the value of their work was disrupted in African-originated societies. It was misrepresented also in the depiction and evaluation of both Aboriginal and Maori women's roles in much the same way. Much of the work of women writers aims to correct this portrayal using women's perceptions, voices and remythologising to do so.

Nwapa equates the creativity of writing with that of motherhood:

> The privileges accorded motherhood within traditional society are counterbalanced by the penalties for childlessness, the failure to marry or simply to conform to social expectations. For a writer who by the very act of writing challenges the patriarchal appropriation of power over the Word, motherhood becomes a site for struggle. Its literary representations, explicitly or implicitly, and exploration by women of the last uncolonised territory are an integral part of a woman's identity as a writer.
>
> Bryce-Okunlola quoting Nwapa in Nasta, 1991, p. 201.

Flora Nwapa's *Efuru* (1966), *Idu* (1970) and *One Is Enough* (1981) show women transforming childlessness into something positive in order to change their roles. Kenyan Rebekah Njau's childless protagonist breaks with convention in *Ripples in the Pool* (1975), which considers the distortion of relationships within Kenyan society resulting from colonialism, especially as they affect constricting social expectations on women. Text and child are conflated in both Njau and Nwapa, who re-examine roles through the images, strategies and behaviour which socially constrict them, that is, motherhood and women's position. In Nwapa's *One is Enough*, the main character, Amaka, leaves her useless husband who cannot make her pregnant, succeeds in business, takes a lover who abandons the priesthood for her, and becomes important in the federal commission as commissioner. For her the term 'Wife' is a social and personal constraint: 'As a wife, I am never free. I am a shadow of myself. As a wife I am almost impotent. I am in prison, unable to advance in body and soul' (Nwapa, 1981, p. 127). She de-centres the role of woman as wife but supports that of woman as mother. For many African women in particular, but other postcolonial women writers in India and elsewhere (see Desai's work), motherhood is a site for debates about power, pain, social links, reproductive issues and identity. Writing about motherhood and its difficulties is seizing power, redefining and valuing it their own way.

In *When Rain Clouds Gather*, *Maru* and *A Question of Power*, Bessie Head problematises motherhood too, reflecting alienation and internal exile. Motherhood is the site where conflicting emotions of anger, frustration, guilt, caring, responsibility and ultimately joyful release coalesce (Bryce Okunlola, quoting Nwapa, in Nasta 1991, p. 214). Though she lacks a mother country and mother tongue, her mothering role brings her back to her senses out of a nightmare world. Motherhood and motherlands are also important driving forces for women writers internationally.

In India, Ranjana Ash writes of 'The search for freedom in Indian women's writing' (1991). The concept of motherland became highly charged before Independence (1947), and images of Mother India bound in chains and waiting for her children to free her appeared in popular literature and art as the freedom struggle continued. Amrita Pritam, Anita Desai and Sahgal lived through and discuss in their work the horrors of Partition in Pakistan and India where, as Pritam notes, much suffering was inflicted upon women in communal riots and mass uprooting. Ranjana Ash explores women's themes which move on from the record of suffering, including the development of self-awareness and identity, and the search for freedom in the family. Historically, women's problems relating to self-image, rights and position in society derive specifically from the 'Code of Manu', which always defines them in relation to male members of the family, and binds them to obedience and subordinate roles:

> She can do nothing independently even in her own house. In childhood subject to her father, in youth to her husband, and when her husband is dead to her sons, she should never enjoy independence.
>
> Basham, 1971, p. 182.

Images of women's roles and the importance of motherhood as a form of identity appear throughout Indian women's writing: witness Desai's Aunt Mira Masi in *Clear Light of Day*, who suffers abuse when her role of wife is undercut at her husband's early death, and the record of crimes of bride burning in *Fasting Feasting*. Motherhood, motherlands and mother tongue are important to women writers such as Anita Desai, Buchi Emecheta and Caribbean writers Lorna Goodison and Grace Nichols. Each explores the tensions between claiming the mothering and mother role on the other hand with identity and expression and the problems of oppression and the limitations of only being seen as a mother on the other.

Mothering and motherhood are celebrated in Glaswegian African Jackie Kay's poem 'Mummy and Donor and Deirdre' (1991). While to *not* be a mother is to be socially criticised and occasionally even treated violently, some mothers, such as Tara in *Clear Light of Day* (1980), seem to be entirely ruled by the timetables and needs of their husbands. Some women characters, refusing the roles of wife and mother, succeed emotionally, financially and socially. Bim in *Clear Light of Day* prefers to teach history and support her brother, Baba, than suffer the deadening control of marriage to Dr Biswas. In Singaporean writer Catherine Lim's work, motherhood is never seen as oppressive and often lasts beyond the grave. In one of her short stories a dead child retains her relationship with her mother even to the point of producing a living grandchild for the (now) grandmother to care for.

Motherhood is a contested position in Buchi Emecheta's *The Bride Price* (1976), however, both for Akunna's mother Ma Blackie, initially strong willed but then somewhat overcome by events in her remarriage to her husband's brother, following the husband's death, and in Akunna's *own* story. Akunna, removed to live with her uncle's family, is only valuable if educated to a limited extent and married off for a bride price. That she elopes with her lover, Chila, the son of an ex-slave, gains Western readership approval but is represented by Emecheta, a diasporan writer, as a local cultural problem. She marries for love but in producing her first child, Akunna dies in childbirth and her story – marriage for love before a bride price is paid – is a cautionary tale to make local girls obedient to the rules of mothering, motherhood, wifehood.

Motherhood is also related to language and to the idea of motherlands. Language becomes a country, a motherland, something with which, and against which, to define oneself. There are often links between women's loss of home and mother with their loss of identity. Motherless, they can be exploited by men (see the example of Soha in Flora Nwapa's story 'This is Lagos'). The idea of motherlands involves both a seeking for roots and identity and a need to define oneself against the motherland as constricting. Mother-tongue is a mode in which to speak of one's own life, yet also potentially restrictive in how much and to whom it can communicate. A new kind of mothering, the act of producing writing, allows women to seek a voice, neither that of patriarchy and the father, nor completely the pre-symbolic interactions with the mother, but their own, exploring the minutiae of the difficulties of being women and mothers. Looking at motherhood as self-image in relation to power or powerlessness is of central importance when looking at postcolonial women's writing.

See also   *Contexts:* Postcolonialism and feminism; *Texts:* Apartheid: anti-apartheid political writing: Head, Bessie (1937–86), Gender and Convention: African women's novels: Emecheta, Buchi.

Further reading

Ash, Ranjana Sidhanta, 'The Search for Freedom in Indian Women's Writing', in *Motherlands* (London: The Women's Press, 1991).

Ba, Mariama, cited in Mineke Schipper, *Theatre et Societe en Afrique* (Dakar: Les Nouvelles Editions Africaines, 1984).

Basham, A.L., *The Wonder That Was India*, trans. from Sanskrit by A.L. Basham (London: Fontana, 1971).

Bryce-Okunlola, Jane, in Susheila Nasta, *Motherlands: Black Women's Writing from Africa, the Caribbean and South Asia* (London: The Women's Press, 1991).

Njau, Rebekah, *Ripples in the Pool* (London: Heinmann, 1978).

Stratton, Florence, *Contemporary African Literature and the Politics of Gender* (London: Routledge, 1994).

Taiwo, Oladele, *Female Novelists of Modern Africa* (London: Macmillan, 1984).

Myths of adapting and replaying

For many writers and storytellers, recuperating and rewriting myths have helped put indigenous people in touch with their heritage and share with those who colonised, ruled and settled some of the hitherto hidden histories and imaginative, mythic, differently informed interpretations of the world held by indigenous peoples. Some peoples who have done this include Aboriginal, Maori, African or those who were forced to move, through slavery, to the Caribbean and the Americas; and some First Nation writers who write of survival in Canada, for example. Poets such as the Ugandan Okot p'Bitek, or the Caribbean performance poets Louise Bennett and Merle Collins, Canadian/Trinidadian fantasy writer Nalo Hopkinson; and self-consciously literary and allusive writers such as Chinua Achebe, Buchi Emecheta, Wole Soyinka or Christopher Okigbo have reconnected with still-vital oral traditions, which explain and convey knowledge through myths.

Other writers have grown up in cultures with histories of writing in the vernacular and focusing on retelling myths. Some of these are Indian writers who use oral storytelling modes, and replay or undercut the constructions and world-views passed on in myths. Using conceptual structures drawn from local tradition, they therefore try to integrate past cultural life with their current issues, problems and developments, so putting people back in touch with their heritage while sometimes updating myth to help interpret current situations, or questioning its fixed interpretations.

Despite a range of efforts from missions and English-based schools to eradicate them, gods, daemons, warriors, strange beasts and origin myths of local legend and oral epic still hold explanatory power. Mythical figures are not merely outworn fetishes but offer a rich resource for people and cultures seeking redefinitions of self and revivals of different world-views and values. Many women writers, such as Suniti Namjoshi from India and Buchi Emecheta and Flora Nwapa from West Africa, question myths in the African and Indian context, for example the faithful wife Sita, revising myths of successful women who do not have children in the example of the water goddess Umahiri, a figure in work by both Nwapa and Emecheta. These newly challenged, recuperated, rewritten myths undercut myths which constrain and disempower.

Some writers reinterpret myths to criticise colonial versions, as Merle Collins does when she exposes Westernised histories in the poem 'Crick Crack Monkey'. Erna Brodber uses the myth of spirit theft in *Myal* (1988) to explain both local daemons and the way Westerners misinterpret and steal histories. In this novel, Selwyn, an American, stages Caribbean Ella's life in a highly artificial performance – stealing her spirit. Some writers also adopt the shape of the original myth to express their tales and arguments. Thus Wole Soyinka, from the start of his career, drew on Yoruba mythic concepts to structure his novels, poems and plays. The god Ogun, destroyer and creator, frequently appears, often as catalyst of action, agent of destiny or purifying force. In the 1950s, Soyinka's fellow countryman Amos Tutuola used Yoruba oral culture for fantastical characters and metamorphoses in stories including *The Palm-Wine Drinkard* (1952) and *My Life in the Bush of Ghosts* (1954). Ghanaian playwright Efua Sutherland in *The Marriage of Anansea* (1967) and Ama Ata Aidoo in the play *Anowa* (1965) used Akan legend, particularly the Ananse story-telling tradition, to shape their work and base it in a familiar cultural background with familiar twists and meanings. R.K Narayan's writings in the 1950s and 1960s are based on the concepts of Karma and Hindu spiritual progression. So, Raju in *The Guide* (1958) embodies the traditional roles of student, householder, hermit and sanyasi (holy man). Salman Rushdie's *Midnight's Children* (1981) not only replays a variety of myths but uses myth forms and a mix of multiple mini-narratives modelled on the digressive form of the *Mahabharata* and *Ramayana*.

Maori writer Witi Ihimaera's novel *The Whale Rider* (1987), perhaps better known as the award-winning film starring Keisha Castle-Hughes, certainly contributed to the opening up of international imaginations in relation to the beauty of New Zealand and the lived everyday myths of Maori. Both novel and film chart the growing up of Kahu/Pikea, a young girl whose twin brother died at birth, followed by her mother. Kahu/Pikea is named after the legendary figure who originally brought the first Maori Melanesian islanders to the shores of New Zealand, riding on the back of a whale. This is significant since Kahu/Pikea's grandfather is fiercely determined to revive the nobility and mission of the Maori, and is disappointed in both his own sons, one able to perform warrior actions but largely unemployed and enjoying life rather than reviving the masculine power-based rituals of strength, and the other a successful international artist. At the death of the male twin all seems lost. Trying to train up local youths in the traditional ways, grandfather (Koro Apirana) is blinded by his misogyny and fails to see that the strongest, most dedicated, able and likely person to revive tradition is his own granddaughter Kahu/Pikea who, although denied the training, secretly learns chants and rituals and naturally adopts the values and dedication needed to be a true leader of her people.

The book and film have been criticised for air-brushing out more modern Maori ways and recreating a rather primitive idyll without problems. Feminist critics have been fascinated by the initially marginalised but strong successful figure of Kahu/Pikea herself, but the portrayal of traditional misogyny has also been seen as representing Maori in a very limited light. However, the sense of a culture which is strongly rooted in location, the earth and sea, ancestral histories and powers, myth and inheritance is vividly portrayed and echoed in other Maori writers' works, such as novels and short stories by Patricia Grace, while the sense of a loss of energies and values is similarly echoed in, for instance, Alan Duff's *Once Were Warriors* (1994). When Kahu/Pikea revives a stranded whale and sets off to sea, with others following her, she simultaneously revives that warrior seafaring spirit and is declared the true new leader of her people. A mythic tale, it engages with cultural differences, Maori tradition and women's roles.

Some writers re-write and re-tell myths, parables and legends. Others reinterpret their implied or stated values, and still others use their forms to explore and expose a link with history and a movement into a post-colonial period and perspectives which have space for, and are enlightened and invigorated by the mythic usage.

Further reading

Brodber, Erna, *Myal* (London: New Beacon Books, 1988).

Ihimaera, Witi, *The Whale Rider* (Auckland: Heinemann, 1987).

Tutuola, Amos, *The Palm-Wine Drinkard* (London: Faber & Faber, 1952).

Nation language

Edward Kamau Braithwaite

One step towards seizing, reclaiming and redeveloping a sense of identity is through language and for some Caribbean poets the term nation language identifies this development. Barbadian poet Edward Kamau Brathwaite (1930–), educated at prestigious Harrison College Barbados, Cambridge and Sussex Universities, turned his doctoral thesis into *The Development of Creole Society in Jamaica 1770–1820* (1971), then a pamphlet *Folk Culture of the Slaves in Jamaica* (1970/81), followed by a study on Caribbean poetry in English, *History of the Voice* (1984), each making a major contribution to recalling history and establishing African roots (largely based on his informative experience of working in Ghana as an Education Officer from 1955 to 1962). Brathwaite was also influenced by American Beat poets such as Allen Ginsberg, Lawrence Ferlinghetti and Gregory Corso, and Black mountain poets such as Charles Olson, Robert Creeley and Robert Duncan, whose focus on the link between oral poetry, use of breath, the rhythm of the spoken word and politics underpinned some of his own contribution to the recognition and development of nation language, the language of the people claiming their national identity. Movements to identify as valid and valuable forms of language spoken and written on a daily basis in the Caribbean led to nation language being coined to define culturally specific forms of Caribbean English. The term has been adopted by many others, including Jean 'Binta' Breeze and Merle Collins. Nation language is heavily influenced by African heritage, and its recognition is a claim for identity and difference. Brathwaite explains that although Jamaican English, for instance, may have the same lexical features as the English of England, 'in its contours, its rhythm and timbre, its sound explosions, it is not English, even though the words, as you hear them, might be English to a greater or lesser degree' (Brathwaite 1984, p. 311). Neither is it 'dialect', usually a critical term for a kind of substandard version of language. Instead, it is a language moulded by specific cultural experience, and based on sound, song, the weather, the hurricane and breath:

> it is an English which is not the standard, imported, educated English, but that of the submerged, surrealist experience and sensibility, which has always been there and which is now increasingly coming to the surface and influencing the perceptions of contemporary Caribbean people.
>
> Brathwaite, 1984, p. 311.

Beyond even the lexical features we find different rhythms and cadences in nation language and in the performance and other poetry of Brathwaite and many Caribbean poets, whose language and forms recreate and evoke at the level of the words, rhythms, metre, sounds and imagery of the poems, the everyday cultural and geographical experiences replayed and explored at the level of storyline, theme and character.

Brathwaite's work comprises two trilogies. The first, *Rights of Passage* (1967), *Mask* (1968) and *Islands* (1969) (compiled as *The Arrivants,* 1973), use and remake African, Afro Caribbean and African American forms, using diasporan musical forms, including work songs and the blues, to explore phases of Black experience in the Americas. These explore also a return to Africa, through migration and the transportation of the Middle Passage to the Caribbean, and revive African heritage in terms both of history and the forms latent in Afro Caribbean archetypes, myths such as Ananse (the storyteller, the spider) and Legba, and expressive forms. The second trilogy, *Mother Poem* (1977), *Sun Poem* (1982) and *X Self* (1987), looks mainly at the male and female histories of Barbados and suggests evolving consciousness and development. *Other Exiles* (1975), *Black + Blues* (1976), *Soweto* (1979), *Third World Poems* (1983) and *Middle Passages* (1992) make further contributions to the development of a Caribbean experience and poetic expression which is politicised, historically based in African Caribbean culture, linguistically engaged, and often experimental. Here, Brathwaite moves beyond commentary on Barbados alone and looks also at South Africa and Third World countries.

Bennett, Louise (1919–)

Louise Bennett, 'Miss Lou', is a Jamaican-born folklorist, educator for the extra mural department of the University of the West Indies (UWI) and performance poet. Although not the first to use vernacular and performance (preceded by Claude McKay and Una Marson), Louise Bennett repopularised the popular and oral forms that Caribbean writers and readers had somehow neglected in favour of written cultural expressions. The revival of performance poetry regained a sense of the flavour of everyday people's lives, and everyday street speech. Louise Bennett received many honours, including an OBE in 1961. Her work mainly appears in *Jamaica Labrish* (1966), and other collections include *Dialect Verse* (1942), *Jamaica Dialect Poems* (1948) and a collection of Anansi stories, *Anansi and Miss Lou* and *Selected Poems* (1982). Many of her poems deal with the confusion of everyday country folk entering the town, and challenges to imperial rule by Jamaican women, whose cunning everyday ways undercut those of the rulers. 'Colonisation in

Reverse' pokes ironic fun at the two-way traffic between Jamaica and England, noting that colonial attitudes and prejudices crisscross the world, and England has become in many ways both very Jamaican and a last colonial outpost.

South Africa has a long tradition of oral poetry which uses the language of local people, although not always termed nation language. It includes the lyric poems of the Khoi and Bushmen, praise poems (izibongo, lithoko), recognising the importance and glory of individuals, songs to the clan, family songs, love lyrics, children's verse, work songs, lullabies, personal izibongo, religious songs, songs to animals and songs of divination. Upon the arrival of the missionaries, forms were influenced by 'the harmonies and poetics of the Christian hymn' (Brown, 1987, p. 123). Sotho women perform poetic narratives (seoeleoele) through songs and dance in shebeens and bars (Copland, 1978, pp. 13–24, in Brown, 1981, p. 123). South African oral poetry remembers that of Caribbean Creole, with its relationship to music and its use of a continuum of language registers, including the Standard English of documents and the vernacular. As is also the case with Caribbean and Aboriginal poetry, orality and performance represent versions of identity, passing on histories and myths. Latterly, the use of oral performance poetry by such as Mzwakhe Mbuli has made a contribution to political activism. Some other African performance poets theorise the connection between the language of the people, identity and place and have developed the idea of nation language, influenced by Louise Bennett.

Further reading

Bennett, Louise, *Dialect Verse* (Kingston: Pioneer Press, 1942).

Bennett, Louise, *Jamaica Dialect Poems* (Kingston: Gleaner, 1948).

Bennett, Louise, *Jamaica Labrish* (Kingston: Sangsters Book Stores, 1966).

Bennett, Louise, *Anansi and Miss Lou* and *Selected Poems* (Kingston: Sangsters Book Stores, 1982).

Brathwaite, Edward Kamau, *Rights of Passage* (Oxford: Oxford University Press, 1967).

Brathwaite, Edward Kamau, *Mask* (Oxford: Oxford University Press, 1968).

Brathwaite, Edward Kamau, *Islands* (1969) (compiled as *The Arrivants*, 1973, Oxford: Oxford University Press).

Brathwaite, Edward Kamau, *History of the Voice* (London: New Beacon, 1984).

Brown, Stewart, 'Dub Poetry: Selling Out', in *Poetry Wales*, vol. 22, no. 2 (1987).

Copland, G. (1978), in Lloyd Brown (ed.), *Women Writers in Black Africa* (Westport, Conn.: Greenwood Press, 1981).

Nationhood and women's equality

For women, an economically subordinated position often adds to that of being a postcolonial subject. Issues of nationhood and women's equality are sometimes in alignment and sometimes at odds in writing by women. Gayatri Chakravorty Spivak's work (1988) problematises women's silenced position as historically subordinated subjects. Discussing a Rani entrusted, upon the death of her husband the Rajah, with the care of both her son and brother, Spivak points out the silencing and absence, the disempowerment which this woman suffers. She was caught between an imperialist and a patriarchal discourse. If she chose sati (to burn as a widow), she was seen as conforming to patriarchal discourse, but if she refused it, she was conforming to the discourse of the English rulers who condemned the practice. There is no space for her, nothing she can be or speak.

Many postcolonial women writers (for example, Anita Desai and Ruth Prabvar Jhabvala) try to find a language for such a subordinated subject. They react against both male-dominated language and colonial languages and representations. As Susheila Nasta notes in her introduction to *Motherlands*:

> The post-colonial woman writer is not only involved in making herself heard, in changing the architecture of male-centred ideologies and languages, or in discovering new forms and language to express her experience, she has also to subvert and demythologise indigenous male writing and traditions which seek to label her. An entrapping cycle begins to emerge
>
> Nasta, 1991, p. xv.

There are many issues concerning women's equality and political changes as postcolonial practices develop. One of these is whether and in what ways struggles for political and national equality run alongside or take precedence over struggles for gender equality. The relationship between the development of a nation state and that of women is interesting and problematic. The struggle between two adversaries – India and Britain – was played out and seemingly settled with Partition, the division of India, a new Nation State and the 1951 General Election based on universal suffrage. However, the ideal of establishing a new national unity meant that oppositional forces had to be contained. Elements of the controlling powers hitherto seen as repressive were redefined as supportive of the State, custodian of people's welfare and champion of economic development and industry. Development action concentrated on the state rather than people, and in the face of this zealous unity, pleas for improvement and equality were sidelined. This situation is similar to the rise of national identity amongst African Americans and Caribbean peoples, where politically the nation or state is considered more crucial than the rights of women, sidelining women's efforts at equality. So, in the instance of India, the equality of women and people of different castes was considered of less importance than the achievement of independence.

Helen Carr indicates ways in which sexual and colonial domination are paralleled:

> In the language of colonialism, non-Europeans occupy the same symbolic space as women. Both are seen as part of nature, not culture, and with the same ambivalence: either they are ripe for government, passive, child-like, unsophisticated, needing leadership and guidance, described always in terms of lack – no initiative, no intellectual powers, no perseverance; or on the other hand, they are outside society, dangerous, treacherous, emotionally inconsistent, wild, threatening, fickle, sexually aberrant, irrational . . . lascivious, disruptive, evil, unpredictable.
>
> Carr, 1985, p. 50.

When Black sexuality, particularly of women, becomes related to the deviant Otherised, so all Black women become labelled primitive: 'the primitive is black, and the qualities of blackness, or at least of the black female, are those of the prostitute' (Carr, 1985, p. 248; in Gilman, 1992, pp. 223–261). Susheila Nasta comments on the development of Black and Asian women's 'feminism' in the context of more general struggles for racial equality:

> In countries with a history of colonialism, women's quest for emancipation, self-identity and fulfilment can be seen to represent a traitorous act, a betrayal not simply of traditional codes of practice and belief but of the wider struggle for liberation and nationalism. Does to be 'feminist' therefore involve a further displacement or reflect an implicit adherence to another form of cultural imperialism?
>
> Nasta, 1991, p. xv.

For work by men and women alike, it is vitally important to avoid merely transient popularity, instead ensuring that the merits of work by postcolonial writers and their contribution to literature is never ignored again. Black British poet, novelist, short story writer and critic Barbara Burford points to the short-livedness of earlier recognition of writing by

Black writers in both the Négritude movement in France and the Harlem Renaissance in the US: 'This time we must not allow ourselves to be turned on and off, and we must not disappear quietly, when it is decided that we as an 'issue' have suffered from over exposure' (Burford, 1987, p. 37). The short-lived celebration of emergent or previously silenced postcolonial writers is often a product of seeing them as only dealing with writing about the pain of being enslaved, silenced, ignored and undermined in the past. Such temporary critical response brings many writers to a wider public but does rather suggest the critics and readers value their work for the novelty of this rage, recuperated history and new perspectives, while for many, the ability to read, write, have some economic stability and recognise a legacy in previous writers and artists has been immensely liberating. Perhaps often the first task is to speak out against inequality. However, writers want to be recognised in their own right for the variety of ways in which they write, and for the issues they want to write about. Black British poet, critic and artist Maud Sulter assesses the need for naming, identity and learning a variety of languages in which to be heard in order both to express women's lives and perceptions and to teach children about the postcolonial experiences, one way of ensuring they are passed on and developed. Maud Sulter's highly politicised writing appears in *Spare Rib* (1985) and *Watchers and Seekers* (1987). In *Zabat: Poetics of a Family Tree* (1989) she calls upon daughters and women generally:

> Daughters, she cries
> learn the tongues
> of this world voices
> teach the children
> of their wonder
> love as only a woman can
> take up the pen, the brush
> explosive,
> and name
> yes name
> yourself
> black
> women
> zami
> proud
> name yourself
> never forget
> our herstory
> ('Full Cycle' Sulter, 1989)

Reassessing her position as a Black woman, a postcolonial feminist, in what is perceived as a hostile society, she also writes:

> as a black woman
> every act is a personal act
> every act is a political act
> ('As a Black Woman', Sulter, 1985, in Wisker, 2000, p. 284)

Jackie Kay writes of adoption (hers and others) in *Adoption Papers* (1991), taking three voices and using three typefaces, and looks also at warrior roles, loving, sexuality, child-rearing, AIDS, artificial insemination and a host of other issues close to the interests of postcolonial feminists but not necessarily directly related to race and equality. In 'Mummy and Donor and Deirdre' (1991, p. 54), the son of a lesbian couple records his first school experiences of making friends and sharing snacks, dealing with the questions of others about his family structure, while the parallel adult voice in the poem considers the difficulty of deciding who goes to parents' evenings when there is a same-sex couple and other parents might feel awkward:

> I said I don't have a daddy;
> I have a mummy and a donor and a Deirdre
> ('Mummy and Donor and Deirdre', Kay, 1991)

Postcolonial feminists write about a range of issues to do with ethnicity and speaking out, but also everyday issues to do with women's lives, mothering, motherhood and relationships.

See also   *Contexts:* Postcolonialism and feminism; *Texts:* Apartheid: anti-apartheid political writing: Head, Bessie (1937–86), Gender and convention: African women's novels: Emecheta, Buchi; *Criticism:* Spivak, Gayatri Chakravorty (1942–).

Further reading

Burford, Barbara, 'The Landscapes Painted on the Inside of My Skin', in *Spare Rib*, no. 179, July 1987.

Carr, Helen, 'Woman/Indian, the American: and his Others', in F. Barker, P. Hulme, M. Iverson and D. Loxley (eds), *Europe and its Others*, vol. 2 (Colchester: University of Essex Press, 1985).

Kay, Jackie, 'Mummy and Donor and Deirdre', in *Adoption Papers* (Newcastle: Bloodaxe Books, 1991).

Mirza, Heidi Safia (ed.), *Black British Feminism* (London: Routledge, 1997).

Nasta, Susheila (ed.), 'Introduction' in *Motherlands: Black Women's Writing from Africa, the Caribbean and South Asia* (London: The Women's Press, 1991).

Spivak, Gayatri Chakravorty, 'Can the Subaltern Speak?', in C. Nelson and L. Grossberg (eds), *Marxism and the Interpretation of Culture* (London: Macmillan, 1988).

Sulter, Maud, *Zabat: Poetics of a Family Tree* (London: Sheba, 1989).

New literatures in English

This term, originating in the 1970s and 80s, is sometimes used as an alternative to Commonwealth Literature and Postcolonial Literature. It avoids the all-embracing and homogenising term Commonwealth, which includes writing from very different cultural and geographical origins, and suggests something fresh, stressing the emergent nature of writing after colonisation, as well as writing in English from other parts of the world not associated with the Commonwealth or Britain's historical colonialism. A difficulty with the term arises from the use of the word new, which in suggesting the emergent somewhat overlooks literary forms, for instance Canadian First Nation writers, or Australian, Indian and South African writing, which has been produced since at least the nineteenth century.

See also *Criticism:* Commonwealth literature.

Further reading

Ashcroft, Bill, Gareth Griffiths and Helen Tiffin, *Post-Colonial Studies: The Key Concepts* (London: Routledge, 2000).

New views of indigenous people – questioning the record

Indigenous people, or the first recorded people of a land, have actually often been erased, misunderstood and silenced by imperial and postcolonial rule. Latterly, many indigenous writers have chosen to rediscover and reunite myths, to claim a history and a legacy in their own terms. Some write in semi-fictionalised autobiography or similar forms that testify to their lives and experiences, using a mixture of realism and historically based writing and also experimental and postmodernist work. The representation of indigenous people has, not surprisingly, often focused both on past ills and on the importance, worth and individuality of the indigenous people, their myths and worldviews. But writers do not necessarily always paint an idyllic picture, and latterly many indigenous writers have exposed tensions, contradictions, the downside of their lives and those of their people. So Jully Sipolo, Samoan poet, writes of wife beating while she also supports national identity. Patricia Grace, Maori writer, exposes the homelessness and excessive drinking of some Maori, while also indicating how they realign themselves with family and history, and Alan Duff, more controversially, emphasises the disempowerment of those who were once great Maori warriors but have, under colonisation, been disenfranchised and in the late twentieth/twenty-first century, like many Native Americans and Australian Aboriginals, find themselves not only marginalised but also increasingly violent.

Alan Duff's hard-hitting and provocative *Once Were Warriors* (1990) depicts contemporary Maori as people with pent-up anger and frustrations, exploding in domestic violence, abuse and fighting. While they demand the lands which were stolen from them historically, they are now seen as having neither voice nor opportunity for the action that would have befitted historical warriors. Alan Duff was born in New Zealand of a Maori mother and a Pakeha father. His point of view and the response his work has evoked – from both inside and outside the Pacific – contributes to any discussion on who can speak with authority for those occupying the margins, those who have been colonised and made invisible. In the Introduction to *Maori: The Crisis and the Challenge* (1993) he describes his reasons for writing *Once Were Warriors* (1990):

> I wrote it in outrage. And quite possibly, in relief that I had not turned out as just another of the losers I portrayed. I wrote because I've lived that life – because I've been on the same path of aimlessness, self destruction and the destruction of others who have been innocents. I wrote . . . as my best protest against that which very nearly destroyed me. And because I want to attempt an understanding of the process that makes for this dreadful disparity between the two races, Pakeha and Maori . . . I write . . . from a history of past failures, past wretchedness, that gives me the qualifications of first hand experience.
>
> Duff, 1993, pp. xii–xiii.

In an interview in *Meanjin* in 1993, Duff tells the interviewer that he spent time in a boy's home during his youth and had an uneducated, volatile Maori mother and an educated, rational white European father (Thompson, 1994, p. 6).

Following the publication of *Once Were Warriors,* Duff was accused of being anti-Maori (Jones, 1993, p. 5) because it exposes Maori family and community wastage and violence. He was seen as attacking 'the very core of Maori culture' (Thompson 1994, p. 406). When the University of Hawaii's Press chose the work in 1994 for inclusion in *Talanoa,* its indigenous Pacific literature series, Vilsoni Hereniko, series editor, suggested Duff had written from a politically incorrect position of blaming the Maori for their own suffering and ruined lives, portraying the hard-drinking, wife-beating Maori father, Jake Heke, as part of a self-inflicted downward spiral of behaviour, instead of identifying the blame as belonging to the Pakeha (white ex colonials). He is often considered to be dogmatic, aggressive and misrepresenting Maori culture. However, it can also be argued that he wants to recognise that some of the blame could lie with Maori behaviour and then to reconnect Maori culture to a more harmonious, uninhibited, forward-looking future. This he does in the novel through the character of Beth, a reflective woman who begins the cultural healing process in Pine Block while simultaneously recognising exactly what Duff is accused of, that is, she calls herself a 'traitor in her own midst' for noticing the violence and destructive Maori lifestyle. Portrayed as ironic, she also represents Duff's ironising of the destructive lifestyles of Maori society.

In his depiction of a woman as the voice for criticisms and change, Duff also challenges traditional Maori views, specifically that women have no right to speak in community affairs. Actually Duff shows the possibility of change, re-viewing lives seen initially as futile. The film version of *Once Were Warriors* met with immense critical acclaim when it appeared in 1994. Maori are all the key players – directed by Lee Tamahori, based on a screenplay by Riwia Brown, it featured Rena Owen and Temuera Morrison, won numerous awards and has been distributed in more than 35 countries worldwide.

Another hard-hitting Maori writer, Keri Hulme, winner of the Booker Prize for her controversial *The Bone People* (1986), has been challenged by New Zealand Pakeha (white) writer C.K. Stead, firstly for only having *one* Maori great-grandparent and secondly for producing inauthentic, self-conscious characters. Another major issue in the novel, which is postmodern in form, circular and lyrical, is that of child abuse (violence) at its core, which does not show Maori in a good light.

Aboriginal writer Ruby Langford exposes the marginalisation of Aboriginal people, traditionally both living and working in close relationship to the land, and then confined on the outskirts of cities in often substandard accommodation, lacking a sense of community. In *Don't Take Your Love to Town* (1988), Ruby undergoes hardship as a mender of fences in the outback, but the family has worse experiences in the urban home where one of Ruby's sons is continually being arrested and imprisoned for disorderly behaviour, something suffered internationally by Black youths more frequently than whites. Other indigenous writers such as First Nation Canadians write of similar hardships, but also revalue myths and link with family histories, themes also common in Maori, Aboriginal and Pacific Islander work.

Further reading

Duff, Alan, *Once Were Warriors* (New York: Vintage, 1990).
Duff, Alan, *Maori: The Crisis and the Challenge* (Auckland: HarperCollins, 1993).
Hulme, K., *The Bone People* (New York: Penguin, 1986).
Thompson, Christina, 'In whose face? An essay on the work of Alan Duff', in *Contemporary Pacific* 6(2) (1994).

Oral-based literature, oral literature

Oral literature and performance poetry have been privileged forms in many lands which have subsequently come under colonial and imperial rule, and one way of maintaining a historical thread with an oral past and refusing to have it obliterated by the imposed scribal or written versions brought by the coloniser, which fix the moment and the expression, is to recuperate the oral in performance poetry and storytelling, and to bring it into the public domain. What is offered by orally based forms of literature, oral storytelling, oral literature and performance poetry is a challenging way of expressing people's thoughts, perceptions, perspectives and feelings and a way which sidesteps or intercepts the heavily scripted tradition of the intellectual and educated West.

Performance poetry is matched in terms of fictionalised narrative by oral literature and life writing, which each use both the language of everyday people and their lives, engaging with roots, in Africa for the most part, but also the many oral cultures which preceded and now continue alongside scribal cultures. They bring to a wider audience both the stories, parables and imaginative representations of everyday people, and the ways in which they express them in their language, fundamentally connected to the experiences themselves, little if at all transformed and so translated for an outside audience. In the African tradition, griots or griottes passed on news and wisdom in tribal cultures in the village, as oral storytellers also do in Aboriginal Australian communities. In many cases, those who have chosen to take the stories of their people to a wider audience through publication have more recently chosen to write down the oral literature, inevitably fixing its usually more dynamic form in the process.

Oral literature and oral storytelling forms are potentially powerful political expressions, inflected by culture and also gender. For silenced colonial Others, and women in particular (doubly silenced as secondary citizens), expression in literary form, first oral and then much later written, has offered a powerful opportunity.

Initially, colonised Black and Asian peoples' expression was largely oral and rooted in storytelling. Some Black and Asian or mixed culture oral storytellers, who deliberately relate to and revive these oral forms, include Indian writers Anita Desai, Jumpna Lahiri and Arundhati Roy, African Americans Toni Morrison and Alice Walker, and Jamaican Erna Brodber. They use oral literary forms to underpin their work, emphasising the circular, repetitive, revisiting moment, so that no stories are fixed and there are several perspectives available; meaning is shared and negotiated. This essentially dialogic expression has been characterised by the theorist Mikhail Bakhtin as offering liberating possibilities to expression as a dynamic form, and by post-Freudian French feminist Julia Kristeva as politically charged, a return to 'the semiotic' or the kind of expression produced between mother and child before the imposition of the mostly male-dominated language of 'the symbolic', latterly largely written forms, publishable, but because so, acceptable and conforming, also curtailed and controlled. Based on this theorising, oral literature is not just the expressions of the ordinary folk culture and the ordinary folk but a deliberate choice of many writers who wish to engage with the lives of their culture, with everyday people, and in so doing to make statements about the different worldviews and expressions which local language, culturally inflected myths, parables and interpretations enable by using oral forms. Achebe's *Things Fall Apart* (1958), for example, utilises oral storytelling formats in the very opening tale of mythical strength and determination, which establishes Okonkwo's right of place in relation to great warriors.

Oral forms, passed on through the generations, were used for communication, news spreading and the development of cultural cohesion in terms of the passing on of moral behaviour and beliefs. Those who used oral forms also used the language of the people from which they sprang and in so doing engaged with cultural difference, location, differing perspectives and the ways in which expression and the construction of folk tales and myths lead to tales that actually reflect on the culture producing them. There might be, for instance, stories of birth, death and love in most societies, but the particular differences for a specific society influence responses readers might have. Readers' interpretations are often deeply embedded in the ways in which a discourse or language form articulates the perspectives and expression of that culture. Achebe points out the power of the culturally located and engaged storyteller, amongst which the oral storyteller is a prime mover:

> storytellers are a threat. They threaten all champions of control, they frighten the usurpers of the right-to-freedom of the human spirit – in state, in church or mosque, in party congress, in the university or wherever.
>
> Chinua Achebe, 1988, p. 30.

One of the most powerful and engaging, and most prolific forms of oral storytelling and expression emerges in performance poetry, largely from the Caribbean; Black British poets Linton Kwesi Johnson, Merle Collins, Jean Binta Breeze, Amryl Johnson and Valerie Bloom, among others, have made an impact, but performance poetry of differing kinds has emerged also in Aboriginal and Maori cultures, and from African Hausa women writers. In South Africa, protests against Apartheid and its economic inequality influenced, amongst others, Mzwakhe Mbuli and worker-poet Nise Malange.

In situations where written literatures are the acceptable forms of expression and act as ways of identifying and continuing the values of specific cultures, oral literature has been characterised as less complex perhaps, more transient, very local and unable to travel beyond the specific context; it has also been seen as ephemeral in so far as oral histories and oral literatures historically tended to be overtaken, usurped and destroyed by written cultures, which were seen by the colonial and imperialist powers as more sophisticated. Latterly, the significance of an oral literature and the vernacular has reasserted itself. Ugandan Okot p'Bitek and Wole Soyinka are among African writers using oral-based forms. In aboriginal cultures, such as First Nation Canada, Australian Aboriginal and many African cultures, a host of oral performers recite, repeat and revitalise the myths of their cultural history. In response to this tradition, published writers include the oral tradition in the myths they use, the language expression of specific characters or in a deliberate adoption of oral characteristics, such as the circling narrative with repetitive motifs used by Anita Desai in *Clear Light of Day* (1980) and the revisiting of stories from different viewpoints seen in Aboriginal writer Sally Morgan's *My Place* (1987). Many writers recognise the importance of myths, local legends and oral epics as ways of reviving their historical past, of recognising the passing on of values and explanations of natural and cultural events. Oral forms and myths repeated by them have revitalised the exploration and expression of culture and cultural identity for a range of writers.

Wole Soyinka uses oral tales in writing of the Yoruba God Ogun, creator and destroyer. Ama Ata Aidoo's play *Anowa* (1965) uses Ananse storytime, which is based on oral storytelling of trickster tales and the supernatural, as does Merle Collins' Caribbean-based performance poem 'Crick Crack Monkey' (1985). Here, Collins extends the characteristics of the trickster motif (lying, deceiving, cheeky character who nevertheless reveals hidden truths) to highlight the ways in which colonialist-biased lies about history have usurped others' versions, notably those of enslaved African and disenfranchised women. In 'Crick Crack

Monkey', the rotten tree branch cracks and nearly drops the monkey each time a lie is repeated. Lies which colonised people have been sold include the 'discovery' of America and the freeing of slaves. America had indigenous people before its discovery, and slaves need never have been freed if they had not first been enslaved. Each twisting of history is exposed in the poem. In her oral performance, Merle Collins invites audience participation in answering and repeating, drawing everyone into the shared experience.

Performance poets introduce audiences to the culture, language and creative forms of their own contexts. Caribbean performance poet Valerie Bloom ensures that her audience learn Jamaican expressions and are aware of the different lexical forms of Jamaican English, such as Dread talk (Rastafarian-influenced Jamaican English) before she performs, to enable them to enter her world and her expression, retrieving power by so doing. Recuperating and moving on with oral literature helps redefine and revalue literary forms of expression, as well as giving voice to cultures and people who have not been widely heard. Performance poetry has also been used to radical ends by the American Beat poets in the 1950s and 60s, by Allen Ginsberg, Lawrence Ferlinghetti, Amiri Baraka and others, and its politicised influence permeates the work of Caribbean Black British poet Linton Kwesi Johnson and Valerie Bloom in different ways.

Notions both of dialogue and polyphony emerge in discussion of the way oral-based forms can express differing views, as speaking in tongues resembling a mother tongue becomes a positive, politicised statement of expression. Bakhtin in *The Dialogic Imagination* (1981) argues that the novel sets up dialogues between many voices (polyphony) and points of view, allowing debate and negotiation. African American Toni Morrison's *Beloved* (1987) offers the language of the community, and of storytelling, set against that limiting, oppressive, dehumanising language of the slavecatcher, setting up such a polyphony in this dialogic novel. Elleke Boehmer (1995, p. 206) finds such polyphony and dialogue in many postcolonial texts where formerly marginalised peoples speak. Jamaica Kinkaid's *Annie John* (1985) is a case in point, as is Erna Brodber's *Myal* (1988). Different perspectives on women's behaviour are also negotiated in writing by African and South African women, notably Flora Nwapa, Buchi Emecheta and Bessie Head, and in Indian writing, particularly that of Arundhati Roy, where often the community view is set in relation to that of an individual, and in some instances that of those traditionally in power, whether chiefs, soldiers, family or colonisers. Sara Suleri identifies two issues in examining Black and Asian women's writing in particular, the first connoting polyphony, multivocality and plurality of voices, and the second signifying intimate, private, inspired utterances. Through their intimacy with the discourses of others, Black and Asian women writers are particularly adept at weaving into their work complementary discourses that seek both to adjudicate competing claims and witness common concerns. They negotiate varied positions for women's relationships to oppression and to speaking out. Suleri comments that 'in their works, black women writers have encoded oppression as a discursive dilemma, that is, their works have consistently raised the problem of the black woman's relationship to power and discourse' (Suleri, 1992, in Chrisman and Williams, 1993, p. 263).

Hierarchical power relations between colonised and coloniser, often Black and white, and the gendered inflection of those relations between (white) men and (Black) women, are reproduced in the patriarchal discourse of master texts or colonial texts that can be seen as conspiring to exclude both colonised indigenous forms and female 'minor' forms from the (scribal, written) literary canon. For subordinated peoples, and in particular women, making any kind of creative or critical statement is making a stand. If tradition decides to hierarchise creative forms, writers tend to write back, revaluing what has been marginalised, and for women this often involves the writing of personalised forms, semi-fictionalised autobiographies, so people such as Aboriginal writers Sally Morgan and Ruby Langford and South African writers Bessie Head and Zoë Wicomb write in forms which allow them to express perceptions. They write down oral poetry and storytelling forms, using the dialogic to negotiate the kind of debates found in communities and families: 'Feminised literary forms such as letters, diaries, and the literature of romance have had the same relationship to the 'Great Tradition' as marginalised oral texts: beyond the pale.' (Cooper, 1993, p. 7, quoting Zora Neale Hurston from *Their Eyes Were Watching God:* 'Well, you know what dey say 'uh white man and uh nigger woman is de freest thing on earth. Dey do as dey please.'). Interestingly, oral forms such as storytelling are now entering professional life as recognised ways of understanding and expressing ways of knowing and seeing. Some performance poets and oral storytellers are deliberately political, others less so, in their wish to bring to popular attention the lives of working people, of women, of colonised Others. Miss Lou is one such performer, while theorists of oral and performance poetry include Edward Kamau Brathwaite, Mervyn Morris and Carolyn Cooper.

See also *Criticism:* Nation language.

Further reading

Achebe, Chinua, 1988, p. 30, in John Thieme *Postcolonial Studies: An Essential Glossary* (London: Edward Arnold, 1989).

Bakhtin, M., *The Dialogic Imagination*, ed. Michael Holquist and trans. Carol Emerson and Michael Holquist (Austin: University of Austin Press, 1981).

Boehmer, Elleke, *Colonial & Postcolonial Literature* (Oxford: Oxford University Press, 1995).

Brodber, Erna, *Myal* (London: New Beacon Books, 1988).

Collins, Merle, *Crick Crack Monkey*, in *Because the Dawn Breaks: Poems Dedicated to the Grenadian People* (London: Women's Press, 1985).

Kinkaid, Jamaica, *Annie John* [1985] (London: Vintage, 1997).

Morrison, Toni, *Beloved* (London: Chatto & Windus, 1987).

Suleri, Sara, in Laura Chrisman and Patrick Williams (eds), *Colonial Discourse and Post-Colonial Theory* (Hemel Hempstead: Prentice-Hall, 1993).

Patriarchy and colonised women

Women can be seen to suffer a triple oppression in terms of patriarchy, the colonial powers and gendered versions of silencing and oppression. Many women writers write *about* speaking out against patriarchy's silencing and that of the coloniser, claiming their own gendered power and expression. Gayatri Chakravorty Spivak's arguments about the 'subaltern' or subordinated woman are important here.

Creativity produces a challenge in Spivak's 'Can the Subaltern Speak?' (1988), itself an answer to the subaltern studies group, which questions the consistent construction of the second class or subaltern citizen for colonised people, particularly for women. For Spivak, women are necessarily subordinated groups, whose expression cannot be other than in the language of the others who have subordinated them and so, in a sense, like Shakespeare's Caliban in *The Tempest*, they cannot speak beyond the language available (cursing or otherwise). Her point is not that the subaltern cannot speak at all but that she is constrained by having to use the discourse of the group in power. She cannot construct an experience or an act of resistance in anything other than the very language which itself casts her into a subordinated position.

However, it can be argued that evidence of postcolonial discourse itself is evidence of subalterns speaking, so postcolonial writers who speak out or express their hybrid perceptions, their alternative versions of the motherland and/or the country of residence and settlement, do speak against the dominant forms, even if they have to use those forms to do so. Whether it is possible to construct expression beyond the constraints of the available discourse, implicated as it is with colonial history and with power and gender, depends on the writer's skills of recuperation and creativity. Indian writer Desai mixes oral storytelling with postmodernist intertextuality. She uses the language (and the imagery) of the colonialists and of her own traditional background in new combinations in order to problematise the very condition of silence or mimicry attributed to the colonial subaltern female subject. In so doing, Desai mixes cultures, visions, versions, images and expressions. She also creates characters whose choices and fates represent culturally inflected debates, offering us Anamika (*Fasting Feasting*) and Miramasi (*Clear Light of Day*), each a sacrificed wife, set against Miramasi in *Fasting Feasting*, the travelling aunt and Bim in *Clear Light of Day*. Each of the latter manages to speak and act away from the limitations of both the colonial language and, for women, the traditional language and constructions which would render them worthless because they don't marry. Instead, each chooses her own way.

Much of Anita Desai's work concentrates on difficulties faced by Indian women trying to balance achievement of identity with family and caste demands. Women in Desai suffer and critique the roles assigned them in Anglo-India. Under the control of patriarchy, they need to find new voices to speak of a potential developing freedom, but for many, any such potential is negated by the constraints of family expectations, second-class citizenship and fantasies based on fictions of romantic love. Aunts are marginalised in *Clear Light of Day*, young brides burned and abused in *Fasting Feasting*, young women married off or considered worthless, and older women just considered supernumerary. However, Desai is not guilty of merely presenting us with impoverished and constrained eternal victims. Instead, she utilises insights into and motifs derived from culturally differing perspectives, from literal, literary and figurative international travelling to enable new readings of lives, world-views, constraints and opportunities. She identifies the mythologies which constrain women:

> Around (the ideal woman) exists a huge body of mythology. She is called by several names – Sita, Draupadi, Parvati, Lakshmi and so on. In each myth, she plays the role of the loyal wife, unswerving in her devotion to her lord. She is meek, docile, trusting, faithful and forgiving.
>
> Desai, 1990, pp. 14–20.

Both *Clear Light of Day* (1980) and *Fasting Feasting* (2000) explore cultural constraints and potential with a particular focus on the lives of women: those who conform to cultural norms – marriage, nurturing, romantic love – those who become victims because of their conformity to social roles, and those who can escape such constraints, not necessarily by leaving but by challenging and reinterpreting the available roles for women. Both novels focus in the main on a single family where the parents are an established, contented couple, and deal with the choices or lack of them open to their children, particularly the young women, each in relation to an aunt. *Fasting Feasting* (2000) deals with the arranging of marriages resulting in farce (Uma), and arranged marriages ending in tragedy (Anamika), while the earlier novel, *Clear Light of Day* (1980), in also dealing with marriages (Miramasi, Tara, Bim – almost), actually offers opportunities for women simply to refuse roles which would constrain and destroy their individual freedoms.

Desai negotiates criticism of the internalised worldviews, myths and systems which oppress women, offering some alternatives, occasional opportunities for recognition within the family and individual self-realisation. She shows us we bring our own versions of India, constructed from our own experiences and imaginations, a mirror in fact, to ourselves, springing from our own ignorance, stereotyping and inability to translate what we might see and experience:

> Was it not India's way of revealing the world that lay on the other side of the mirror? India flashed the mirror in your face, with a brightness and laughter as raucous as a street band. You could be blinded by it. Not if you refused to look into it, if you insisted on walking around to the back, then India stood aside, admitting you where you had not thought you could go.
>
> Desai, 1988, pp. 85–6.

In *Clear Light of Day*, Desai explores the different choices made by an Indian family during and after partition. Tara, the younger sister, left, married and lived abroad, but her husband, Bakul, who has a minor ambassadorial role, projects a honeyed, touristic version of India embodied mainly in the Taj Mahal. His sister-in law, Bim, the elder sister who remained in old Delhi, is quick to point out that only someone living *out* of the country could so conjure it up for international consumption. Initially, the household managed by Bim seems entirely archaic and stagnant. Redolent with memories, it is exemplified by the behaviour of the baby of the family, Baba, who continually plays old 1940s music on a record player left behind by the fleeing local Muslim family of Hyder Ali, whose daughter married the other brother, Raja. The latter crossed cultural boundaries in his allegiances and fled, Tara entered a diasporic existence where her own desires were secondary to the maintenance of a successful appearance (her ambassadorial marriage), and Bim and Baba remained at home – but Desai cleverly reverses this seemingly cautionary tale about stagnation: Bim has been able to choose her own life, she refused a marriage to Dr Biswas (named after Naipaul's character in *A House for Mr Biswas* [1961]) and his oppressive mother (it would indeed have been more of a marriage to the mother) and developed her caring career as a teacher.

Desai gives us a variety of versions of Indian women's lives. She notes that myths are 'the cornerstone on which the Indian family and therefore Indian society are built': they keep women 'bemused, bound hand and foot' (Desai, 1990, pp. 14–20). We would expect, then, that her treatment of the conditions and experiences of women would be no mere simplistic revelation of arranged marriages and patriarchal controls, although indeed these are also exposed and critiqued in her work. Instead, Desai celebrates new liberated ways: she looks at power and freedom, self-actualisation in context, and the ability or otherwise of women to rise above stereotypical and real social constructions. Bim in *Clear Light of Day* is Desai's example of a most successful woman and, ironically, it is Bim who stays still, does not fly off to the US but instead remains, looking after the family and the home. But it is also Bim who avoids marriage, becomes highly educated and uses this education. Desai enables some of her women characters to move out from under their subaltern, marginalised positions and find a new voice, while others remain silenced. Other writers, such as Grace Nichols in *The Fat Black Woman's Poems*, give a voice to hidden women, as does Buchi Emecheta for African women, Bessie Head for South African, and Aboriginal writers Sally Morgan and Glenyse Ward for otherwise silenced Aboriginal women.

See also *Contexts*: Postcolonialism and feminism, Independence; *Criticism*: Spivak, Gayatri Chakravorty (1942 –).

Further reading

Ashcroft, Bill, Gareth Griffiths and Helen Tiffin *Post-Colonial Studies: The Key Concepts* (London: Routledge, 2000).

Desai, Anita, *Clear Light of Day* (London: Vintage, 1980).

Spivak, Gayatri Chakravorty, 'Can the Subaltern Speak?', in C. Nelson and L. Grossberg (eds), *Marxism and the Interpretation of Culture* (London: Macmillan, 1988).

Performance poetry

Performance poetry is largely known in the forms produced by Caribbean poets and African American poets, the latter clearly influenced by the radical politics of the 1950s/60s Beat poets Allen Ginsberg,

Lawrence Ferlinghetti, Gregory Corso and Amiri Baraka (Leroi Jones). It is a key feature of racial and politicised expression internationally for its potential to politically engage audiences in large numbers and convey a message which the poem on the page, absorbed silently by an individual, cannot hope to do in the same way. Much performance poetry is overtly political, as is that by worker-poets in South Africa.

Within these performance traditions lie the powerful political poems of South African Mzwakhe Mbuli, Nise Malange and Alfred Qabala, who have performed their work to large workers' groups. A gathering of workers at the Jabulani stadium in July 1985 united workers and worker poets against oppression, expressing their desire to seize their own culture and cultural futures. They endeavour 'in Durban to build alongside our union organisations a cultural movement . . . over the last three years, choirs, dance-teams, plays, poems, written pieces are becoming important activities within the workers' struggle' (Qabala, 1986, p. 59). Performance poetry is vibrant and evolving, it changes with the audience, and involves mood, repetition and coherence. It is usually performed in an energetic way, with facial gestures punctuating each line.

Exploration of the development of Caribbean performance poetry reveals its links with the politics and expression of African-influenced history and identity at every turn. It also reveals links with the Rastafarian movement, calypso and other popular musical forms such as reggae, and in particular the music of Bob Marley. Bob Marley arguably brought Caribbean culture, Rastafarian lifestyle and belief, and reggae almost single-handedly to a large Western audience in the 1970s and 80s, and his home in Jamaica is a testimony to his status as cultural icon and inspired, energetic, creative fuser of music and poetry. Other influential performance poets include Mutabaruka and the performance and nation language poet, the late Mikey Smith (1954–83), who was stoned to death after a political rally in Kingston. Mikey Smith's *Me Cyaan Believe It* (1982) and the volume *It a Come* (1986) use nation language, the sounds of the street, such as revving motorbikes, and a highly controlled use of breath and voice to pour out dismay and anger at poverty, violence, oppression and social inequalities in Jamaica. There is rare taped footage of his powerful performance, some of which appears in the 1991 TV programme on Caribbean Black British poetry as part of the Open University's A 306 course, 'Literature in the Modern World'.

Arguably, University of the West Indies Emeritus Professor and distinguished poet Mervyn Morris (1937–) is much to be thanked for bringing Caribbean performance poets not only to the notice of Western listeners and readers, but actually to Britain to perform, and into the public gaze as critically worthy of recognition. His work is occasionally definable as performance poetry but more recognisable as sensitive comment on social, philosophical and cultural themes, such as growing up, moving on, travel, family and education, and is collected in *The Pond* (1973), *Shadowboxing* (1979) and *The Examination Centre* (1992). As spokesman and critic of Caribbean poetry, particularly performance poetry, his work has been crucial in enabling the growth of a wider audience able to appreciate the poetry beyond localised entertainment:

> If the poem in print does, however minimally, alter with the specific context of its reception, the 'performance poem' is even more difficult to fix, dependent for its meanings on the variable interaction between text, performer, audience and occasion.
>
> Morris, 1988, p. 19.

Those listening learn the stories and the words, joining in. The next stage is fame, achieved by dub poetry, reggae and rap-influenced performance poetry.

Mervyn Morris and others suggest that there can be a problem with transforming rage into entertainment and that the sophisticated performance poet's work will go beyond protest, fire and blood, concentrating on making individualised statements. Poetic expression should use rather than be carried away by the beat or the moment.

There is a difference, Mervyn Morris notes, between dub poetry (of which Linton Kwesi Johnson is considered a master) and performance poetry, where there is often a sense of chant, of different voices, of the accompaniment of body language and emphases to make the poem dramatic and varied. What characterises good performance poetry is the conjunction of word and beat, of a sense and sound of attitude, movement and atmosphere, using tags from ring games and chants, folklore and legend, myth and ironic wit. Dub poetry grew from the 1960s Jamaican dance culture and used Black Power rhetoric, Rastafarian ideals, and the language of Jamaican English. The themes are often about politics, poverty, revolution, and the point is to dub or add music into a poem.

Breeze, Jean 'Binta' (1956–)

Another great Caribbean Black British performance poet is Jean 'Binta' Breeze. Often seen as having developed oral performance forms deriving from Louise Bennett, Jean 'Binta' Breeze lives and works in both the UK and the Caribbean. Her roots are in the Rastafarian movement; she is drama trained and offers workshops on performance poetry. She has appeared on television and sees her work as being politically derived from her multiple experiences as a Black woman and single mother in an extended family and wider community. Like Merle Collins, she uses music, song, mime and dance to produce electrifying performances, and to highlight the experience of those who might never otherwise be heard – the working classes, poor women – but she also celebrates hidden histories of immigration (settling in England, missing home), following the settling of those who came on the SS Empire Windrush in 1948 and on subsequent ships to work in what they felt to be the motherland.

A particularly moving poem in her first collection, *Riddym Ravings and Other Poems* (1988), features a pregnant country woman, depressed, mentally ill, lost in the streets of Kingston, Jamaica. 'Riddym Ravings (The Mad Woman's Poem)' shows this displaced woman's oppression by a variety of others, particularly the landlord and the doctors, figures of control who would take the radio, the voices out of her head and lock her up, when these voices, although voices of mania, are her sense of identity. Jean Breeze uses the street language of everyday people to dramatise their perspectives and views. 'Hustler Skank', in particular, uses street talk, exposing arrogant male speakers. These are tightly controlled poems concentrating on recognising a woman's lot in life. Jean Breeze's poetry is powerful, vibrant, oral performance work capturing the rhythms of monologues and dialogues, the personal and the lived experiences of Caribbean people in the UK and back home.

Breeze chooses to write and perform without any of the musical accompaniments, for example reggae or calypso, chosen by male performance poets such as Linton Kwesi Johnson, but instead to re-create the lilt and rhythms, the individuality of the speech patterns and concerns of ordinary women faced with passing wisdom on to daughters, sharing lovers, and some ordinary men talking with their partners. Occasionally she sings her work, and then returns to speech. Dramatising the lives of everyday folk, Jean Breeze argues that her words are fluid, released from the mechanical rigidity of the beat and from the fixity of the page. She makes a distinction between the poet as maker and the poet as performer, as explained by Caroline Cooper of the University of the West Indies:

> For not only are the works in motion, unbroken by the beat, but the poet/performer, uncontained by the boundaries of the book, speaks face to face with an immediate audience. In the act of performatic transference, the speaker gets across the closure of the printed page.
>
> Cooper, 1993, p. 82.

Because the performance is a privileged reading of the text, each performance is original, partly fired and inspired by audience engagement and response. You can't tell how wonderful it is going to be by just reading it on the page; instead, it comes alive in the uniqueness of each performance, 'somewhat like a musical score, the poem pressed to the page encodes performance' (Cooper, 1993, p. 82). Breeze uses audio, visual and kinetic power and watching her perform is riveting.

Like Mikey Smith, Breeze uses the words and rhythms of children's play, adopting the persona, tones and speech of ordinary folk. She articulates different Jamaican and English voices and versions of English, from standard English with inflections of the biblical (in 'Spring Cleaning') to everyday street language ('Riddym Ravings', 'The Madwoman's Poem'). Moving between the values of city and countryside Jamaica, and the lives of those who live in the UK communities, she dramatises the ageing immigrant looking back on her arrival, as the young girl sent to the UK from Jamaica by her mum, now long settled in London, in *The Arrival of Brighteye* (2000). In this she brings a community of individuals to life.

Some of her work interweaves oral and scribal characteristics and sources so we can read as well as hear it, although the written language is often quite difficult to follow unless read aloud, and it is decidedly better to get hold of one of her published tapes and listen along with the written word. She mixes conversational language and tone, the repetition of speech rhythms and more formal language, moving between registers, so sometimes she will use the more colloquial 'ah' and later shift to a more formal, distanced poet's voice, using 'I'. Her poems are also about both Jamaica and Britain, everyday relationships and exchanges, meetings in the street, chatting to each other in the market, women giving each other advice, mother to daughter, friend to friend, bewailing the behaviour of men and advising cunning, and also about colonisation and the examples of arriving, settling, living and loving. In this, they reflect her everyday life and her diasporan existence, moving between at least two countries.

Performance poets produce and perform specific versions of oral-based literature in order to bring the language of ordinary people alive, and to capture the breath, rhythms and talk of everyday life. Some, such as the South Africans Mzwakhe Mbuli and Nise Malange or Caribbean Black British Linton Kwesi Johnson, have a specific political aim: they enact the culture from which their work springs, and by doing so share with a wider audience at the same time as providing another potentially marginal or silenced group with a voice. Discussions of oral literature and performance poetry engage with issues of identity, culture, heritage, discourse, power and history. Oral-literature-influenced work is wide ranging compared to the otherwise relatively canonical literary text which just uses some oral characteristics, myths and 'native' forms, such as we find in the work of Aboriginals Sally Morgan and Glenyse Ward, Indian Anita Desai, some of Nigerian Buchi Emecheta, South African Bessie Head's short stories, and the performance of Jamaican Rastafarian poet Mikey Smith, who uses street language and street sounds in a political manner in his performance.

Johnson, Linton Kwesi (1952–)

One of the great Caribbean Black British performance poets is Linton Kwesi Johnson, who frequently performs with the Dub band whose musical scores emphasise and intertwine with the rhythms of his words, the beat underscoring key points and engaging with youth (and older) culture in so doing. Coming to Britain when he was eleven, Johnson achieved a Sociology degree at Goldsmiths College, London, and first gained popularity in his 1970s concert performances, touring with Dennis Bovell's Dub band. This led to several records: *Dread Beat an' Blood* (1978, book 1975), *Bass Culture* (1980), *Tings an' Times* (1991, and book) and *LKJ A Cappella Live* (1996). Other written work includes *Inglan is a Bitch* (1980) and *Mi Revalueshanary Fren* (2002). His work, always engaged in an exposure of racism and social inequalities, appeals across culture, age and racial divisions. He was a founder member of the 'Race Today' collective, arts editor of their magazine, and produced a TV series on Jamaican music which also intertwined some of his own work. He recognises the influences of Brathwaite in his writing and performance, but his unique focus on beat and rhythm in the performance and emphasis of his lines marks him out as going beyond the dub poet, to be a spokesperson for dispossessed Black youth and someone who changed the face and sound of performance poetry and poetry more generally.

Bloom, Valerie (1956–)

Jamaican-born Valerie Bloom studied English, African and Caribbean Studies at the University of Kent, producing her first book of poetry, *Touch Mi Tell Mi*, in 1983. She has carried on the work of Caribbean performance poet Louise Bennett (Miss Lou) as folklorist, lecturer and teacher, with her performance poetry and her strategy of teaching the audience how to pronounce and use Jamaican words. Of *Touch Mi, Tell Mi* (1983) and other work, Maggie Humm comments that:

> Bloom's Black British dialect is a technical and rhythmic innovation. It is a self-conscious attempt to subvert the traditional language of

poetry and insist on a merciless difference. These poets refuse embellishment or camouflage. They are linear poets who write free and open verse which works directly from example to example to make designs upon the world.

Humm, 1991, p. 59.

Like 'Miss Lou', Bloom tends to use dramatic personae addressing other characters through dialogue and four-line rhyming stanzas. In 'Dyuh hear about?', a discussion about absence, silence and racism is initiated through the questioner asking whether there has been any reporting or word going round concerning the beatings of young Blacks, faeces through the letterboxes of Asian families and other evidence of everyday racism. That no such events ever hit the white middle-class-controlled press and media is evidence of British society's attempts to silence and obliterate large numbers of its population. Casual conversation reveals prejudice and enables the articulation of a critical view.

Johnson, Amryl (1944–2001)

Caribbean Black British writer Amryl Johnson writes poetry and prose, recording her experiences in the UK and the Caribbean, and journeying between the two. Her collection *Long Road to Nowhere* (1985) was inspired by her second trip to the Caribbean and return to the UK, which highlighted her diasporan position as someone who lives in two locations and cultures, feels influenced by and part of both, yet also feels torn between the two. She sees the flaws as well as the beauties of the Caribbean: 'The Caribbean isn't all exotic fruit, white sands and coconut palms against a blue sky. The gulf between those who have and those who do not is too blatant to be ignored' (in Johnson, 1988, p. 38). Like several other performance poets, including The Mighty Sparrow, she uses the rhythms of the calypso to explore her arrival and to celebrate recovery of her cultural origins, but she also notes poverty and artifice, a kind of performance for the tourists:

> Whitewash the face of hunger
> When all the features have been removed
> Paint on the smile, the laughing eyes
> Show the tourists what they want
> But not too close
> Behind the grinning facade are slums
> Which rob the people – of all dignity.
> ('Blowing in a Random Breeze', Johnson, 1985)

Julie Pearn says of her work: 'Amryl's earlier poems are full of a sense of bleakness and cold which is spiritual as much as physical. The British environment offers her images of thorns, dead leaves and brackish waters. These are not abstract images but reflect the hostility she feels from the society towards herself and all black people, and a general absence of love and creativity' (Pearn, 1985, p. 46).

Mbuli, Mzwakhe (1959–)

South African, Mzwakhe Mbuli's work has sometimes been compared to that of Linton Kwesi Johnson in terms of its power to evoke dispossession, its rallying call to insurgence, and its use of the spoken word and breath. Mbuli came to prominence in the late 1970s and early 1980s when his riveting performances engaged his audiences, Black and white, in a dialogue about the cruelties and inequalities of apartheid as a lived experience. Hunted himself by the police for his performances' ability to rally political fervour and unify expressions against oppression, he was jailed several times and his wife was forcibly questioned. In an interview in his video from the 1980s, he talks of always having to go in and out of the back door for fear of arrest and reprisals. He is filmed against a backdrop of chickens pacing on the arid ground and, much more terrifyingly, the brutalising attacks of soldiers, Black and white, on civilians, including children, riots in Soweto, and massacres some of which occasionally appeared in edited versions on TV screens at the time. The beat underlying his poem 'I have been accused' is staccato, emphasising the harsh movements of gunshots, tanks and jeeps as well as the beatings of Black women, young men and children by the brutal forces of Apartheid. His poems are in many ways a call to arms, so in 'The Spear Has Fallen' he urged everyone to 'pick it up', and like the Beat poets, he reels off a list of names of those who have died for the cause of equality, including white and Black, from 'yesterday it was . . . and Ruth First . . . '. Today, he suggests, it will be you unless you do something about it. Mbuli's language is also influenced by the imagery and cadences of the Bible, as in 'I have come unto', and everyday individual speech.

Malange, Nise (1960–)

Nise Malange's poetry is worker and performance poetry, and it concentrates equally on praising political colleagues who have fought for recognition of self-worth and the economic, political cause and on lamenting the suffering of children, women and families in South Africa.

In 'I, the Unemployed' she uses repetition and a call to action and unity. She dramatises, using the figure 'I', and testifies, but uses a persona or dramatic voice, and in so doing avoids the merely personal, reaching out to the experience of so many others and speaking for them:

> I am here dying of hunger
> And my country is also dying
> My children are dying too
> Look at them:
> How dull their eyes
> How slow their walk and the turning
> of their heads
> Nothing for them to eat
> Can you hear?
> They are crying.
> ('I, the Unemployed', Malange, 1986)

The suffering of children is immediate, as is her call for others to become involved and change social injustices. Her poem concentrates on sound and vision. Although fellow South African performance poet Mzwakhe Mbuli talks of arrests, on the whole many poets were somehow unscathed by their role as spokespeople, and were able to reach out and call to others to rally for change:

> For reasons that are hard to explain the poets and their writing enjoyed a form of official tolerance not accorded to any other kind of writer. This poetry became the only outlet for the increasingly grim experience of the 1960s and 1970s. For the first time literary expression in our writing took on a completely political perspective.
>
> Ngcobo, 1989, p. xiv.

See also *Contexts:* Apartheid, Diasporan writers, 'SS Empire Windrush'; *Criticism:* Colonial discourse, Nation language.

Further reading

Bloom, Valerie, *Touch Mi, Tell Mi* (London: Bogle-L'Ouverture, 1983).

Breeze, Jean 'Binta', 'Hustler Skank', 'Riddym Ravings (The Mad Woman's Poem)', in Mervyn Morris (ed.), *Riddym Ravings and Other Poems* (London: Race Today, 1988).

Breeze, Jean 'Binta', *Spring Cleaning: Poems* (London: Virago, 1992).

Breeze, Jean 'Binta', *The Arrival of Brighteye* (Northumberland: Bloodaxe Books, 2000).

Humm, Maggie, *Border Traffic* (Manchester: Manchester University Press, 1991).

Johnson, Amryl, 'Blowing in a Random Breeze' in *Long Road to Nowhere* (London: Virago, 1985).

Johnson, Amryl, *Let It Be Told* (London: Virago Press, 1988).

Johnson, Linton Kwesi, *Dread Beat an' Blood* (London: Bogle-L'Ouverture, 1975).

Johnson, Linton Kwesi, *Inglan is a Bitch* (London: Race Today, 1980).

Johnson, Linton Kwesi, *Tings an' Times* (Northumberland: Bloodaxe Books, 1991).

Johnson, Linton Kwesi, *Mi Revalueshanary Fren* (London: Penguin, 2002).

Malange, Nise, 'I, the Unemployed', in Ari Sitas (ed.), *Black Mamba Rising: South African Worker Poets in Struggle* (Durban: Culture and Working Life Publications, 1986).

Mbuli, Mzwakhe, 'The Spear Has Fallen', in *Change is Pain* (Cambridge, MA: Rounder Records, 1992).

Morris, Mervyn, *The Pond* (London: New Beacon, 1973).

Morris, Mervyn, *Shadowboxing* (London: New Beacon, 1979).

Ngcobo, Lauretta, introduction to Miriam Tlali's *Soweto Stories* (London, Pandora Press, 1989).

Pearn, Julie, *Poetry in the Caribbean* (London: Hodder & Stoughton, 1985).

Qabala A., in Ari Sitas (ed.), *Black Mamba Rising: South African Worker Poets in Struggle* (Durban: Worker Resistance and Culture Publications, 1986).

Smith, Mikey, *Me Cyaan Believe It* (1982), in *It a Come: Poems by Michael Smith* (London: Race Today, 1986).

Postcolonial Gothic

The process of mutual postcolonial abjection is, I suppose, one that confronts us every day in the ambiguous form of a series of uncanny returns.

(Punter, 2000, p. vi)

As David Punter has pointed out, there is a distinct similarity and conjunction between the postcolonial and the Gothic, each focusing on the return of the repressed, on alternative hidden histories and versions of the present. For both coloniser and colonised the experience of disgust, rejection or abjection (otherising) takes place. Postcolonial landscapes are filled with the histories and spirits of a past of colonialism, the silencing of alternative visions, and hidden violence. The Gothic offers the potential to explore how such tales and hidden histories can represent themselves. A well-known postcolonial and Gothic text is *The Piano* (1993), written and filmed by Jane Campion. The story, set in New Zealand, both reproduces and questions northern hemisphere, European notions of the other side of the world, that is, Australia or New Zealand, as places to exploit and to export what does not fit in, whether convicts or mute piano-playing single mothers (in the case of *The Piano*). Australasia has been considered a Gothic location and beneath Europe physically on the globe, which positions Europe on top. Australasia is seen as terra nullius, whose primitive peoples, if any, were to be managed or killed off by colonisers. Images of undergrowth, artistic endeavour, silencing and being able to articulate are all both Gothic and postcolonial in so far as they show expression leaking out from conformity and insisting on different perspectives.

For African American and Afro Caribbean women, for example, repression and silencing is deeply affected by gender as well as by race. The imaginative worlds and lived realities, past and present, are made tangible and realised in the work of African American and Afro Caribbean postcolonial women who are fantasy Gothic horror writers, who produce a hybrid form, transformed into the speculative to suggest that life might be imagined otherwise.

Canadian/Trinidadian postcolonial Gothic fantasy writer Nalo Hopkinson establishes the use of a radical power, emphasising the groundbreaking nature of contemporary postcolonial Gothic fictions by women, whether horror, fabulist, sci-fi or speculative – whichever label fits (and most often the works are new mixes of at least two of these). Postcolonial Gothic writers, far from remaining with life-writing and testimony, can be seen to utilise and further develop the characteristics of the literary Gothic (and horror) using death/life boundaries – duppies, zombies, and especially the figure of the vampire and other werebeasts or 'skin folk'. Nalo Hopkinson, Caribbean Olive Senior, Australian/ Malaysian Beth Yahp, Malaysian Tash Aw and Singaporean Catherine Lim explore racism, the history and legacy of slavery, sexism, and women's roles and conditioning; to do this they use location and African, Caribbean, Chinese and Malaysian myths. They often move between horror and speculative endings which posit alternative ways of being and living in new racial and gendered harmonies.

African American Toni Morrison urges a recognition of the importance of expressing the imaginative life as well as the factually historical, and this valuing of the imaginative life of which the Gothic is an element equally underpins postcolonial Gothic writing by others. Morrison seeks:

> the tone in which I could blend acceptance of the supernatural and a profound rootedness in the real time at the same time with neither taking precedence over the other. It is indicative of the cosmology, the way in which Black people looked at the world, we are a very practical people, very down to earth, even shrewd people. But within that practicality we also accepted what I suppose could be called superstition and magic, which is another way of knowing things. But to blend these two works together at the same time was enhancing not limiting. And some of those things were 'discredited' only because Black people were 'discredited' therefore what they knew was 'discredited'. And also because the press upward towards social mobility would

mean to get as far away from that kind of knowledge as possible. That kind of knowledge has a very strong place in my world.

Morrison, 1985, p. 342.

Meanwhile, Tananarive Due, an African American Gothic writer, points out the difficulty of writing in the Gothic and fantasy/horror: 'I needed to address my fear that I would not be respected if I wrote about the supernatural' (Tananarive Due in interview, 17 March 2002, at www.tananarivedue.com/interview.htm accessed 19/09/02).

A history of critical myopia regarding such work by Black writers is being somewhat redressed by two recent collections which extend the timeline for Gothic horror and speculative writing into earlier twentieth century work from greats like W.E.B. Du Bois and George Schuyler, and which expand the sense of a geographic spread. These are Sheree Renee Thomas (ed.), *Dark Matter: A Century of Speculative Fiction from the African Diaspora*, and Nalo Hopkinson (ed.), *Whispers from the Cotton Tree Roots: Caribbean Fabulist Fiction*, which includes among its women writers Marcia Douglas, Jamaica Kincaid, Olive Senior, Opal Palmer Adisa and Pamela Mordecai.

These authors write postcolonial Gothic against a critical context which exposes fact-based texts built on life writing and recuperation of history so that their work, along with that of Salman Rushdie and Malaysian Tash Aw, is quite radical in its mix of genres and refutation of more conventional versions of postcolonial writing. Cultures infused with the supernatural and the spiritual, maintained across centuries and continents by oral storytelling and song, coded myths and tales, frequently express themselves in the Gothic, the speculative, the fantastic, the magical and, like all good Gothic, provide spellbinding insights into people's ways of constructing and imagining their lives, coping with and moving beyond constraints and denials. Gothic writing by postcolonial writers is written against attempts to shackle the imagination and it offers powerful, liberating, celebratory cultural critiques of, in particular, gendered and cultured oppression.

Postcolonial history is a common feature in postcolonial Gothic. The meeting of myths, fables, fantasies between cultures, and the building on African-originated or derived myths, equally with Western-derived myths, is a feature of the work of Nalo Hopkinson, who rewrites the fairytales 'Bluebeard' and 'The Snow Queen' with Afro Caribbean/Canadian characters, settings, culture and fears, and relocates African Anansi stories in Canadian city life. Gothic tropes of split selves, werebeasts and liminal spaces address the concerns of American/Canadian daily life.

David Punter (*Postcolonial Imaginings*, 2000) talks of voids, ghosts and hauntings as a necessary product of the postcolonial. The horrors of rape, murder, dispossession of indigenous peoples and slavery are the silenced memories of those who suffered gaps in their histories, of ancestors who died and whose stories cannot be or have not been discovered and passed on. There are also hauntings of the colonisers. They, implicated directly or not, carry the secrets, the whisperings of ghosts, part of that great oppressive history of transportation, uprooting from home, and abuse. Colonisers were, he argues, like capitalist vampires, taking the ownership of their own bodies from the people they enslaved and from those whose lands they stole, emptied or developed. Colonisers were also psychic vampires, removing history from people, taking away their own sense of ontological identity and security, so the tales of the dispossessed were not written down.

However, the tales of those colonised *were* passed on in folk tale and oral storytelling from mother to child and throughout communities. Contemporary postcolonial writers, descendants of colonised and colonisers, slaves and slave owners, transported and transporters, distant and close beneficiaries and victims, now seek to free these hauntings and ghostings and to let the ghosts speak, the spectres emerge, so that there can be some reconfiguration of the history and the value system we all share, some eventual laying of that ghost of the abused, unjust past which haunts all of us. This manifesto of freeing, embodying, seeking out and exorcising is the trajectory of African American Toni Morrison's *Beloved* (1987), and it is equally the trajectory of many postcolonial hauntings by other postcolonial Gothic writers.

Punter's arguments identify postcolonial imaginings as 'fictions of a new world order':

as the great globalising project of modernity, which has its own controlling relationship to the postcolonial, rolls on, one of its more curious current effects is that, perhaps against expectations we live increasingly in a world of ghosts, spirits, phantoms.

Punter, 2000, p. 61.

Postcolonial Gothic horror writers use the characteristics of the genre to reclaim the past, to revision a lived present and to speculate upon a future. Several of their tales deal with issues of difference, acceptance and Otherising, springing from a need to address and redress racism and effectively reinstate the histories and myths of a largely hidden ancestry. For some, this takes the form of developing complex, mythic histories located in Africa, for others recuperating the use of African and

Caribbean myths which explain behaviours in the world, selfishness, greed, inability to achieve maturity, power and oppression, seeking out and asserting identity, nurturing, solidarity and so on. These critiques and explorations take the form of a variety of myths, some of which are specifically Caribbean or African, like Crick Crack Monkey and the Lagahoo (Trinidadian myth), while others are transferable across cultures.

Jamaican born, Toronto resident Nalo Hopkinson was influenced by Caribbean speculative fiction writer Olive Senior. Hopkinson's own imaginative history is a fusion of the Caribbean/African folk tale and the British-influenced classroom and culture, interpreted anew with Anansi story time, and the 'Crick Crack Monkey' story of the monkey cracking the bough it climbs when lies are heard. These are tales of power and usurpation, of devil women who sap the strength of young men, tales to accompany, explain and warn against the dangers of deceit as one crosses the threshold between childhood and adulthood, and tales which explain the draining of energies of children by those of the older generation and of the older generation drained by the younger. Soucouyants are favourites of hers, vampires who enter the windows of children's rooms and drain the child. Nalo Hopkinson defines her own work:

> The stories invoke a sense of fable. Sometimes they are fantastical, sometimes absurd, satirical, magical, or allegorical. Northern science fiction and fantasy come out of a rational and skeptical approach to the world: That which cannot be explained must be proven to exist, either through scientific method or independent corroboration. But the Caribbean, much like the rest of the world, tends to have a different worldview: The irrational, the inexplicable, and the mysterious exist side by side each with the daily events of life. Questioning the irrational overmuch is unlikely to yield a rational answer, and may prove dangerous. Best instead to find ways to incorporate both the logical and the illogical to one's approach to the world, because you never know when life will just drop you down in that hole, into a ceiba space where none of the rules you know operate.
>
> Hopkinson, 2000, pp. xii–xiii.

Hopkinson is concerned with reclaiming, reinscribing and reconfiguring the geographies of place, the Caribbean and Canada, and the geographies of the mind linked with place and history. In her original mix of Caribbean folk legend, Canadian setting and the contemporary, she brings an entirely new critical, Gothic, speculative fiction to the fore. For Hopkinson it provides an opportunity to see life, people, things and events from very different viewpoints; it enables different sets of rules and values to govern a therefore quite differently felt world. In this respect, it is a perfect fit for the engaged African/Afro-Caribbean, American and postcolonial critical venture, because it destabilises fixed complacencies and recognises of the validity and equal worth of difference, both currently realised and potential. Writing within speculative Gothic horror, Hopkinson knows she is confronting racial stereotyping.

In 'A Habit of Waste' (1999) Hopkinson explores how a young Black woman, attracted and convinced by versions of a culturally acceptable body shape, would feel in a totally differently shaped white body, after a 'body swap'. The myth of the soucouyant, a vampiric figure, is used to explore how a young woman, Jacky Connor, comes to terms with her ageing and flies nightly to vampirise the young, especially babies, but is taught social values by her grandmother who refuses Jacky re-entry into her sloughed human skin, peppers it, and points out to her that this is *very* antisocial behaviour.

Another example of the postcolonial literary Gothic is Jamaican Erna Brodber's powerful novel of spirit theft, *Myal* (1988), which characterises as zombies those colonised people who have been disabled from expressing their own histories and writing their own stories. Ella, mixed-race child and talented singer, has her history literally taken from her by the relatively well-meaning Selwyn Langley, who marries her, puts her home village and herself onstage and believes this celebrates Ella's life. In fact, he creates a 'coon show'; the lead woman is blonde and blue-eyed. He totally misunderstands the landscapes and community, representing the fruits and flowers at once in a pantomime performance of someone else's interpretation of Jamaican life and values. And he further debilitates Ella by avoiding a sexual relationship, which would feed his fear of miscegenation – mixed-race children. Eugenics underlie hospitable, patronising colonial attitudes. Ella becomes a teacher but is horrified at the propagandist children's book *Mr Joe's Farm*, which she is expected to teach and which indicates allegorically that colonised or enslaved people can escape only temporarily but can never be really free and self-governing. All succumb, at least temporarily, to a paralysis due to the internalisation of the colonial oppressors' view of themselves as second rate and voiceless. For another character, Anita, spirit theft is gendered, sexual, her spirit is stolen by Mass Levy. Released from a form of zombieism gives these people clarity of self-image and a movement towards a voice. Then the non-linear, non-chronological, magical and realist, mixed voice of *Myal* is influenced by the celebratory Jamaican-African-influenced religion, Myalism, and in its mix of postmodern form and circular, oral, mythic form it is an exciting hybrid novel.

In postcolonial Gothic, ghosts and were-creatures express a suppressed past and enable empowering versions of the future. Malaysian/Australian Beth Yahp in the novel *The Crocodile Fury* (1992), reimagines a history of colonial theft and disempowerment in Malaya, where the radical energies are embodied in a creature of the seas and jungle, a mythical crocodile, who has also been a bandit who invokes ostensibly secure situations and identities. The protagonist is a young girl growing up in her mother's workplace, a convent, once owned by a rich plantation owner and importer to whom her grandmother was a bond-maid. The girl's gradual imaginative alignment with the radical crocodile figure parallels the twisting sea beast into whom the rich plantation owner's stolen indigenous lover turns to seek escape. Local myth is used to indict colonial history and reimagine other futures. The Gothic strategies are used to leak dreams, alternative selves and metamorphosis into the story and events.

Malaysian Tash Aw, author of *The Harmony Silk Factory* (2005), mixes recuperation of hidden historical moments with postcolonial Gothic. His novel uncovers a moment in the history of Malaya just before the Japanese invasion during World War II. Focusing on a notorious, wealthy local man, Johnny Lim, through the eyes of his son Jasper, who retells Lim's history and his own, Tash Aw uses postmodernist and oral storytelling strategies to indicate that there are *always* multiple versions of history – many lies, facades, pretences and hidden horrors. Johnny Lim, seeminly a kind of local Mafia type, a self-made man, an entrepreneurial shop owner who murdered the opposition – that is, the first shop owners – also fabricates versions of himself which make him out to be a legendary hero. Lim's own version of his life is more charitable. At the same time, Tash Aw systematically unpicks Jasper's certainty that 'Death erases all traces, all memories of lives that once existed'.

Johnny Lim was, according to Jasper whom he raised, a thief, opium smuggler and black marketeer, murderer and 'monster'. While Jasper's version of his father is hateful, what he shows and what Lim tells us is actually/apparently different. Born in 1920 and surviving the contradictions of life during the Japanese invasion of British-administered Malaya in the 1940s, Johnny was the inarticulate but entrepreneurial son of southern Chinese immigrants. He survives bullying in a British-run tin mine with racist, incompetent white managers – 'No. 1 Sir' and the equally obnoxious Nos 2, 3, 4 and 5. Johnny trains himself to be a genius with machinery, moving out of mining into salesmanship, close in time to the suspicious death of No. 2 Sir. When he becomes an equally brilliant salesman at the Tiger Brand Trading Company, Tiger Tan, the kindly owner, also dies, without warning, after a suspicious fire. Johnny is a romantic, seems gentle, but is surrounded with the dubious mystery of the deaths.

Snow, Johnny's lovely wife, narrates the second part of the novel in a diary, and the third part is narrated by Peter Wormwood, elegant, sexually ambivalent English aesthete. Parts two and three describe, from different viewpoints, a belated honeymoon trip that Snow and Johnny take with Peter Wormwood and Mamoru Kunichika, a highly intelligent, artistic Japanese professor, actually a military man, a vanguard of the invasion. They sail to a mythical/real place where realities and relationships become increasingly confused. The Seven Maiden Islands are mistily visible, shifting in time, space and prime location for a melodramatic affair and suspicious death.

In the final section of the book, the opera-loving, elderly Wormwood, living in an Oriental old people's home, depicts an innocent Johnny who plans to plant a paradisal garden in his honour. Multiple unreliable narrators emphasise the difficulty of pinning down history, identity and experience. Versions slip through cracks in the tales of each narrator and myths and lies predominate.

The Harmony Silk Factory itself is a front for gangster dealings. Harmony is only fabricated and the stories are held together delicately, like skeins of silk, as Snow describes music – 'the notes seemed to weave in and out of each other, no longer discernible, like a length of shot silk held up close to your eyes'. Wormwood also describes shifting, indecipherable memories like 'sensations that the years have layered on top of the initial emptiness, like sheet after sheet of silk covering a bare table'. The central question about identity and history is actually more *who* Jasper's father was, a mystery similar to the versions of politically charged histories of the period.

Postcolonial Gothic writers utilise and further develop the characteristics and strategies of the literary Gothic and horror, taking these into new territory and new realms of experience. They explore racism, suppressed history, the legacy of slavery, apartheid, the subcultures of gangstas, drug dealers, sexism and women's roles and conditioning. In so doing, they use spaces somewhat new to Gothic fictions: Africa, the Caribbean, Malaysia and underground Canada. And they deploy familiar Gothic figures, tropes and spaces, such as the death/life boundary, inflecting them with African American, Afro Caribbean, Chinese and Malaysian traditions and concerns. Figures and tropes include the duppy, the zombie, the vampire and other were-creatures or, as Hopkinson calls them, 'skin folk'. Metamorphosis and the exposure of contradictory selves are common. They offer the opportunity to imagine that our world might be otherwise. Their mix of horror and speculative fiction enables the construction and projection of alternative futures and alternative future relationships. Their work suggests that the insights provided by horror, the postcolonial and the Gothic can lead to an exorcism of restrictive and repressed histories and imaginative versions, and to a construction of a new set of relationships, in the case of much of these works, relationships which recognise and value equality and difference. As such, then, they exemplify what David Punter has described as 'becoming' characteristics, significant in postcolonial texts, moving beyond lament and indictment to alternative possibilities. They are also hybrids in terms of genre, moving constructively beyond indictment and guilt to new unities.

Storytelling is powerful. For women and those whose ancestors have suffered under colonialism and imperialism, postcolonial Gothic storytelling is a valuable link with a denied and silenced past, a way of evoking the imaginary in the present, and a way of looking forward to other futures, and to creating them.

See also *Criticism*: Postcolonial Gothic.

Further reading

Hopkinson, Nalo (ed.), *Whispers from the Cotton Tree Roots: Caribbean Fabulist Fiction* (Montpelier, VT: Invisible Cities Press, 2000).

Hopkinson, Nalo, in conversation with Alondra Nelson, *Social Texts*, Vol. 71 (Durham, North Carolina: Duke University Press, 2002).

Morrison, Toni, 'Rootedness: The Ancestor as Foundation', in in Mari Evans (ed.), *Black Women Writers* (London/Sydney: Pluto Press, 1985).

Morrison, Toni, *Beloved* (London: Chatto and Windus, 1987).

Thomas, Sheree Renee (ed.), *Dark Matter: A Century of Speculative Fiction from the African Diaspora* (New York: Warner Aspect, 2000).

Yahp, Beth, *The Crocodile Fury* (Sidney: Angus & Robertson, 1992).

Postcolonialism and feminism

There are many issues in common between postcolonialism and feminism, most particularly the interest of both approaches in rediscovering hidden work by people considered subordinate in the past, in concerns with finding and valuing difference and different voices, and in recognising and empowering expression about lives and perspectives previously erased or marginalised. Feminist critical theory recuperated the work of silenced Other, Black and Asian women, its basis in challenging the notion of subordinate positions and Otherising being fundamentally similar to that basis within postcolonial criticism. However, Westernised feminism has been criticised (see Parmar and Amos, 1997; Mohanty 1988; Davis, 1982) by Black and Asian feminists as being too dependent upon the comfortable economic position of white women in the US and UK, and too liable to ignore the very different social, cultural and material economic positions of the diversity of Black and Asian women. In short, Westernised feminism's focus has been seen as oppressed, silencing, sometimes even racist.

See also *Contexts*: Postcolonialism and Feminism.

Further reading

Mohanty, Chandra Talpade, 'Under Western Eyes: Feminist Scholarship and Colonial Discourse', in *Feminist Review*, 30 (Autumn) (1988).

Parmar, Pratibha and Valerie Amos, 'Challenging Imperial Feminism', in Heidi Safia Mirza (ed.), *Black British Feminism* (London: Routledge, 1997).

Postcolonial settler writing

Settlers are people who have literally settled into another country, although the term initially suggested they settled something empty or disruptive. In the former settler colonies such as Australia, New Zealand, South Africa and Canada, the period of decolonisation represented a time of growing cultural self-assertion and national self-consciousness, what George Woodcock, the founding editor of *Canadian Literature* (1959), called 'the rising up of national pride' ('Possessing the Land', 1977). Except for Ireland and the US, the predominantly white settler nations did not take up the weapons of political resistance and there was little if any anti-colonial struggle or fight for independence. But Australian, New Zealand, South Africa and Canadian writers also gradually sought to shake off and change the relationship of colonial dependency. They debated and still debate issues of national identity or the lack of it, about the nature of belonging and of being considered as local or native in what was actually originally perceived as alien land. Many settler writers have chosen to rewrite history from their own perspectives, seeking identity as other than British in their work.

Settler colonials often saw themselves as cultural migrants, who had inherited ill-fitting values and attitudes belonging to an older or Other world. Although they reviewed and maintained the education, religion, law and fashion of 'back home', they increasingly challenged and recuperated the presence of the lands from which they and their forefathers came. Thomas Keneally once remarked, 'All the books we read were full of trees we had never seen', 'Australians are educated to be exiles'.

Settling new lands, colonial writers who became settlers write of hardships endured, the surprising newness of the landscape, the culture, the perceived hostility of both landscape and indigenous peoples, and the difficulties of adjusting and making the new place their own. In postcolonial writing, settler writing is revisited, so in the work of Canadian Margaret Atwood, the journals of the settler Susannah Moodie reappear in *Alias Grace* (1996), which rewrites a period of Canadian history when life was harsh and poor and Irish immigrants entered service in richer households. Atwood's text, with its postmodernist, postcolonial twisting and turning narratives and shifting versions of reality and truth, highlights ways in which all forms of response to and recording of a particular moment in history could mislead, betray or misrepresent lived experience. Through the narrative point of view of Grace Marks, a convicted murderess whose testimony never reveals either guilt or innocence, Atwood recognises the ways in which tales of colonial imperialism are constructed from fragments of journals, articles, newspapers, testimonies – all as constructed as is Grace herself when interviewed by Freudian-influenced psychoanalyst Simon Jordan. We can only unpick the fragments, putting them together into new stories. But the task is a worthy one, especially as so much about the misrepresentation of stories of all kinds is exposed en route, histories both large-scale and individual, and constructed from fragments and interpretations, influenced by the background, reading practices and perspectives of teller and listener.

Early settler women's writing in Canada, Australia, New Zealand and indeed traveller writing from across the colonies, such as Cyprus and the near and middle east, is often largely in the form of diaries, letters, memoirs and journals, recording the hardships of life in strange inhospitable surroundings, in some cases in the bush. Accounts of women's experiences in Australia, for instance, such as those by Kay Daniels and Mary Murnane (*Uphill All the Way*, 1980), help build up and recuperate a picture of women's lives. Early settlers wrote fictionalised and autobiographical writing. Some women left their diaries, amongst them convicts – for example Margaret Catchpole, twice sentenced to death for horse stealing, Eliza Brown, Georgiana Molloy and Rachel Henning – and women pioneers – such as Elizabeth Macarthur, who testified to hardships in the wool colony. Accounts of hardships in early colonial life in Canada and Australia are remarkably similar. Other forms of women's writing fell into a more nineteenth-century romance tradition, engaging issues of women's work and independence, and these include Elizabeth Murray's *Ella Norman Or a Woman's Perils* (1864), one of many novels dealing with the perils of drunken men and women's vulnerability in the late nineteenth and early twentieth century.

The first Australian woman's novel was by Anna Maria Bun, *The Guardian* (1838), followed by Catherine Spence's *Clara Morrison* (1854). Barbara Baynton's *Bush Studies* (1902) was a series of short stories using realism to record abuse, racism, sexism and callousness. These early pioneer writers are not postcolonial but the critics who have recuperated their work are employing a traditional postcolonial writing tradition of discovering radical voices which both began to portray those hidden histories and to question the established complacencies and orthodoxies of colonial, imperial or settler ways of life – the radical edge creeping in in a period before that of the postcolonial.

Drusilla Modjeska's *Exiles at Home: Australian Women Writers 1925–45* (1981) and *A Time to Write* by Kay Ferrers (1984) discuss work by Miles Franklin, Flora Eldershaw, Marjorie Barnard, Eleanor Dark, Katherine Susannah Pritchard, Jean Devanny and the critic Nettie Palmer, all of whom, as settler writers, problematised a complacent view of living in Australia and New Zealand, thereby/thus beginning to undermine colonial complacencies. Pritchard and Devanny were committed communists. Pritchard wrote *Coonardoo* (1929), dealing with a relationship between an Aboriginal girl and a white station owner, whose son she bears. Jean Devanny's *Sugar Heaven* (1926) focuses on terrible cane-cutting working conditions, while *The Butcher Shop* (1926) looks at New Zealand country life.

More recently, Australian novelist Peter Carey has repositioned settler writing and rewritten settler history. *Oscar and Lucinda* (1988) tracks the lives of the two protagonists through gambling and travel, depicting the fragile and troubled importation of the old colony's ways into that of the new, using the vehicle of a glass church which Oscar steers upstream. Carey's *True History of the Kelly Gang* (2001) and *Jack Maggs* (1997) also rewrite fictional and real aspects of history. Ned Kelly was a notorious outlaw, while Jack Maggs is the figure Magwitch, the convict in Charles Dickens' *Great Expectations* (1861), who is transported to Australia, makes a future, but cannot question the notions of what it means to be an English gentleman, even though it is these hypotheses which led to his poverty. Settler writers' work suggests that readers need to ask in what ways it challenges colonial voices and presents new versions of identity and place.

See also   *Contexts*: Settler Societies.

Further reading

Atwood, Margaret, *Alias Grace* (London: QPD, 1996).

Modjeska, Drusilla, *Exiles at Home: Australian Women Writers 1925–45* (Sydney: Angus & Robertson, 1981).

Recuperating and rewriting history

For those who move on from imperial and/or colonial rule, there are several key themes and several forms of expression which emerge in literature and oral literature and which offer the opportunity to rewrite, write anew and express the writers' own now postcolonial experiences. One of the key themes is that of rewriting and recuperating histories which have been erased, hidden, silenced or just completely overlooked in the Enlightenment trajectory which cast colonial and imperial rulers, European for the most part, as progressive and developed, and those they ruled as primitive, secondary, in need of development and control, their histories to be subsumed beneath histories of those in power, their perspectives similarly overlooked. Two key early figures who emerge in the rewriting and recuperation of hidden histories are Chinua Achebe, the Nigerian writer of novels, short stories and criticism, and Jean Rhys, white Dominican-born novelist and short story writer. Each develops their versions of rewritten histories through using literary echoes, inter-textuality and recognition of the ways in which literature represented, misrepresented or erased the perspectives of colonised peoples, whether indigenous, immigrated, transported or settled.

Mitchison, Naomi (1897–1999)

Early in the twentieth century, Naomi Mitchison rewrites versions of history. Rephrasing W.H. Auden's 'history of the defeated must say alas but cannot help or pardon', Naomi Mitchison's Vercingetorix, the defeated Gallic chief in her story 'Vercingetorix and Others' (1924, p. 85), says, 'The conquered is always forgotten'. Mitchison is known for her versions of myths (*The Corn King and the Spring Queen*, 1931) and her politically charged historical fantasies or historical, culturally sensitive recuperations of ancient times, particularly Caesar's Gallic wars in, for example, *The Conquered* (1923) and *Cloud Cuckoo Land* (1925). She had learned, through her boys' school education and early reading of Kipling, great author of the British imperial age, to use allegories as interventions on the history of her time. Her work offers a sustained attempt to remember the conquered. By focalising her narratives through the eyes of outsiders, slaves, children, women and colonised peoples, she offers a view from beneath which undermines and rewrites the histories of imperialist Rome and Greece; those, through a form of a '"classical education" offered by the public school system, underpinned Britain's own ideologies of empire' (Wallace, 2005).

Rhys, Jean (1890–1979)

Jean Rhys' novel *The Wide Sargasso Sea* (1966) also rewrites history and does so by rewriting a foundation text, Charlotte Brontë's *Jane Eyre* (1847), in which Bertha Mason, Creole heiress, madwoman in the attic, is portrayed as the dark alter ego of quiet, straightlaced governess Jane, and representative of the hidden colonial history of imperial Britain. The novel is for many readers the first postcolonial text they encounter and the issues it raises are central to postcolonial literature more generally. Jean Rhys was a colonial in terms of her history but postcolonial in her attitudes and writing strategies.

Jean Rhys was born on Dominica in 1890 and moved to Britain when she was 16. Her father was Welsh and her mother's family were historically linked to the Caribbean history of plantation and slavery, as they had been based there throughout the nineteenth century and had once owned slaves. Jean Rhys' relationship with those whose ancestors were slaves, the white plantation-owning class and those among whom she lived a bohemian existence in Britain, was confused by this mixed background. Confusion led to a sense of displacement which appeared mostly in her earlier works in the 1930s, and then latterly informed her great work, *The Wide Sargasso Sea* (1966). As a Dominican-born white woman she never considered herself fully British, but her position as part of the Caribbean contribution to Britain's historical imperial wealth and hidden histories enabled her to reveal such histories in the Caribbean and in Britain, where she was an uneasy immigrant with an unusual perspective.

Jane Eyre is seen as an indication of repressed sexuality and the cultural labelling of women's striving for identity as hysteria. By demonising Bertha, the Creole heiress, as a madwoman who nearly brings down Rochester's home and is a threat to Jane, she replays the ways in which colonial history was silent about the origins of British wealth. Silence and denial hid nineteenth-century guilt over the history of slavery, which underpinned much of the wealth of individual Victorians and the grand buildings of British cities: Liverpool, Hull and Bristol among others. Bertha has come to stand for a construction and re-creation of Other, women's sexuality as abject, and those from countries other than Britain as exotic, frightening, abject Other (different, disgusting and rejected). Through using the twin perspectives of Rochester and Antoinette (latterly Bertha), Rhys can express some of the problematic characteristics of the imperial and colonial period, such as the marginalisation of the second son who must seek his fortune abroad and marry a woman from another country, somewhat transporting Bertha's sexual energies, then taming their products (see McLintock's *Imperial Leather*,

1995). This Rochester in *Wide Sargasso Sea* finds Antoinette/Bertha's ways as exotic, dangerous and worrying as her location. But most of all, Rhys dramatises the sense of alienation, denial, silencing and marginalisation of Antoinette herself, whose inherited madness as a mixed race Creole heiress is triggered and dangerously nurtured by her uprooting to the dark enclosed spaces of the northern hemisphere and Victorian Britain.

In some respects, Rhys' own two positions were similar to that of Bertha Mason/Antoinette Cosby. Bertha's father is Jonas Mason, a planter merchant, and member of the colonising community in Jamaica. Both Bertha's mother and Rhys' mother were Creoles; both Bertha and Rhys left the Caribbean for England as young women. By foregrounding Antoinette/Bertha's story, Rhys establishes her perspective and position, giving other silenced, colonial voices the opportunity to be heard by placing Bertha centre-stage. Given her historical location, Bertha cannot achieve selfhood and awareness but must emerge a victim of cultural disempowerment. However, the rewritten narrative, Rhys' version of *Jane Eyre*, gives an insider exploration of Antoinette/Bertha's view, one view produced by colonised peoples, literally enabling readers to re-read history and cultural expression through the lens of the marginalised, disempowered, maddened and silenced Other.

Achebe, Chinua (1930–)

Considered the finest, groundbreaking African novelist (sub Saharan) of his generation, Nigerian born and university educated, Achebe became Professor of Literature at the Nigerian university in Nsukka and editor both of *Okike*, an African journal of new writing, and of the Heinemann African Writers series. Following a serious car accident in 1990 he moved to the US, becoming professor at Bard College, New York. Like African American Toni Morrison, Achebe is concerned to recuperate a very different African version or versions of the past, which avoid the Westernised interpretations of African activities, rituals and behaviours as primitive. He notes that he wishes to 'teach my relatives that their past – with all of its imperfections – was not one long night of savagery from which the first Europeans acting on God's behalf, delivered them' (Achebe, 1988). His trilogy deals with different moments of African history's relationship with Europeans and Westernisation. *Things Fall Apart* (1958) is set in 1888 following the Berlin congress, which formulated an imperial 'scramble for Africa'. Okonkwo, a warrior of the old kind, is dangerously outdated because his tribe's ways are changing, as the missionaries and European transport law and ways are arriving, discrediting and undermining the ways of his people. *Arrow of God*

(1964) is set in the 1920s, when England was introducing a system of indirect rule in Iboland, while *No Longer at Ease* (1960) focuses on the post-independence 1960 days. Later novels *A Man for the People* (1966) and *Anthills of the Savannah* (1987) depict new colonial systems and state corruption, and incorporate criticisms of the political situation. These outspoken works and words earned Achebe threats. In all these texts, Achebe is at pains to retrieve historical moments from the point of view of African, specifically Ibo, people.

Levy, Andrea (1956–)
Andrea Levy is a child of the 'SS Empire Windrush' generation, the daughter of one of the pioneers who sailed from Jamaica to England on the SS Empire Windrush in 1948. Her father and later her mother came to Britain in 1948 in search of a better life. For the British-born Levy this meant that she grew up Black in a very white England. This experience has given her a particular perspective on the country of her birth – neither feeling totally part of the society nor a total outsider.

In her novel *Small Island* (2004) she uses this perspective and examines the experiences of her father's generation, who returned to Britain after being in the forces during the Second World War. Hers is a very balanced and sensitive tale, both the story of the Jamaicans who came looking for a new life in the Mother Country, and the experience of the white society which they entered. It suggests the misleading expectations, the adjustments and problems faced by English people, among whom those Jamaicans came to live. The experience of immigration changes everyone's lives and in *Small Island* Andrea Levy examines the conflicts of two cultures thrown together after a terrible war and also the kindness and strength which people can show so that we can go on to create a better future together. *Small Island* was the winner of the Orange Prize for Fiction, the Whitbread Novel Award and the Commonwealth Writer's Prize.

Thiong'o, Ngugi Wa (1938–)
A Grain of Wheat (1967) tackles biased history and rewrites the stories of the Kenyan Mau Mau insurrections and guerrilla activities of the 1950s from the inside. Informed by a grounding in political economics and his own brand of Marxism, Thiong'o analyses the cultural imperialism of colonialism:

> Colonialism imposed its control of the social production of wealth through military conquest and subsequent political dictatorship. But its most important area of domination was the mental universe of the

colonized, the control, through culture, of how people perceived themselves and their relation to the world.

Thiong'o in Childs and Williams, 1997, p. 61.

Thiong'o's collection of essays, *Decolonising the Mind* (1986), focuses much argument in postcolonial studies on the issues of altering the mindset of colonised peoples, re- placing, restoring, in Thiong'o's case, European with African culture, literature and education. Crucially, Thiong'o argues both for decolonisation and decentralisation, shifting the centralised structures of power and expression controlled by Western or national beliefs, expressions and culture. Thus in his collection of essays, *Moving the Centre* (1993), he argues that humanism, a love of diverse humanity, is more important than being rigidly naturalistic, that is, supporting only those from the same origins and location as yourself.

Rewriting history is something African American writer Toni Morrison also does and her arguments are that silenced and absent peoples need to look back through history and re-place their ancestors and their history in order to develop a sense of identity and legacy.

See also *Contexts:* Postcolonial discourse, Rewriting history, SS Empire Windrush; *Criticism:* Nation language.

Further reading

Achebe, Chinua, *No Longer at Ease* (London: Heinemann, 1960).

Achebe, Chinua, *Arrow of God* (London: Heinemann, 1964).

Achebe, Chinua, *A Man for the People* (London: Heinemann, 1966).

Achebe, Chinua, *Anthills of the Savannah* (London: Heinemann, 1987).

Achebe, Chinua (1988) in John Thieme, *Postcolonial Studies: An Essential Glossary,* (London: Edward Arnold, 1989).

Bronte, Charlotte, *Jane Eyre* [1847] ed. and intro. Margaret Smith (Oxford and New York: Oxford University Press, 1998).

Gilbert, Sandra M. and Gubar, Susan, *The Madwoman in the Attic* (New Haven, CT: Yale University Press, 1979).

Levy, Andrea, *Small Island* (London: Hodder Headline, 2004).

McLintock, Anne, *Imperial Leather: Race, Gender and Sexuality in the Colonial Context* (London: Routledge, 1995).

Mitchison, Naomi, *The Conquered* (London: Jonathan Cape, 1923).

Mitchison, Naomi, 'Vercingetorix and Others' in *When the Bough Breaks and Other Stories* (London: Cape, 1924, 1927).

Mitchison, Naomi, *Cloud Cuckoo Land* (London: Jonathan Cape, 1925).

Mitchison, Naomi, *The Corn King and the Spring Queen* (London: Jonathan Cape, 1931).

Rhys, Jean, *The Wide Sargasso Sea* (Harmondsworth: Penguin, 1966).

Thiong'o, Ngugi Wa, *A Grain of Wheat* (London: Heinemann, 1967).

Thiong'o, Ngugi Wa, *Decolonising the Mind* (London: Heinemann, 1986).

Thiong'o, Ngugi Wa, *Moving the Centre* (London: Heinemann 1993).

Thiong'o, Ngugi Wa, in Peter Childs and Patrick Williams (eds), *An Introduction to Post-Colonial Theory* (Hemel Hempstead: Prentice-Hall, 1997).

Wallace, Diana, *The Woman's Historical Novel: British Women Writers, 1900–2000* (New York and Basingstoke: Palgrave Macmillan, 2005).

Semi-fictionalised autobiography

Semi-fictionalised autobiography and life writing are powerful forms of rediscovering hidden histories in postcolonial societies, as South African Betty Govinden notes: 'Telling our stories, using the 'self as subject', shows the intersection between the individual and the larger forces of our history. In telling our stories we attempt to understand both intellectually and emotionally.' (Govinden, 1995, pp. 70–183). In testimonies of the past and reclamations of the individual voice through semi-fictionalised autobiography, writers of South Africa give power and voice both to their personal lives and to the changing, shaping identity of South Africa itself. Writing directly from personal experience and testifying has a history in African American slave narratives, such as Harriet Jacobs' *Incidents in the Life of a Slave Girl* (1861) and latterly the many part, semi-fictionalised autobiography of contemporary African American writer Maya Angelou. Writers, particularly women, from Australian Aboriginal groups and South Africa have developed life writing and semi-fictionalised autobiography to emphasise this truth of their histories. The entry on Aboriginal writing explores several Aboriginal versions, while this entry looks mostly at South African examples.

For people silenced and dispossessed, writing back against that silence often involves the crucial need to explore and express history and, most importantly, the self. Semi-fictionalised autobiography and life writing have been particular favourites of many women writers in response to the double experience of silencing, the subaltern position of being female as well as a colonised Other. Using this form, writers can both explore parts of their own life and also distance themselves through the fictional elements which help others identify similar experiences. It is more than a diary or autobiography; it is shaped and reflected on. In this respect, African American Maya Angelou can be seen as an example, where she explores her childhood in a Southern state which still lynched young Black men on a regular basis and where the local dentist would rather stick his hand in a dog's mouth than in her own, because of her colour. The stories are based on remembering herstory, the growing self, culture and truths now selectively formed into narratives and testi-monies to lives of both suffering and gradual self-assertion.

We can also find work by numerous South African women, such as Farida Karodia and Zoë Wicomb who were enabled to produce life writing, perhaps a less fictionalised form of testimony of their lives than Angelou's. Sally Morgan, Glenyse Ward and several other Aboriginal women testify to their lives, coming to terms, in Morgan's case, with her Aboriginal heritage, which was hidden from her by her mother (*My Place,* 1987) and in Glenyse Ward's case, her tale of being brought up on a Mission away from her family, and taught to be a domestic servant. The highly complex, literary Janet Frame's experimental modernist/postmodernist *An Angel at My Table* (1984) recounts her upbringing, breakdowns and breakthroughs in a novel which is a mixture of the autobiographical and the fictional. Similarly, South African Bessie Head in *A Question of Power* (1974) uses the semi-fictionalised character of Elizabeth to explore her own breakdown.

The pain of enforced removals and enforced establishments of tempo-rary living spaces is a very destructive influence on women's lives. Attempting to bring up families, with the dangers and deprivations of dispossession and transience, and the conflicts between the values of the town and the rural village, are subjects explored and dramatised by Bessie Head, Miriam Tlali, Zoë Wicomb, Gcina Mhlope, Ingrid de Kok and others, including the writers of COSAW (the Congress of South African Writers) collective, whose work appears in *Like a House on Fire: Contemporary Women's Writing from South Africa* (1994). But even these transient living spaces, through being inhabited by people, have become communities whose existence enables a sense of identity to develop. In the apartheid period, a community developed which engendered revolt and direct political action.

The creative human spirit, under pressure, identifies with and occu-pies space unrecognised as nurturing by others, an example of which is explored by Gcina Mhlope in her short story 'The Toilet' (1987). She liter-ally wrote in the confined but enabling dry, secure space of a Johannesburg toilet:

> I was really lucky to have found that toilet because the winter was very cold. Not that it was any warmer in there but once I'd closed the door it used to be a little less windy. Also the toilet was very small – the walls were wonderfully close to me – it felt like it was made to fit me. I enjoyed that kind of privacy.
>
> Mhlope, 1987, p. 3.

Under stress and denial, her creative spirit finds unusual spaces and ways in which to express itself.

Zoë Wicomb's 'A Clearing in the Bush' (1987) is a semi-fictionalised, autobiography-based short story featuring Frieda, Wicomb's protagonist, first a young girl then a student, who falls in love with a young white man. The larger story sequence itself, *You Can't Get Lost in Cape Town* (1987) combines personal testimony with the creativity and shape of fictional form in order to speak to, from and about a community from the life of an individual. In 'A Clearing in the Bush' Frieda is studying Thomas Hardy's *Tess of the D'Urbervilles*, and like Ruby Langford's mixing of English Romantic and local poetry, and the view from her school window, she interprets her own situation and context as if in Hardy's novel, and the novel in terms of her experience and location:

> Wessex spread like a well-used map before me, worn and dim along the fold-lines... The scuffed greenstrop is the chase where God knows what happened. Seduced, my notes say. Can you be seduced by someone you hate? Can trees gnarled with age whisper ancient ecstasies and wave of darkness in dark lap until the flesh melts? I do, of course, not know of these matters, but shudder for Tess.
>
> Wicomb, 1987, p. 41.

Both Tess and Frieda consider a clearing in the bush which betrayed Tess, while for Frieda the landscapes of the coloniser fill her imagination, contrasting with her own surroundings, in which 'blue gum trees, and behind them the bush stretches for miles across the Cape Flats. Bushes, I imagine, that send out wayward limbs to weave into the tangled undergrowth, for I have never left the concrete paths of the campus' (p. 41). Frieda's university correspondence notes provide a reading of the novel which is in disagreement with her own (Tess was raped, not 'seduced'). She is to explore her own reading and experience, but this is denied by the concrete rigidity of the university campus paths and paths of reading she must trace to conform and pass exams. Her experience is denied as an African woman in her own country. She is as restricted in experience as Tess, with whom she identifies, though ironically Hardy's novel is British, one of the colonial powers affecting a legacy of inequality and exclusion.

In 'A Clearing in the Bush', Wicomb engages with political dimensions, the collusion and rejection of the values of apartheid in an academic environment, and political and social dimensions of class and origin. The protagonist, Frieda, is studying literature but finds her views on *Tess of the D'Urbervilles* undermined in the academic system. She is meant not to respond as a Black woman to the abusive elements of the text, but to merely repeat the accepted readings passed on by her teachers. Another character, Tamieta, a working-class African cook, not a student, is unaware of the student boycott of the memorial service for Vervoerd, the architect of apartheid. Because a worker, Tamieta is not informed; she attends, and then feels she is an interloper:

> Tamieta had no idea that the ceremony was for white people only. Oh, what should she do, and the shame of it flames in her chest. Wait until she is told to leave? Or pick up the bag of working clothes she has just tucked under her chair and stagger off?
>
> Wicomb, 1987, p. 57.

Underpaid and overworked, she is isolated from the intellectual community of the university because of class and economic position rather than colour. More subtle, then, is her awkward position. She is vulnerable in the clearing (of the title), a space used in other contexts for protests, or to suggest clearing away dead ways and beliefs, clearing out and moving on. The 'clearing in the bush' is both the university (an intellectual clearing for students) and the space in which the university holds Vervoerd's remembrance service. There are gender/cultural/political/economic dimensions to this clearing and this tale, including the effective silencing of the student narrator's response to the novel she studies.

In another story the protagonist, Frieda, seeks an abortion as the union between her and her white lover is discredited in South Africa. Experiences of the intersection of race and gender fill Wicomb's short stories, which interweave different perspectives, constructing a dialogic relation between different versions of life in South Africa. In 'Behind the Bougainvillea' (1987), Frieda, returning from her UK education, must wait in the yard at the white doctor's because of her colour, which relegates her to a secondary position. Wicomb revalues women's roles and reclaims language from the coloniser who would sanitise it of local references:

> Her writing bears witness to a history of deprivation, yet it also suggests ways which subvert this history: not through political or economic change but through a psychological change whose major route is in re-writing representation.
>
> Driver, 1996, p. 45.

Aboriginal writers and writers from South Africa, among others, use semi-fictionalised autobiography to establish a sense of their own identity and history, and to show up how they have been marginalised and silenced. Some use the strengths of oral storytelling, some of realist testifying (Morgan, Narrogin, Langford), while others (Head, Wicomb, Coetzee) mix the telling of their own histories in semi-fictionalised forms with strategies more frequently found in experimental and postmodernist writing, enacting breakdown and breakthrough (for example, Head), or emphasising how *all* narratives are constructions. There is no particular hierarchy in terms of chosen forms. Those who prefer to use life-writing or oral-based forms might well be closer to the expression used by their community or ancestors, but it is still fiction. Those who choose more experimental postmodernist forms have not necessarily committed a politically unacceptable treasonable act by not sticking to the absolutely accurate facts. Each form has its pros, cons and achievements.

See also   *Contexts:* Land rights, Settler societies, *Terra Nullius; Texts*: Aboriginal writing: tale-telling and women's experience.

Further reading

Frame, Janet, *An Angel at My Table* ((London: The Women's Press, 1984).

Head, Bessie, *A Question of Power* (Oxford: Heinemann, 1974).

Mhlope, Gcina, 'The Toilet', in Ann Oosthuizen (ed.), *Sometimes When It Rains* (London, Pandora, 1987).

Morgan, Sally, *My Place* (Fremantle: Fremantle Arts Centre Press, 1987).

Wicomb, Zoe, 'A Clearing in the Bush', in *You Can't Get Lost in Cape Town* (London: Virago, 1987).

The last outpost of colonisation: rewriting the coloniser's homeland, from the inside

Salman Rushdie's comments about 'outsiders' – that is, immigrated people – as having 'beady eyes and without Anglo-Saxon attitudes' (1982) introduces the idea of how powerful the perspectives of immigrated, postcolonial people can be wherever they have settled and particularly if it is in the land from which originated the colonisers or imperial rulers. Jean Rhys from the Caribbean, Salman Rushdie, whose origins are in Pakistan, Linton Kwesi Johnson and many other Caribbean performance poets, and Andrea Levy, whose *Small Island* (2005) is focused on exactly that topic, that is, settling into a changing and ever-changing 'motherland', each provide very different versions of, in their cases, Britain than any constructed by any relatively untravelled indigenous British writer.

Jean Rhys' *Voyage in the Dark* (1934) interleaves scenes of urban spiritual dereliction with homesickness for the West Indies. Filled with a yearning and loss for the wholeness promised by the Dominica of Rhys' childhood, the novel recreates a Caribbean exotic on the basis of an insider's memories while in the city, in Britain. The imperial capital is observed and detailed at once from both within and without: the coloniser's homeland is seen from a colonial perspective to be inhospitable, to be strange, and to have no place for those who settle there from the colonies or ex colonies.

From the time of the First World War, colonial artists and writers working in London, who included Claude McKay, Aimé Cesaire, Katherine Mansfield and Mulk Raj Anand, explained and expressed cultural difference within European culture and exposed new perspectives in Britain, particularly London, while simultaneously creating exiles' memories and perspectives of their own land of origin. Mansfield's 'undiscovered country' leapt into readers' minds, and a version of the strangeness and beauty of New Zealand entered British consciousness. Like Rhys, Mansfield and Anand haunted Bloomsbury circles between the wars and re-created distant homelands in their fiction. This all challenged established perceptions, thought patterns and forms, as did Aimé Césaire who more radically in the 1930s, used surrealist techniques based on Freudian and Jungian ideas. Césaire helped to create a radical expression in content and form, producing 'insurrectional', 'hell-bound' poetry which undercut imprisoning forms of Western thought and perspectives. More recently, several postcolonial immigrated or second generation writers have used comic forms to explore their lands of adoption or birth.

In *Anita and Me* Meera Syal constructs a diasporan character aware of her own constructedness and performativity. She deals ironically with various myths of arrival, the poverty-stricken Indians blinking in the cold light of Heathrow as they land, welcomed into the UK, only to find jobs scarce, and improvisation a key – sharing beds, using a drawer lined with newspapers as a cot. In Syal's version, theirs are simple origins and they meet ignorance, silence, class prejudice and, later in Meena's growing up, a new kind of exoticism. So, Syal faces a mixed readership with its own confusions and prejudices, and dramatises some of the decisions and issues facing British Asians: racism, assimilation, multiculturalism and erasure. Meena's mum's neighbour, Anita's mother, says she hardly notices the family are different – but this merging in would not necessarily be welcomed – difference is something to celebrate as a component of identity. Not everyone living in the diaspora seeks assimilation. In *Life Isn't All Ha Ha Hee Hee* (2000), the lives of three young women offer examples of varied alternatives. Using the international, traditional, mythical formula of a comparison of three girls, Syal represents the conformist motherly Sunita, a totally domesticated wife, (Chila who falls for romance) and Tania, whose life as a journalist enables her to straddle cultures and present versions of her own Asian culture to large audiences, often to the detriment of those whose lives she transforms to represent. In these novels, now both films (*Anita and Me* [2002] and *Life Isn't All Ha Ha Hee Hee* [TV, 2005]), in her other plays, films and TV comedy, Syal explores and dramatises cultural stereotypes in a manner of rewritten myths, satire, irony and farce, which causes those portrayed and those viewing to question their own cultural confusions and contradictions. Her characters also deal with issues of contorting versions of their own cultural hybridity as British Asians.

Other writers who explore the diasporan existence include Hanif Kureishi, whose *The Buddha of Suburbia* (1990) and *My Beautiful Laundrette* (1985) negotiate cultural stereotypes and interracial interactions and relationships among adolescent young men growing up – in *The Buddha of Suburbia,* coming to terms with his father, and in *My Beautiful Laundrette*, exploring a same-sex mixed-race relationship. Some diasporan writers develop both a hybrid identity, each their own individual, and an enlightened, often satirical or gently humorous way of exposing ways of life in the country now their home.

See also *Contexts:* Diasporan writers; *Criticism:* Cosmopolitanism.

Further reading

Boehmer, Elleke, *Colonial & Postcolonial Literature* (Oxford: Oxford University Press, 1995).
Kureishi, Hanif, *The Buddha of Suburbia* (London: Penguin, 1990).
Kureishi, Hanif, *My Beautiful Laundrette* (London: Faber & Faber, 1996).
Rhys, Jean, *Voyage in the Dark* [1934] (London: Penguin, 1987).
Syal, Meera, *Anita and Me* (London: Flamingo, 1997).
Syal, Meera, *Life Isn't All Ha Ha Hee Hee* (London: Black Swan, 2000).

3 Criticism: Approaches, Theory, Practice

Introduction

Postcolonial criticism is a branch of Postcolonial Studies. Research in Postcolonial Studies, including postcolonial literary criticism, is growing because postcolonial criticism engages with a wide-ranging investigation into a variety of power relations. Postcolonial Studies more broadly concentrates in the main on the history of empires and colonies, how colonisation impacted on the history of indigenous peoples, and subsequently how people have reacted against it and established their own versions of history and society, identity and values, considering issues of the economy, science and culture. It looks at the cultural productions of colonised societies, and moves in more specialised ways into the study of differences, especially in the case of feminism and postcolonialism, of gender. Postcolonial Studies is not just focused on the problems and issues, the ongoing concerns, but also on ways in which colonised peoples, once they have entered the postcolonial context, are involved in agency, whether they are marginalised or not, and the state of the ex- and post colony in contemporary economic and cultural contexts.

Postcolonial criticism has produced a myriad of debates around contexts, issues and definitions, practices and texts. It generally concerns itself initially with defining the term postcolonial and arguing whether this means a radical revolt against colonialism and its impact during the time of the colonisers or a temporal description referring to work produced after the end of colonisation and imperialism. In the first definition, only radical voices would be heard, while in the second it could be said that all voices are heard, but they would need to move on from colonialism and imperialism in terms of ideas and arguments, even if, as many critics note, writers are, necessarily, frequently writing in the language of the coloniser. Indeed, finding a voice which does more than merely mimic that of the colonisers and all their values is a crucial step for many postcolonial writers and therefore a major issue in postcolonial criticism. In this respect, postcolonial criticism engages with issues of whose language is being used, whether meanings can be redefined, and reclaiming and revaluing the language of indigenous peoples, first peoples, and those who suffered forced immigration.

The definition of postcolonial literature and criticism we will use here is of work which is in reaction to, and a response against, the oppressions and constructions of colonisation and imperialism and which was produced during but mostly after the end of colonialism. In this respect, we could recognise E.M. Forster's *A Passage to India* (1924) as postcolonial or proto postcolonial in its tendencies to critique oppressive worldviews and explore the differing experiences of Indian peoples, not merely through the eyes of the British Raj. But we would also recognise, with Maori women writers, for example, that much of New Zealand is still not readily definable as a postcolonial country since the Maori view themselves as disenfranchised and de-nuded of their land in many respects.

Postcolonial theory has been seen as 'depressingly difficult' by Chrisman and Williams (1993, p. ix). I agree with them and with Ania Loomba (1998) that it should not necessarily always have to be so, and I hope, in clarifying, that I am not merely simplifying reductively. Postcolonial criticism can fall into several other traps. It might substitute the topical term 'postcolonial' as an avoidance of difference in terms of context, historical and economic conditions, origins, ethnicity, religion, gender and so on, homogenising what is in fact clearly a different set of experiences for a wide variety of diverse peoples. These attempt to theorise what are sensed as common or shared issues, such as the similar past of imperialism or colonial rule; imposition of the language of the coloniser as the discourse of acceptable expression; erasure of or denial of language of origin; and imposition and normalisation of the worldview of the coloniser over that of the indigenous people, first settlers or forcibly immigrated peoples. Theory and criticism tend to focus on issues of identity, location in history and, in terms of nationhood, the importance of finding discourses with which to speak and speak out. Theory and criticism also consider and theorise ways in which people and their literary products can end up merely mimicking what has gone before, staying somewhat infected and affected by the feelings and forms of colonialism and imperialism. Postcolonial criticism looks also at ways in which those who produce literature can challenge what is considered a literary tradition, preferring perhaps the oral form over the written and the remythologising of mythical forms which have been silenced under colonisation, and it considers how writers can challenge what are considered to be (by those historically in power) fit or acceptable subjects for literature and fit or appropriate forms of written discourse and expression.

This section introduces both many of the major themes and issues in postcolonial criticism and key postcolonial theorists whose work underlies postcolonial literary criticism. One such key theory was originated by Edward Said (1978) who developed the notion of 'Orientalism' to explain how and in what ways Western people and writers constructed a version of eastern people (and often those of the Southern hemisphere) as different, other, exotic but dubious. He argued that this has been the basis of much misunderstanding, hierarchy and racism. Homi K. Bhabha developed the idea of mimicry to explain how colonised and ex-colonised peoples mostly mimic or copy the ways of those who have ruled them, but find it almost impossible to do otherwise, having only those models produced by colonisers upon which to build. Taking a specific feminist view of the joint pressure of gender and ethnicity in postcolonial writing and criticism, Gayatri Chakravorty Spivak (1988) has explored how subordinated or 'subaltern' women speak out against racism and sexism, finding their own empowered voices in the postcolonial context.

Other theorists and critics who debate power and freedom (Freire) and power and language (Foucault) or a variety of issues to do with gender and expression (Suleri, Gunew, Smith, Henderson, Lorde) are also introduced in this section, along with a range of critics who interpret these theorists in practice, looking at literary production.

Postcolonial literary critics frequently consider, analyse and celebrate a diversity of forms of expression and particularly those which deviate frequently from the classical, canonical forms more commonly found in literature and criticism courses in European, Australian, US and English universities. They focus on ways in which knowledge of the cultural contexts is essential for an informed reading of the texts, noting that these texts will be in response to, products of and reactions against elements of the context historically and culturally produced and maintained by colonisers and imperialists. Postcolonial critical practices and practitioners might well critique practices which seem to hierarchise forms of literary production, presenting those from the previously colonised as always speaking out against marginalisation and victimisation, and in so doing perpetuating that 'subaltern' position, that is, all they can write about is their victim history rather than moving on. More often, as postcolonial writing develops, writers are seen to seek instead to celebrate difference and the ability to speak out in differing forms about different world views and experiences, that is, to move on from challenging the coloniser, or 'talking up to the white woman', as aboriginal women writers succinctly put it (Moreton-Robinson, 2000).

Some of the major issues

Some of the major issues include the following: How did the experience of colonisation affect those who were colonised and how did it also affect the colonisers? Who gained control over such a large part of the world, how, and what affected the colonised and/or indigenous peoples or those who were forcibly immigrated to other lands? What are the legacies of colonialism – what are the traces left by colonial language, education, science, government, bureaucracy and technology in the various postcolonial societies? How do these legacies affect decisions about development, modernisation and subjects for literary or other artistic expression in those ex-colonies? What forms of resistance against colonial control existed in the past and were expressed in literature and the arts? How did the laws, education and language influence the culture and identity of colonised people and how do they express their thoughts and feelings about this? Was knowledge constructed through a Western point of view in terms of science, technology, medicine, business, values, religion and so on, and what did it affect or change in the ways of colonised peoples, about which they are now writing? What emergent forms of postcolonial identity are developing after the departure of the colonisers? How successful has decolonisation and any reconstruction free from colonial influence been? Has it been possible? How might decolonisation proceed? Is it a return to a pre-colonial past or a fusion of pre- and postcolonial ways and expressions? Is this actually unavoidable anyway? Is such a fusion actually yet another problematic influence of colonisation? What can be made new? How can the material, economic, geographical, historical and cultural differences for the many postcolonial peoples be engaged with in any form of postcolonial studies, and the kinds of homogenising or generalising resulting from calling it 'Postcolonial Studies' or 'postcolonial writing' be avoided? How do gender, race, culture, class and economic influences function and express themselves in colonial and postcolonial discourse? In the postcolonial period, are there new forms of imperialism developing, perhaps by multinationals or the work of the G8 summit, among others, and how? And how is exploration, expression and resistance to this being expressed by writers? How do people construct, represent and write about their identities in a postcolonial context? Seeking recompense? Expressing a sense of diasporan existence? Mimicry? Hybridity? Cosmopolitanism? Metropolitanism? These questions inform our discussions in this section as we consider some of the works by the better-known postcolonial critics, and by some hitherto less well-known critics, exploring the major areas and issues with which they deal, and the light they have shone on our study and reading.

There are some very good collections of postcolonial writing which often have interesting critical introductions, such as John Thieme's *The Arnold Anthology of Post-Colonial Literatures in English* (1996), selections and critical works such as Rutherford, Jensen and Chew's *Into the Nineties* (1994) and Walder's *Post-Colonial Literatures in English* (1998), and on women's writing by those of African descent, such as Margaret Busby's *Daughters of Africa* (1992). There are also some fine critical engagements with the various issues involved in postcolonial writing and the range of the field, such as Childs and Williams' *An Introduction to Post-Colonial Theory* (1997) and Mongia's *Contemporary Post-Colonial Theory* (1996).

Into the Nineties (1994) is one of the very few collections of both primary and critical materials focusing on women's writing and with an Australian emphasis. There are now many useful books exploring the terms used in Postcolonial Studies, theory and literature, dealing with versions of the range and providing critical introductions to postcolonial writing, however it is defined. These include Ashcroft, Griffiths and Tiffin's *The Empire Writes Back* (1989), Tiffin and Adam's *Past the Last Post* (1993), and Tiffin and Lawson's *De-scribing Empire* (1994). Latterly, there are some good books which focus on the historical and contextual influences, such as Robert Young's massive *Postcolonialism* (2001) and his tiny Oxford University Press book of the same name (2003). Others locate postcolonial writing in the context of colonialism and imperialism, taking both a historical development view and a way through which emphasises literary trends – these include Ania Loomba's *Colonialism/ Post Colonialism* (1998) and Elleke Boehmer's *Colonial & Postcolonial Literature* (1995), each of which highlights issues and concerns about identity changes caused by treaties, independence and the like, and looks at the impact on the imperial and colonial as it moves into the postcolonial, recognising ground-breaking texts such as those by Chinua Achebe. There are several other books which explore postcolonialism or postcolonial theory and studies in a manner resembling this book, only using alphabetical author/editor, issue-oriented entries (see below).

Further reading

Ashcroft, Bill, Gareth Griffiths and Helen Tiffin, *The Empire Writes Back* (London: Routledge, 1989).

Ashcroft, Bill, Gareth Griffiths and Helen Tiffin, *Post-Colonial Studies: The Key Concepts* (London: Routledge, 2000).

Boehmer, Elleke, *Colonial & Postcolonial Literature* (Oxford: Oxford University Press, 1995).

Boyce Davies, Carole, *Black Women, Writing and Identity* (London: Routledge, 1994).

Busby, Margaret, *Daughters of Africa* (London: Vintage, 1992).

Childs, Peter, and Patrick Williams, *An Introduction to Post-Colonial Theory* (Hemel Hempstead: Prentice Hall, 1997).

Chrisman, Laura and Patrick Williams, (eds), *Colonial Discourse and Post-Colonial Theory* (Hemel Hempstead: Prentice-Hall, 1993).

Forster, E.M., *A Passage to India* [1924] (Harmondsworth: Penguin Books Limited, 1998).

Loomba, Ania, *Colonialism/Post Colonialism* (London: Routledge, 1998).

Mongia, Padmini, *Contemporary Post-Colonial Theory* (London: Arnold, 1996).

Nasta, Susheila, (ed.), 'Introduction', in *Motherlands: Black Women's Writing from Africa, the Caribbean and South Asia* (London: The Women's Press, 1991).

Rutherford, Anna, Lars Jensen and Shirley Chew, *Into the Nineties* (Armidale, New South Wales: Kunapipi, Dangaroo Press, 1994).

Said, Edward, *Orientalism: Western Conceptions of the Orient* (London: Penguin, 1978).

Spivak, Gayatri Chakravorty, 'Can the Subaltern Speak?', in C. Nelson and L. Grossberg, (eds), *Marxism and the Interpretation of Culture* (London: Macmillan, 1988).

Thieme, John, *Postcolonial Studies* (London: Edward Arnold, 1989).

Thieme, John, *The Arnold Anthology of Post-Colonial Literatures in English* (London: Edward Arnold, 1996).

Tiffin, Chris and Alan Lawson, *De-scribing Empire* (London: Routledge, 1994).

Tiffin, Helen and Ian Adam, *Past the Last Post* (London: Harvester Wheatsheaf, 1993).

Walder, Dennis, *Post-Colonial Literatures in English* (London: Edward Arnold, 1998).

Wisker, Gina, *Insights into Black Women's Writing* (London: Macmillan, 1993).

Wisker, Gina, *Postcolonial and African American Women's Writing: A Critical Introduction* (Basingstoke: Macmillan, 2000).

Young, Robert, *Postcolonialism* (Oxford: Blackwell, 2001).

Young, Robert, *Postcolonialism* (Oxford: Oxford University Press 2003).

Carnival

People under imperial or colonial rule might well want to argue or act against it, criticising the rulers and their behaviours and turning them upside down. Such a spirit of revolt appears in the notion of 'carnival'. Homi Bhabha's notion of there being a polyphony of voices in society is also implied in Mikhail Bakhtin's idea of the carnivalesque. Often this also includes varieties of Rabelaisian carnivalesque, a form of expression which challenges constraint and order and has its historical roots in carnival in the Middle Ages, when working-class people celebrated in a manner which disrupted the power structures of the times, turning values and hierarchies upside down, and temporarily refusing the controls of those in power. The temporary nature of the carnivalesque means it can be seen as a legitimate and controlled escape space – but it can also be seen as a necessary mode and space for the construction and expression of alternative energies from hitherto economically or culturally subordinated peoples. Examples of carnival in society include saturnalia such as twelfth night, circuses, travelling fairs and, very important in postcolonial contexts, calypso music and carnivals in such locations as Trinidad or Notting Hill in Britain. In Earl Lovelace's *The Dragon Can't Dance*, the carnival on Calgary Hill offers opportunities for singing, dancing, performance and different versions of identity and power to people otherwise impoverished, but it also fuses rival groups of Calypsonians and releases violent and creative energies. One of the main features of the carnival, apart from excess energies and challenging power, is the temporary nature of the defiance and excess; soon it is shut down and order restored.

Further reading

Bakhtin, Mikhail, *Rabelais and His World* [1965] (Cambridge, MA: MIT Press, 1968).
Lovelace, Earl, *The Dragon Can't Dance* (London: André Deutsch, 1979).

Colonial discourse

This is a term used by Edward Said in *Orientalism*, building upon the work of Michel Foucault, who identified a discourse as a system of expression influenced and derived from representing a range of values and practices, in this case, colonial practices. Foucault notes that dominant groups in society impose knowledgeable beliefs and disciplines deriving from the dominant position upon those who are controlled by the discourse and unable to speak, in most cases beyond and outside it. Said considered the ways in which colonial discourse acted as a vehicle for power. Homi Bhabha's use of the term reorganised 'contradictions within colonial relationships, such as hybridity, ambivalence and mimicry, which revealed the inherent vulnerability of colonial discourse' (Ashcroft, Griffiths and Tiffin, 2000, pp. 41–2). Colonial discourse, controlled by those in power, excludes critiques which identify the exploitation of those colonised peoples it describes.

Hence, the task of colonised peoples becomes one of challenging colonial discourse, finding instead their own expressions, whether in image and sound, to articulate independently. They can salvage from their history the different experiences and worldviews they create, find space and power to express. Hence the poet Edward Kamau Brathwaite argues that 'the hurricane does not roar in pentameters' (*The History of the Voice*, 1984). Caribbean Black British performance poets Valerie Bloom and Benjamin Zephaniah insist on enabling their diverse audience to enter the language or discourse community of the Caribbean, through changing various words and phrases such as 'overstanding' instead of understanding; this highlights in a highly accessible way the importance of ensuring that discourse is claimed, constructed and used by postcolonial peoples.

See also *Contexts*: Postcolonialism and feminism, Postcolonial discourse; *Texts*: Language, discourse, culture and power: reclaiming/rewriting language and power *Criticism:* Said, Edward (1935–2003) and Orientalism.

Further reading

Ashcroft, Bill, Gareth Griffiths, and Helen Tiffin, *Post-Colonial Studies: The Key Concepts* (London: Routledge, 2000).
Said, Edward, *Orientalism: Western Conceptions of the Orient* (London: Penguin, 1978).

Commonwealth literature

Now rather an outdated term, replaced by, for example, 'New Literatures in English' (which, however, avoids the geographical and political history of Commonwealth literatures) or more recently 'postcolonial' (which might be seen as determining that everything is affected by colonialism and can only be considered after the end of colonialism – an ideological, political, historical stance), the term Commonwealth literature developed initially as a way of recognising writing, for the most part written in English, produced by writers from the former British Empire and the developing Commonwealth, that is, the colonies/ex-colonies and dependencies. Ashcroft *et al.* argue that Commonwealth literature 'has sometimes included literatures written in "local" languages and oral performance; and it has been used to include the literatures of Wales, Scotland and Ireland' (2000, p. 51), these latter on the grounds that they have been under English rule. In the case of writers from these locations, they would need to self-identify as being part of Commonwealth writing and this would depend on whether they felt they were part of the Commonwealth – that is, separate and joining the larger grouping – or part of the British Isles. The term remains more popular than the term 'postcolonial' in India.

Writing by Caribbean poet Una Marson might be labelled in this way, as she contributed to the development of literary modernism (earlier part of twentieth century), and so, too, could early work by African writers such as Chinua Achebe or Wole Soyinka, but most writers would now neither recognise nor use the term, preferring postcolonial to denote a political and cultural change.

See also *Texts*: New literatures in English.

Further reading

Ashcroft, Bill, Gareth Griffiths and Helen Tiffin, *Post-Colonial Studies: The Key Concepts* (London: Routledge, 2000).

Cosmopolitanism

Since 2000 discussions about culture, particularly in Britain, have focused not on multiculturalism and minority arts but on a redefinition of concepts of culture arising from growing 'cosmopolitanism', a term largely coined by Homi K. Bhabha, which suggests that people, including writers, are now more used to mixing with different cultures and races and that we are all influenced by this mixing, citizens of a kind of global city, neither insisting on our specific cultural difference nor being assimilated and pretending we are all the same. As Bhabha puts it, there are now:

> concepts of culture and community that emerge from the *hybrid* cosmopolitanism of contemporary metropolitan life. Culture and an authenticating/identity-bestowing function, expressive of the past tradition, or that customary belief, is of limited relevance to the cosmopolitan condition.
>
> Bhabha, 1999, pp. 40–1.

Bhabha claims that in the 1980s, multiculturalist thinking sought to revisit and undercut the homogenisation of different cultures by emphasising the range of identities of class, race and gender in the people in Britain, and in so doing also showed not only how Englishness itself had been constructed discursively over time, but also that it was in flux, a changing construct. Since then, locating the problem of identity at the centre has moved on, changed, and a new cosmopolitanism has transformed the public sphere. But if we are all now cosmopolitan, in reinventing Britain, there is still a problem in the assumption that postcolonial writers, first or second generation, focus entirely on identity and on difference. British Asian critic Susheila Nasta points out that this just perpetuates the problem, since it recreates the discourse of mainstream and margin, and fails to redefine something new. It is all too easy, then, to emphasise cultural difference in a historically hierarchising manner.

Theories of multiculturalism and celebrations of difference are indeed in need of revision. The most resistant white British person, for example, has had his or her experience changed through the presence of a more cosmopolitan multicultural Britain. Genuinely, in the case of Britain in particular, it is not just those who have settled here, or whose parents settled here, who have had to change. Everything has changed, and the younger Asian and Black British writers reflect this, first negotiating their own identities, through the seventies and eighties, then entering into a new perception of Britain that does not always place them, tolerated, exotic and a little entertaining, on the margins of some all-encompassing definable Britishness. Hybridity redefines Britishness because it is more inclusive. Some of this negotiation of identity, involving experience of the diaspora, hybridity and cosmopolitanism, is articulated in the works of Asian and Afro-Caribbean British writers. Similar arguments about hybridity and cosmopolitanism emerge in writers from other ex-colonial powers such as France and Germany.

As British Asian writer and actress Meera Syal's Meena (*Anita and Me*, 1997) recalls, any representation of Asian British people used to be a rarity, so historically, Asian, African and Caribbean people settling in Britain hardly ever saw themselves in the media or in literature: in effect, they seemed not to exist. Syal deals with this in a comic manner, portraying the family watching (performed – not genuine as it happens) Asian characters on TV:

> According to the newspapers and television, we simply did not exist. If a brown or a black face ever did appear on TV, it stopped us all in our tracks. 'Daljit! Quick!' pap would call, and we would crowd round and coo over the walk-on in some detective series, some long-suffering actor in a gaudy costume with a goodness-gracious-me accent. ('So Mr Templar, you speak fluent Hindustani too! But that won't stop me stealing the secret formula for my countrydom where I will soon rule the world. Heh heh heh . . .') and welcome him into our home like a long-lost relative.
>
> Syal, 1997, p. 165.

In this example, a white British actor is playing a stereotypically wicked, untrustworthy Oriental in a decidedly non-postcolonial piece. Syal laughs at and exposes this while also making the point about the absence of Black and Asian people in the media. But TV is increasingly providing opportunities for cultural exchange, representation, understanding and hybridity. One of Meera Syal's great gifts to multiculturalism, hybridity, cosmopolitanism and the dialogue between cultures lies in the popularisation of the forms of expression of British Asian people through the medium of TV and film. Here, her work, though very different, comic and visual, can be aligned with that of the Caribbean performance poets and with author Zadie Smith, whose *White Teeth* (2000) has been televised.

The theorist and critic Stuart Hall speaks of relating the writing of what we might call an im/migrant genre or im/migrant imaginary to a context in which that literature 'stages the experience of exile, immigration and deterritorialization' (Hall, 1992), so it deliberately focuses on these experiences of immigrated people instead of hiding or erasing them. This can be arguably seen as a situation that may be postcolonial. Both Nasta and Hall identify ways in which the explorations of many postcolonial writers showed, through their imaginative expression of historic and lived experience, that they contributed early onto debates about the defamiliarisation, new configurations and articulations which define not only the postcolonial but also more generally the postmodern condition. This is seen as a condition of fragmentation or new combinations in terms of identity, and what forms of expression might be used for negotiating identity and multiple versions of reality and world views. In their literary strategies, writers who negotiate versions of postcolonial realities and identities translate and transform the rigidity of oppositional racial and national categorizations, intervening in and subverting traditional ways of narrating identity. In the case of writers with whom both Nasta and Hall deal, these are likely to be Black or Asian British. Nasta is speaking below about early twentieth-century writers but the description fits more recent writers also. So each writer – Syal, Breeze, Kureishi, Rushdie, Merle Collins and Zadie Smith among others – has

> set in motion a discourse for diaspora in which the experience of im/migration could be seen as an active process, marking a stage on a continuum which was to develop into a poetics of migrancy within subsequent writings in the 1980s and 1990s.
>
> Nasta, 2002, p. 69.

In *The Buddha of Suburbia* (1990), Hanif Kureishi argues that the 'figure of the "immigrant" becomes the physical sign and symbolic trope of late twentieth-century modernity, a professional mutator' (Nasta, 2002, pp. 178–9), the 'Everyman of the . . . century' (Kureishi, 1990, p. 141), so in his argument the immigrant learns to perform and transform, as indeed everyone needs to and must in our very changing world where we are expected to perform a whole raft of roles. Kureishi's Asian British family in *The Buddha of Suburbia* work out a variety of relationships between father and son, male and female friends, sexuality, and social positions.

In the light of these arguments about the problematising of an Enlightenment view – which is one which defines colonised people as secondary and savage, and colonisers as developed, cultured and enlightened – we can read much work by diasporan cosmopolitan writers. Grace

Nichols, for example, has written a diasporan poem of the 'Middle Passage' or slave crossing between Africa and the Americas, which can perhaps be read as one celebrating new dialogues between the past and the present, between differing selves, a new expression of hybridity:

> I have crossed an ocean
> I have lost my tongue
> from the root of the old one
> a new one has sprung
> ('Is a Long Memoried Woman', Nichols, 1983)

Writers who engage with the ideas of changing identity following chosen or forced immigration or colonisation raise a range of issues to do with performing different kinds of roles in a culture which immigrated people are themselves changing or which colonised peoples are conspiring to change. A major point here is that as coloniser and colonised, immigrated or indigenous, side by side, people are metamorphosing, developing different, more mixed hybrid identities, reliving histories but also changing their sense of location, identity and language – it is all in flux.

See also *Contexts:* Diasporan writers; *Criticism:* Global citizenship and cosmopolitanism, Hybridity.

Further reading

Bhabha, Homi K., 'Reinventing Britain', *Wasafiri,* Spring 29 (1999).
Hall, Stuart, *Modernity and Its Future* (Cambridge: Polity Press, 1992).
Kureishi, Hanif, *The Buddha of Suburbia* (London: Penguin, 1990).
Nasta, Susheila, 'Reinventing Britain', *Wasafiri,* Spring 29 (1999).
Nasta, Susheila, *Home Truths: Fictions of the South Asian Diaspora in Britain* (Basingstoke: Palgrave, 2002).
Nichols, Grace, *I Is a Long Memoried Woman* (London: Karnak House, 1983).
Smith, Zadie, *White Teeth* (London: Penguin, 2000).
Syal, Meera, *Anita and Me* (London: Flamingo, 1997).

Critical issues: location and difference

Walter Mignolo, using the language of poetics, points out the importance of recognising location as it affects knowledge, construction and world view:

> Despite all of its ambiguities and potential hazards, however, the notion of the 'post colonial' ultimately foregrounds the politics and

ethics of location in the construction of knowledge: first, because it clarifies the theorizing of colonial experiences as non-neutral with respect to where the act of theorizing is (ethically and politically, not necessarily geographically) located or performed, and second, because it inserts the personal signs of the understanding subject (her or his ability 'to be from' and 'to be at') into an imaginary construction.

Mignolo, 1994, p. 508.

As readers of postcolonial writing, we need to negotiate our own expectations and imaginary versions of the lives and meanings of others in order to make contact with and begin to understand and respond to them. One problem here for white Western European readers is the issue of misinterpretation and of appropriation. Lauretta Ngcobo reduces the chances of a superficial white response of genteel liberalism to texts by Black and Asian, African American and postcolonial writers, noting:

We as Black writers at times displease our white readership. Our writing is seldom genteel since it springs from our experiences which in real life have none of the trimmings of gentility. If the truth be told, it cannot titillate the aesthetic palates of many white people, for deep down it is a criticism of their values and their treatment of us throughout history.

Ngcobo, 1987, p. 4.

Often the tone and subject matter of postcolonial writing specifically focuses on Black/white relations and the effects of racism. It can indict white societies, seemingly casting readers and critics from a Western European background in the light of oppressors, when this is the last thing a writer might intend. Sometimes in a direct, overt fashion and sometimes in a covert fashion, it records, revises and challenges the ways in which racism, or a history of genocide or of slavery, the mass extinction of Aboriginal peoples in Australia, Apartheid in South Africa and the transportation and forced settlement of Africans to the Caribbean and America have operated. In so doing, writing can indict the historical perpetrators of these injustices but for white Western readers, it can be argued that this criticism should produce neither avoidance nor merely stunned, speechless guilt from those who perhaps confusedly recognise an involuntary but inherited complicity in such terrible racist histories (and their contemporary legacies). Instead, while white readers need to ensure they do not speak *for* Black and Asian people, they can appreciate and respond *to* their work.

Further reading

Mignolo, Walter, D., Introduction to *Poetics Today,* 215, 4 (Winter) (1994).
Ngcobo, Lauretta (ed.), *Let It Be Told: Black Women Writers in Britain* (London: Virago, 1987).

Essentialism

This is a term relating to the construction and representation of people as if each individual were the same as the next and that people belong in categories. It is a reductive way of labelling people and a strategy used by colonial and imperial powers to stereotype and denigrate colonised peoples, focusing on similarities and flaws and identifying these as natural, normal, to be expected and routinely found amongst (colonised, subordinate) Other peoples. Because the term involves both Otherising and homogenising, and because it removes individuality and can lead to racial and gender stereotyping, it is criticised alike by both postcolonial and feminist critics. However, some protest movements built on self-esteem also use essentialism in a positive sense, as in the many varieties of Black pride or gay pride movements, because here it is important to insist on basic background and behaviours in common. An early example of such claims is perhaps the concept of Négritude, which was developed by Frantz Fanon, among Caribbean and African writers living in 1930s and 40s Paris. Fanon was deliberately identifying what African-originated people had in common in order to raise a sense of shared and definable identity and solidarity. There is a real tension between the need to identify similarities for reasons of solidarity, based on ethnicity and political identity, and the difficulty of being essentialised by *other people*. This is the clue to the positive possibilities of essentialism: should a group identify its own characteristics and use them as a way of recognising and celebrating difference? This kind of positive use of essentialism can be set against the essentialising done to others by those who claim power and would wish to denigrate, reduce and stigmatise. Fanon is a key figure in this debate.

See also *Contexts*: Fanon, Frantz (1925–61); *Criticism*: Fanon, Frantz (1925–61), Négritude.

Further reading

Fanon, Frantz, *Black Skin, White Masks* (London: Pluto Press, 1952).
Fanon, Frantz, *The Wretched of the Earth* [1961], preface by Jean-Paul Sartre, trans. Constance Farrington (Harmondsworth: Penguin, 1990).

Fanon, Frantz (1925–61)

Martinique-born psychiatrist and activist for the Algerian National Liberation Front, Frantz Fanon produced two highly influential texts, *Black Skin, White Masks* (1952) and *The Wretched of the Earth* (1961/90), and two collections of essays which develop further the construction of Négritude, which originated in the 1930s in the work of Aimé Césaire, one of his school teachers. Fanon recognises culture as being both a product of nationhood and the anthropological and makes statements about reclaiming cultural identity and nationhood. *Black Skin, White Masks* made a considerable contribution to postcolonial studies because it explored how colonised peoples internalise versions of themselves which are actually built on the values, histories and discourse of the colonisers. Fanon sees one of the greatest destructive activities of colonialism as being the act of translation – translating the difference of others' cultures, language and ways into that of the coloniser. This erases any differences but, on the way, usually finds those translated to be hierarchically subordinate. Of translation, distinguished postcolonial historian Robert Young argues that, 'Under colonialism, the colonial copy becomes more powerful than the indigenous original that is devalued. It will even be claimed that the copy corrects deficiencies in the native version' (Young, 2003, p. 140).

Fanon highlights the deceptions of translation of different cultures into that of the coloniser – the history of colonised peoples and their different worlds are redescribed in the colonisers' terms, reinterpreted and revalued and usually found to be secondary to the worldviews and values of the coloniser. Cultural translation redescribes and falsifies perception, culture, history and identity. In 'On National Culture' (1961), Fanon argues that colonialism works to define and express the present and future of colonised peoples and also to reshape their past, leading to cultural erasure, defamiliarisation and estrangement: 'By a kind of perverted logic, it turns to the past of the oppressed people, and distorts, disfigures and destroys it' (1990 [1961], p. 265), leaving only warped, translated remains. For colonialists and colonial histories, the lands of these colonised were always seen as *terra nullias*, where primitive peoples needed taming, so the 'vast continent was the haunt of savages', and all Black people were homogenised into 'the Negro' (1990 [1961], p. 266), a savage.

Fanon explains this reasoning and rejects its premises. His theorising builds on that of Jacques Lacan and Sigmund Freud, identifying moments of identity construction. He recognises that for many Black people it is necessary to adopt a white 'mask', and to conform to white values and versions of their behaviour. This enables their entrance into the colonisers' culture but along the way it also erases their own identities. Fanon urges them to recognise the damage of hiding behind such a mask and the need to seize and shape their own identity. Around him in Algeria he saw Arabs estranged from their identities in their own land and criticised French assimilationist policies.

Fanon's argument is that contemporary Black people need to rediscover history and reaffirm African identity and culture. He argues that today's natives (his label) exploring their history are probably amazed at the 'dignity, glory, solemnity' that they find there (1990 [1961], p. 266). Fanon identifies the movement towards culture reclaiming a version of parts of the past, in which the Negro intellectual, in particular, will emerge as central. It is important to fight for the nation first and then to see culture as one aspect. Updating histories and re-establishing identities are crucial, as Black people shake off the stranglehold of colonialism on the history and culture of its subjects and ex subjects.

See also   *Contexts*: Fanon, Frantz (1925–61); *Criticism*: Essentialism, Négritude.

Further reading

Fanon, Frantz, *Black Skin, White Masks* (London: Pluto Press, 1952).
Fanon, Frantz, *The Wretched of the Earth* [1961], preface by Jean-Paul Sartre, trans. Constance Farrington (Harmondsworth: Penguin, 1990).

Global citizenship and cosmopolitanism

Global citizenship suggests that instead of emphasising differences and hierarchising them, we are all citizens of the world. It is a goal of liberal education, which springs from the belief in cosmopolitanism (Bhabha), as further developed and advocated by philosopher Martha Nussbaum in *For Love of Country: Debating the Limits of Patriotism* (1996), and *Cultivating Humanity* (1997). Nussbaum initially directs her thoughts at the liberal education of students but they have a wider application as theories and practices leading to equality without hierarchy. The students she aims at are Americans and hers is a particularly American-focused set of theories, being aware of the richness, reach and insularity of the greatest, richest, most powerful and culturally imperialistic nation in the world, which thrives on immediate media information and a belief in the right to take imperial decisions over distant countries. Nussbaum breaks down the tendency to hierarchise cultures, a tendency based on post-Enlightenment philosophy which saw Westernised culture as further developed than eastern, or African in particular. She believes that local and national identities should be subject to debate, critique and comparison with others so that students and the population more widely can become sufficiently experienced in the ways of diverse cultures, and can reflect and clarify or 'bracket' their own frames of identity and belief, while being able to appreciate and value alternative beliefs and behaviours and culturally inflected multiple perspectives. Nussbaum's concept of cosmopolitanism therefore leads further into the ideal of a kind of global citizenship in which the view of the world is that it is filled with equally valuable people whatever their differences. This echoes arguments from African American critics and poet Audre Lorde and is differently developed by Anthony Appiah, author of *Cosmopolitanism* (2006), and by Homi Bhabha.

Anthony Appiah is a Professor at Harvard and Princeton. In *The Ethics of Identity* (2004), on the philosophy of individuality and cosmopolitanism, he explores how 'while we do have responsibilities to certain identities and that we're not free to do, as it were, absolutely anything in terms of them, people are responsible themselves in the management of different identities and their priorities in different contexts.' His 'rooted cosmopolitanism' seeks specific commonalities in an age of ideological, material and metaphorical differences. He argues that we live best on a smaller scale, that is, from within our familial, religious, cultural or national 'circles'; through our legitimate locations of country and our personal and professional loyalties we develop our rooted identities and from this location we can identify and act out broader moral concerns.

While Appiah argues for a rooted cosmopolitanism, arising from awareness of and comfort with one's own location, history, nationality and cultural differences, Homi Bhabha builds on the mobility of the world populations enabled by global migrations of refugees and guest workers, and on our growing awareness of other subaltern populations. He seeks to identify and explore cultural differences and richness from bottom up, bringing in from the margins those marginalised others, those condemned to a silenced subaltern position (see Spivak's notion of the subaltern) and placing them as equals, in a kind of rich cultural mixture which neither hierarchises cultural values of one group over another nor homogenises their differences. Bhabha's version of cosmopolitanism is an alternative to Nussbaum's universalist model with a model of equality, diversity and overlapping consensus.

Bhabha brings a postcolonial, class-oriented perspective to bear on cosmopolitanism, advocating a 'vernacular cosmopolitanism' that sees from the margins, from the peripheries of global centres of power and wealth. He sees no one knowledge system or epistemology as superior to another and instead advocates the recognition of different constructions and representations of knowledge, seeing knowledge construction as rich with overlapping perspectives, experiences and culture.

Appiah's chapter on 'Rooted Cosmopolitanism' can be used to explore different readings of practices and situations, which depend for each of us on the limitations or experiences of our own lives from our own contexts. This affects how a writer might reference or judge different cultures and their practices and how a reader might read about such difference. Appiah discusses apparent contradictions based in local practice. One of the examples is that of comparing female circumcision, which most people outside specific kin and ethnic groups regard as abhorrent, with male circumcision, which is universally tolerated. He argues that though forced circumcisions might cause harm they do support the identities of some African communities and this needs to be taken into consideration. He is here citing some of the specific difficulties dealt with in short stories such as those by Buchi Emecheta, Bessie Head, Flora Nwapa, Ama Ata Aidoo and Gcina Mhlope, who expose culturally contrasting values of city and country, the Westernised set of seemingly liberal values with respect to women's emancipation and not only the difficulty of operating these practices in certain African institutions but also/even the danger. In the case of female circumcision, for instance, those choosing to leave the village, ignore the rituals and ties, and refuse genital mutilation (a feminist description of the practice) might well find themselves ostracised with no place to be at all.

Such is the contradiction faced by African American Alice Walker in *Possessing the Secret of Joy* and the accompanying Arena TV production. In her work, Walker showed that the desire to remove little girls from female circumcision practice cannot work because they are themselves rooted in their own culture and location, and even though removal would be enlightened (the practice is dangerous) it would also be culturally imperialist because it imposes values of one powerful culture – America in this instance – on another. In *Possessing the Secret of Joy*, Tashi, an African woman who moves to the US, is so scarred emotionally as well as physically that she takes revenge on her mutilator with fatal consequences. The novel suggests that while the practice might be recognised as abhorrent, you cannot easily refuse, punish or stamp it out unless those practising it *in context* choose to do so. Appiah wonders how the liberal cosmopolitanism he advocates 'might justify tolerance for illiberal practices that are grounded in local traditions'. Cosmopolitanism in the view of Appiah, Nussbaum and Bhaba is a form of global citizenship which recognises variety and difference in a non-hierarchical fashion and rejects the idea of one culture imposing knowledge, laws and behaviours on another. We are equal but different cultures in the world.

See also *Criticism*: Cosmopolitanism; *Texts:* Forms of writing – identity and subjectivity.

Further reading

Appiah, Anthony, *The Ethics of Identity* (Princeton, NJ: Princeton University Press, 2004).
Appiah, Anthony, *Cosmopolitanism* (New York: W.W. Norton, 2006).
Nussbaum, Martha and Joshua Cohen (eds), *For Love of Country: Debating the Limits of Patriotism* (Boston: Beacon Press, 1996).
Nussbaum, Martha *Cultivating Humanity* (Cambridge, MA: Harvard University Press, 1997).
Walker, Alice, *Possessing the Secret of Joy* (London: Jonathan Cape, 1992).

Hobson, John A. (1858–1940)

Early critic of the effects of colonial and imperial rule, John Atkinson Hobson explored the links between imperialism and international conflict in *War in South Africa* (1900) and *Psychology of Jingoism* (1901). In his greatest work, *Imperialism* (1902), he argued that imperial expansion is driven by a search for new markets and investment opportunities overseas, gaining Hobson an international reputation. His ideas influenced both Lenin and Trotsky.

Hobson's opposition to World War I led to his joining the Union of Democratic Control and advocating the formation of a world political body to prevent wars, explored in his piece *Towards International Government* (1914). He was, however, opposed to the League of Nations, and expressed hope that America would join World War II.

Further reading

Hobson, John Atkinson, *The War in South Africa: Its Causes and Effects* (London: Macmillan, 1900).
Hobson, John Atkinson, *The Psychology of Jingoism* (London: Grant Richards, 1901).
Hobson, John Atkinson, *Imperialism: A Study* (New York: James Pott & Co., 1902).
Hobson, John Atkinson, *Towards International Government* (London: Macmillan, 1914).

Hybridity

The term hybridity began in horticulture, and refers to the cross-breeding of two species by grafting or cross-pollination to form a third, 'hybrid' species. In postcolonial theory it is both widely used and disputed, referring to the creation of new transcultural rather than multicultural (crossing and fertilising rather than fragmented) forms within the space produced by colonisation where people, indigenous, immigrated, settled, colonising and colonised, live and move.

Hybridisation involves new mixes of linguistic, cultural, political and racial beliefs and forms. Linguistic examples include pidgin and creole languages, which are local versions of a language brought by colonisers. Hybridity recognises a polyphony of voices, narrative forms and viewpoints underlying forms of expression. Hybridity aligns itself with a sense of a cultural equity despite difference, through these varieties of voices.

Homi Bhabha's analysis of coloniser/colonised relations stresses their interdependence and the mutual construction of their subjectivities (*mimicry* and *ambivalence*). Bhabha contends that all cultural statements and systems are constructed in a space that he calls the 'Third Space of enunciation' (1994, p. 37). Cultural identity always emerges in this contradictory and ambivalent space which, for Bhabha, makes the claim to hierarchical 'purity' of cultures untenable. For him, the recognition of this ambivalent space of cultural identity may help us to overcome the exoticism of cultural diversity in favour of the recognition of an empowering hybridity within which cultural difference may operate:

> It is significant that the productive capacities of this Third Space have a colonial or postcolonial provenance. For a willingness to descend into that alien territory . . . may open the way to conceptualizing an *inter*national culture, based not on the exoticism of multiculturalism or the *diversity* of cultures, but on the inscription and articulation of culture's *hybridity*.
>
> Bhabha 1994, p. 38.

Hybridity as a concept and lived experience is rich with cultural meaning drawn from the varieties of culture which are affecting any individuals or groups. It is more than just a cross-cultural exchange since for those included there is a wealth of expected issues to do with language, politics, values and identity.

Hybrid is a term which since the mid 1990s has begun to change its meaning dramatically. In the times of the British Empire hybrid it was used as a stigma related to colonial ideas about racial purity and a horror of miscegenation (mixed race relations producing children). In colonial and imperial days, children of white male colonisers and female 'native' peoples were given a different (and inferior) status in colonial society and often shunned by both the coloniser and colonised as not fitting into either group. Hybridity also affects language, food, music, art and other aspects of culture, so in terms of language, food and music, the term 'creole' was used, initially in the Spanish and

French Caribbean and parts of the US – for example, New Orleans is used to describe 'mixtures' of European and African culture, considered inferior *because* mixed. From this horror at impurity or mixture, the fear of hybridity and creolisation appears in racist political language, especially when immigration seems to be likely to affect culture, behaviours and heredity. When the postwar migration of people from Africa, the Caribbean and Asia began to reach Europe, then when Kenyan, Ugandan and Asian people came to live in England M.P. Enoch Powell talked, for instance, of 'rivers of blood' and the terrible threat of dark hordes swamping the country, taking jobs and intermixing. Margaret Thatcher spoke of the fear of being 'swamped' by the different cultures of immigrant communities. Even more insidious is the successful campaign to return to 'English' history at the expense of learning about the rest of the world.

In Meera Syal's *Life Isn't All Ha Ha Hee Hee* (2000), Tanya, a British Asian journalist and media person, stands at the crossroads of a spot in North London and notes how very mixed and hybrid the culture is in terms of food, clothing and language. She perceives herself to have her own particular individual hybridity. In the face of racism, Millat, the British Asian teenager in Zadie Smith's *White Teeth* (2000), realises that as a 'Paki' he will be excluded from certain jobs and stereotyped by many, but he and his friends have actually developed their own unique hybrid cultural mix in a positive sense. Elsewhere, a less positive view predominates in the figure of the genetically engineered 'Future Mouse', which is bred by another character. Millat and his friends, and Caribbean Black British Irie and hers, are used to foods, music, clothes, values, language and behaviours from the full variety of their mixed parentage and the cultural diversity in which they live in London. This comic spirit of the novel goes inside some of the confusions and much of the richness of hybridity for its new generation. Characters' exploration of cultural hybridity as a lived experience appears also in the work of Hanif Kureishi, Salman Rushdie and Michael Ondaatje, who refuse to see themselves as in exile and begin to embrace the rich wealth of a new cultural mixture: cultural and individual hybridity in all its differences.

See also *Criticism*: Global citizenship and cosmopolitanism, Mimicry.

Further reading

Syal, Meera, *Life Isn't All Ha Ha Hee Hee* (London, Black Swan, 2000).

Mimicry

The term mimicry has been developed by Homi Bhabha to explore the ambivalence of colonial experience and discourse. In India, Macaulay's 'Minute' (Macaulay, 1835) supported providing Indians with a European education to help develop 'civilised' ways in these 'savage' foreigners. But a European education helped produce people who rejected much that was India but were somewhat different from Europeans. For Bhabha the consequence of the 'Minute' and other Europeanising strategies is mimicry. Mimicry is the process by which the colonised subject is reproduced as 'almost the same, but not quite' (Bhabha, 1994, p. 86). Colonised people are seen as copying the coloniser and in so doing both mock and 'menace' them, 'so that mimicry is at once resemblance and menace' (p. 86). Mimicry upsets the authority of colonial discourse, which is reproduced, altered and undermined. Naipaul's novel *The Mimic Men* (2001) explores the destructive, confusing effects of mimicry. Characters represent people in society who mimic others, the colonial ex-powers. In so doing they are clearly troubled and unable to establish their *own* voice. The descent of the 'mimic man', which starts with Macaulay's writing, Bhabha notes, is traceable also through the works of Kipling, Forster and Orwell. It is the product of 'a flawed colonial mimesis in which to be Anglicized is *emphatically* not to be English' (1994, p. 87). Mimicry is a menace to colonial power because it produces writing which exposes the ambivalence and ambiguity of colonial discourse, both undermining and questioning it.

We are reminded of Merle Collins' powerful performance poem 'Crick Crack Monkey' (1985), in which colonial discourse and history are undermined and reinterpreted at the moment when the colonised (in her poem the hunted lioness) speaks out using the forms of the coloniser (the hunter) and tells a different story. This is a positive version of mimicry, while Naipaul's was one which seemed to undermine and reduce those seen as mimic men.

See also *Criticism*: Global citizenship and cosmopolitanism, Hybridity.

Further reading

Bhabha, Homi H., 'The Other Question: Sterotype, Discrimination and the Discourse of Colonialsim', in *The Location of Culture* (London: Routledge, 1994)

Collins, Merle, 'Crick Crack Monkey', in *Because the Dawn Breaks: Poems Dedicated to the Grenadian People* (London: Women's Press, 1985).

Macaulay [1835] in S.I. Choudhury, 'Rethinking the Two Englishes' in F. Alam, N. Zaman and T. Ahmed (eds), *Revisioning English in Bangladesh* (Dhaka: The University Press Limited, 2001).

Nation language

Nation language is Edward Kamau Brathwaite's term for culturally specific forms of Caribbean English. Brathwaite sees nation language as heavily influenced by the African heritage in Caribbean cultures, and suggests that while the language used in, for instance, Jamaica, may be English in terms of its lexical features, 'in its contours, its rhythm and timbre, its sound explosions, it is not English, even though the words, as you hear them, might be English to a greater or lesser degree' (Brathwaite 1984, p. 311). Brathwaite argues that this language is the result of a specific cultural experience when he says,

> it is an English which is not the standard, imported, educated English, but that of the submerged, surrealist experience and sensibility, which has always been there and which is now increasingly coming to the surface and influencing the perceptions of contemporary Caribbean people.
>
> Brathwaite, 1984, p. 311.

Brathwaite distinguishes nation language, a positive term claiming identity, from 'dialect' which, he argues, is considered 'bad English'. Nation language is based on an *oral* tradition; the language is based in sound, breath, song and noise. So, in Brathwaite's own poetry we find a vital use of vernacular, of breath and rhythm in speech, and of local sounds. In the work of Mikey Smith, performance poet, Dread talk, a Rastafarian variant of Jamaican English, revving motorbike sounds and Smith's own pace of breathing reproduce the language, tone, mood and perspective of ordinary people whose voices have been silenced.

Louise Bennett, Caribbean performance poet, fully expresses the sense in which colonised peoples, migrating, bring with them language built on the coloniser's, but also develop nation language of their own. In her 'Colonisation in Reverse', she explores the immigration to Britain of Caribbean folk in the 1940s and 1950s, celebrating the return to the mother country this suggests, and the ways in which both Jamaicans settling in England and the English they settle among will change as a result.

> Wat a joyful news, Miss Mattie,
> I feel like me heart gwine burs'
> Jamaica people colonizin
> Englan in reverse.'
> ('Colonisation in Reverse', Bennett, 1966)

The language is vernacular, a version of the coloniser's English, and the views of 'de mother land' and perspectives will indeed 'tun history upside dung'. Populating 'De seat o' de Empire' will make radical changes.

The use of nation language gives a voice to silenced ordinary people. It is a variant of Standard English and couples thoughts and feelings. It is used by Caribbean poets, particularly performance poets, to characterise the lives and people they know, the history and culture they feel is not heard of in poetry or the media, and which brings changes to all concerned.

See also *Texts:* Nation language, Oral-based literature, oral literature, Performance poetry.

Further reading

Bennett, Louise, 'Colonisation in Reverse', in *Jamaica Labrish* (Kingston: Sangsters Book Stores, 1966).

Brathwaite, Edward Kamau, *The History of the Voice* (London: New Beacon, 1984).

Négritude

Négritude was a Black consciousness movement which began among African and African diaspora students in Paris in the 1930s, and established a sense of pride in African cultural values, emphasising the worth and distinctiveness of African personality and culture, so it was somewhat essentialist, but in a positive sense to encourage solidarity. African Francophone writers including Leopold Sédar Senghor and Birago Diop, and Caribbean theorist Aimé Césaire, studying in French universities, developed the theory of Négritude in Paris, building on their views, origins and experiences of exposure to influences from African-American movements such as the earlier Harlem Renaissance (1930s). Négritude emphasised the similarities between those of African descent and developed the notion of 'race', suggesting the concept of a specifically 'African personality'. Influential intellectuals such as Jean Paul Sartre embraced the ideas, and Négritude fed into the kind of cultural exchange which influenced both politics and art, such as that between American Booker T. Washington and Caribbean Marcus Garvey. Frantz Fanon latterly developed the theory further and it fed into the 1960s American 'Roots' movement where African Americans sought their African roots.

Issues and practices of subject formation converge with postcolonial studies in Fanon's work, which starts by revising and reviewing the

Lacanian mirror stage when the infant, seeing himself in the mirror, constructs a version of self, or subject, as opposed to that of Other, not-self. In gendered terms, this identity recognition results in woman being seen as the Other, since both Freudian and Lacanian psychoanalysis consider the norm to be male, and here there is a convergence of ideas equally useful for feminist critics eager to challenge a gendered norm of identity, history and discourse. In terms of culture and ethnicity, this recognition results in the Black person being defined as Other, which clearly constitutes a negative deconstruction which Fanon, writers and theorists would wish to slough off. In terms of ethnicity, Fanon argues:

> When one has grasped the mechanism described by Lacan, one can have no further doubt that the real Other of the white man is and will continue to be the black man. And conversely, only for the white man is the Other perceived on the level of the body image, absolutely as the not-self – that is, the unidentifiable, the unassimilable. For the black man . . . historical and economic realities come into the picture.
>
> Fanon, 1967, p. 161.

As Ania Loomba points out (1998, p. 144), in this essentialist and negative construction, the Black man becomes defined by his 'limitless sexuality' (related we assume to the racist argument that animal nature is more predominant in a Black than a white man, the latter being thought to be inevitably 'civilised', that is, in control of his libido because of his pale skin colour). For 'the black subject' however, the white Other serves to define everything that is desirable, everything that the self desires. This desire is embedded within a power structure, so 'the white man is not only the Other but also the master, real or imaginary' (Fanon, 1967, p. 138, quoted in Loomba, 1998, p. 144). Therefore 'blackness confirms the white self, but whiteness empties the black subject' (Loomba, 1998, p. 144). Faced with the ostracism and Otherness of their self image, Black people adopt white masks. Recognising this alienation of self, this translation can lead to resistance and retranslation, recuperation, and redefinition. While Fanon's *Black Skin, White Masks* is concerned with the psychologies of the oppressed, in line with his own developing political activism, *The Wretched of the Earth* urges the revolt of the oppressed.

Some see Césaire and Fanon's assertion of Négritude as a version of a limited, perhaps dangerous, nationalism, and Fanon also critiqued its tenets as potentially leading to a simplistic, celebratory Negroism, an unconditional affirmation of African cultures beyond the European. Such an assertion of similarity, in this instance of African cultural features and characteristics, however, is possibly a necessary first step to independent thought, identity and history. Fanon is a key postcolonial theorist and an author of revolutionary fervour, arguing for agency, the recognition of a unified Black self released by valuing the cultures which colonialism denigrates and subordinates.

Fanon's work enables engagement with debates about how ex-colonial subjects develop and seize their own identities, sloughing off the destructiveness of colonial experiences and perceptions which represent them in a negative light. In this respect, his work can be fed into the theorising of, for example, Caribbean performance poetry, and the work of Edward Kamau Brathwaite, who celebrates the rhythms – Calypso, dub, reggae – indigenous to the Caribbean. It can also feed into the language which helps reclaim a sense of varied national identity – from Jamaican, Trinidadian, Barbadian, etc, Creole to Dread talk (the language of Rastafarians, a mix of Jamaican English and Creole – the Caribbean performance poets are commented on in *Texts*). It can also usefully underpin our thoughts about the ways in which Achebe recuperates histories of African people, which replace a different historical perspective to that of the white imperialist, and Ngugi deliberately writes in Gikuyu, each establishing or re-establishing a sense of national cultural identity using language and form, historical recuperation and differing perspectives. In our reading of Erna Brodber's *Myal* (1988) there is a specific exploration of how a woman of Caribbean/African origin – Ella – has her story retold and re-presented in a staged musical performance by her writer American husband Selwyn Langley. Ella sees someone else as a white mask of herself – and is temporarily completely silenced, but eventually in recognising this pretence, this misrepresentation of her history and self as a form of theft, is able to retell histories and re-educate other children; she seizes power without revolution.

See also   *Contexts*: Fanon, Frantz (1925–61); *Texts:* Forms of writing – identity and subjectivity; *Criticism*: Essentialism, Fanon, Frantz (1925–61).

Further reading

Brodber, Erna, *Myal* (London: New Beacon Books, 1988).
Fanon, Frantz, 'On National Culture' (1961) in D. Walder (ed.), *Literature in the Modern World* (London: Edward Arnold, 1998), and 1967, quoted in Ania Loomba, ed., *Colonialism/Post Colonialism* (London: Routledge, 1998).

Postcolonial Gothic

Postcolonial Gothic mixes these two destabilising, questioning influences – the Gothic and the postcolonial. The latter ensures readers are presented with cultural difference and the demand that the gaps in their knowledge be at least a little filled with contextual information, and some understanding of different worldviews beyond the facts of the everyday reality of the differences posed by geography, climate and history.

Postcolonial texts are strange, sometimes even to those whose cultures have produced them. Because of their postcolonial nature, they query, undercut, question and problematise the imposed values and interpretations of history and of the colonisers' worldviews; they are challenging and disturbing. Already we are, oddly enough, assigning similar words to the descriptions of the Gothic. If we and our students need to learn to problematise seemingly fixed comfortable versions of everyday life, authorised histories, normalised readings of relationships of power and of values when reading the Gothic, or reading the post-colonial, how much more so must we ensure this kind of insight, imaginative freedom, sense of alternatives and diversity of underpinning values of representation and interpretation is nurtured when reading, studying and articulating arguments about the postcolonial Gothic, doubly defamiliarised, doubly entrenched and duplicitous.

One area of danger in reading and studying the postcolonial Gothic is the possible tendency to view these strangers from strange places as naïve, folk tale, the fantasy ways in which a maybe simpler (because foreign) or merely different people try to explain events they cannot fully comprehend. Those attitudes come dangerously close to some of the statements made by colonisers, imperialists and settlers, who saw both an empty space before them and very primitive cultures, and set about reinterpreting both space and culture within their own frameworks of interpretation, affected as those were by their own histories, locations, perspectives and worldviews. If you don't understand something you try and fit it in with what you are familiar with and by so doing are very likely to misunderstand and misinterpret, moving between simplifying, to grasp and feel secure in your new knowing, and some sense of disgust or repulsion at the elements which don't fit your scheme of things.

Interestingly, the reading practices involved in studying the Gothic seem here to be emerging as very similar to those involved in studying the postcolonial. There is a tendency to Otherise the strange and confusingly different, finding this Other fascinating and dangerous, in need of reduction to a comprehensible scheme of interpretation, a zone with which we are familiar, and which probably only temporarily, if at all, disturbs our comfort zones, our tendencies to produce conventional readings within a framework of acceptable values, beliefs and interpretations. Students approaching the postcolonial can also be somewhat dismayed by the vast array of critical approaches and terminology –

hybridity, metropolitan theory, whether there is a hyphen in postcolonial or not (and what it actually defines) and the very minefield of linguistic and value-related articulations which it uses (is hybridity OK to use, or is it insulting? What about Black?). It's an uncharted territory navigated by clever folk who like to impress and exclude. Postcolonial theorising emphasises the exclusion of those who don't fit into a scheme and set of interpretations, a linguistic register and critical worldview whose arcane rules and regulations seem frequently to be there to obfuscate and confuse rather than lead towards enlightened attempts at making some kind of sense of what is being read and discussed.

In reading and teaching postcolonial Gothic the two absolutely key elements are the theory they share – that of Otherising, excluding and destroying, or recognising the rich differences of the Other we construct in order somehow to feel clearer and more secure about our own stable identities, however individual or national. Kristeva is central to this. In her *Powers of Horror* (1982), she identifies abjection of that which is Other than ourselves, therefore both fascinating and disgusting, in need of exclusion from us so that we might recognise ourselves as whole. Here, and later in *Strangers to Ourselves* (1991), she shows that the Other is a monster of our own making. We have, of course, constructed it from what we desire and fear in order to recognise ourselves and the very limited, complacent, confined, conventional self; one which finds it difficult, perhaps, to recognise that here could be a diversity of versions of self and events, a diversity of perceptions and interpretations, and that what is strange provides a challenge to some visioned complacency rather than something which must be destroyed, colonised or redescribed. The Gothic fractures comfortable surfaces and complacencies, retains contradictions, compromising what seems given, as does the postcolonial.

For certain readers this wealth of ambiguity and exposure of the relatives of value systems and systems of interpretation can be terrifying, threatening and definitely to be avoided. Others luxuriate in the possibilities offered, generous, imaginative-minded travellers in a strange country. They need enough familiarity not to feel alienated entirely, enough accessible theory to begin to try and interpret, and some creative free imaginative space to experience the different ways in which histories, worldviews and interpretations could be perceived and constructed, represented and negotiated. It is challenging and it is absolutely fundamental to our reading practices, even beyond the postcolonial or the Gothic, and the postcolonial Gothic. These kinds of issues and strategies are at the heart of studying literature itself – structures, presentations, significances, differences, varied perspectives and challenges to the status quo.

The postcolonial Gothic can be found within some aspects of novels which themselves could not be described as Gothic. Forster's *A Passage to India* (1924) is a case in point, not postcolonial in terms of its dates, but postcolonial if we read its problematising of the rigid conventional Imperial British worldviews at the level of descriptions of and interpretations of location – laid out with roads intersecting at right angles in a grid system, which would attempt to contain and reduce the foreign world in which it sits like a club on the brow – both allegorical description (the Club sits on the hill), and an indication of the violence deemed necessary to control Indian natives. Meanwhile, Chandrapore, with its rich, fertile, rotting, shapeshifting qualities refuses the translations, the systematisation, simple description and rule of the imperialists.

Introduced at the start of the novel as unknowable and indefinable, the Marabar caves can be seen through the lens implied by the postcolonial Gothic. Indescribable, untouched by human and time, they are mythic, like the Otherness at the heart of a different culture. Any attempt to label and reduce them to the comprehensible systems we bring with us for those purposes merely renders them utterly dull and meaningless, or a threatening place where you are confronted with Otherness and your own fears of the indefinable, whether it be of great issues such as identity, or values or why we are here. Mrs Moore has a dark night of the soul because of her encounters with what? In the caves – all systems of power being thrown into relativism seem no longer to sustain any sense of values – she stares into an abyss. The more prosaic Miss Quested possibly merely stares into the meaningless abyss of her own sealed self and how the future she has constructed with Ronny has been undermined by his pomposity and her lack of a role in Imperial India. But the caves being Other, growths both of a foreign country and of a foreign mythology, are examples of the postcolonial Gothic and so open up for us as readers and students rich opportunities to problematise, question and not necessarily translate into the value systems of the prosaic and the familiar something indescribable and incomprehensible by realistic description and the systems of interpretation and language of imperial colonial Britain. Postcolonial Gothic writer Beth Yahp's *The Crocodile Fury* (1992) mixes a recuperated version of Malaysian history, where the coloniser is seen as a powerful, dominant, destructive then reclusive figure, with the oppressed energies of colonised people, which emerge in the invasion of a bandit figure and of a crocodile or sea serpent, each of which is both person and creature (were beasts).

See also *Text*: Postcolonial Gothic.

Further reading

Kristeva, Julia, *Powers of Horror* (New York: Columbia University Press, 1982).
Kristeva, Julia, *Strangers to Ourselves* (London: Harvester Wheatsheaf, 1991).
Yahp, Beth, *The Crocodile Fury* (North Ryde, NSW: Angus & Robertson, 1992).

Postcolonial theory

By distinguishing between manifest and latent Orientalism, Edward Said's *Orientalism* allowed the process of constituting European culture from the margin to be a partially unconscious one (see Said, Edward (1935–2003) and Orientalism. pp. 260–3). In other words, evidence for the colonial reflex need not involve awareness on the part of Europeans. Postcolonial theorists have argued that the colonial or postcolonial margin is constitutive of Western culture more generally insofar as defining a margin between Western culture and postcolonial, affects many other definitions and categories.

Indeed, one of the most vibrant areas of postcolonial thinking has involved the reinterpretation of canonical works of European literature that are not ostensibly concerned with colonialism at all. Writers like Gayatri Chakravorty Spivak and Edward Said have analysed texts by 'neo-colonial writers' (Jane Austen, Mary Shelley, Charlotte Brontë, Baudelaire, Kafka, Shakespeare) as constituted by the colonial margin. Others have explored the ways in which the intertwining of core and periphery has shaped other aspects of European culture. Paul Rabinow suggests that the colonies were crucial for experiments in modernism that were difficult to carry out in the (French) metropole. Several writers (such as McClintock) have reconstructed the impact of colonialism on the evolution of the modern ideas of race and social evolutionary theory, starting in the eighteenth century, and on European understandings of sexuality, gender and social class. Others have examined the ways in which intra-European class dynamics were displaced on to the colonial field. The new colonial studies have also started to disrupt entrenched ways of thinking about processes that are not colonial in any conventional sense.

For centuries, Europeans viewed their intellectual and pedagogical relationship to the colonised and postcolonial periphery as a one-way street. Missionaries, colonisers, social scientists and development agencies understood the flow of knowledge in similar ways. Postcolonial studies have finally started to reverse this entrenched mode of relating to the periphery. The first generation of postcolonial critics, such as Hobsbawm, came disproportionately from colonial and postcolonial countries themselves. Some have criticised these critics for working within universities in Europe and the United States while attacking the core, but this seems less important than the fact that these writers were able to come up with startlingly new insights. But now these insights are available to all.

See also *Criticism:* Colonial discourse, Said, Edward (1935–2003) and Orientalism.

Further reading

McLintock, Anne, *Imperial Leather: Race, Gender and Sexuality in the Colonial Contest* (London: Routledge, 1995).
Said, Edward, *Orientalism: Western Conceptions of the Orient* (London: Penguin, 1978).
Spivak, Gayatri Chakravorty, 'Three Women's Texts and a Critique of Imperialism', *Critical Inquiry* 12 (1985).

Said, Edward (1935–2003) and Orientalism

Edward Said is the author of the colonial concept of 'Orientalism', in which Western, particularly European, colonisers historically have constructed the East, the Orient as exotic, strange, exciting, dangerous, to be exhibited, tamed, silenced. Their imperialistic response always Otherises the East and people from the East (or the Southern hemisphere). Once Said's term is understood, the behaviours which it describes can be challenged.

Born in Jerusalem, Palestine, Edward Said, a Christian Arab, moved to Cairo in 1947 during the partition of Palestine, where he and his family lived as refugees. He was educated in America. When the Arab–Israeli war broke out (1967), he reviewed his own identity as a Palestinian – his cultural origins, literary scholarship and Palestinian rights. In 2002, with Dr Mustafa Barghouthi, Dr Haidar Abdel-Shafi and Ibrahim Dakak, he helped to found the Palestinian National Initiative, or Mubadara, a democratic opposition movement in Palestinian domestic politics.

Influenced by Michel Foucault and Antonio Gramsci in his concern with the ways in which discourses construct and replicate power formations, Said's work is underpinned by beliefs in the links between culture, geography, politics and history. He is best known for *Orientalism: Western Conceptions of the Orient* (1978), in which he argues that the West's view of the Middle East and the Islamic world is distorted by Otherising. He is sometimes seen, with Frantz Fanon, as producing a founding text for postcolonial studies. Said bases his critical work on literary examples influenced by culture and power, and shows how language in postcolonial writing holds Oriental people and ways at a distance, for celebration and denigration as Other. Said discusses Orientalism as a Western institutional way of dealing with the Orient, the East, and as he uses discourse analysis inspired by Foucault, he notes the Orient is dealt with 'by discourse, describing, teaching, ruling, settling: in short, Orientalism as a Western style for dominating, restructuring, and having authority over the Orient' (*Orientalism*, 1978). It is 'a *distribution of* geopolitical awareness into aesthetic, scholarly, economic, sociological, historical and philological text; it is an *elaboration* not only of a basic geographical distinction (the world is made up of two unequal halves: orient and occident) but also a whole series of "interests"' (Said, 1985, p. 12), creating prejudices, and political power differences, and thus hierarchies of value.

Some critics argue that, problematically, by speaking for the silenced, Said inevitably became something of an Orientalist himself, though this was far from his intentions:

> My idea in Orientalism is to use humanistic critique to open up the fields of struggle, to introduce a longer sequence of thought and analysis to replace the short bursts of polemical, thought-stopping fury that so imprison us. I have called what I try to do 'humanism', a word I continue to use stubbornly despite the scornful dismissal of the term by sophisticated post-modern critics. By humanism I mean first of all attempting to dissolve Blake's 'mind-forg'd manacles' so as to be able to use one's mind historically and rationally for the purposes of reflective understanding. Moreover, humanism is sustained by a sense of community with other interpreters and other societies and periods:
>
> Said, *Al-Ahram Weekly*, 2003.

While Orientalism is mainly a study of how the Western colonial powers of Britain and France represented North African and Middle Eastern lands in the late nineteenth and early twentieth centuries, 'the orient' is also used to suggest the Far East and the treatment of others who are culturally not white and Western imperial/colonial. Said concludes that Orientalism continues today in Western media reports of eastern, especially Arab, lands, and the media coverage of Iraq, when under American and British invasion, would be a case in point. Non-Western people are depicted as ill-educated, violent, savage, less than human and also, often, fascinating because exotic.

Said also evidenced ways in which representation common to colonialism continues after decolonisation. Orientalism is a Western fantasy, a construction, an imposition of a Western vision and set of values on eastern peoples in a way which builds on the binary division it makes between the Orient and the Occident (the West). Each is constructed as in opposition to the other, so the Orient is represented as everything that the West is *not*, its 'alter ego'. The Orient, fabulous and temptingly different, is also the poor relation, a threat to Western homogenising and stability, and secondary in a hierarchical relationship.

Ironically, Orientalism (Said argues) leads to 'postcolonial studies', which focuses on differences. In his *The World, the Text and the Critic* (1983), the essays 'Travelling Theory' and 'Criticism Between Culture and System' argue links between reading well, literature and cultural context. His political and polemic books include *The Question of Palestine* (1979), *Covering Islam* (1981) and *After the Last Sky* (1986).

Said's views of US/Arab relations and misconceptions 'come out of a long dialectic of US involvement in the affairs of the Islamic world, the oil-producing world, the Arab world, the Middle East – those areas that are considered to be essential to US interests and security' (Said, *Al-Ahram Weekly*, 2003). The US has played a distinct role in this political history, while Arabs view the US both as a fascinating place to send their children for education and yet a location of armies and interventions against Palestine and the Arab world.

Said was very critical about the perpetuation of versions of Othering based in Orientalism following the destruction of the Twin Towers on 9/11. His oppositional role is, in his words, 'to sift, to judge, to criticize, to choose so that choice and agency return to the individual'. He envisions a community that doesn't exalt 'commodified interests and profitable commercial goals' but values instead 'survivability and sustainability in a human and decent way. Those are difficult goals to achieve. But I think they are achievable' (from a phone interview in late September after the 9/11 tragedy). On 11 September 2001, the attack on the Twin Towers in Wall Street, Manhattan, New York, in which thousands lost their lives, not only shocked the world but led, in the minds of some, to a kind of cultural polarisation between Muslims and Christians. This was based on the popular conception that Fundamentalist Muslim revolutionary leader Osama bin Laden had masterminded the event as a deliberate attack on Western powers and specifically on the US, its ways and its power. Key to that US power was colonial power and the contemporary commodity-oriented version of capitalism. Theorists and thinkers such as Said recognised cultural differences but tried to defuse culturally based violent reactions.

See also   *Contexts:* Postcolonialism and feminism, Postcolonial discourse; *Texts:* Language, discourse, culture and power: reclaiming/rewriting language and power. *Criticism:* Colonial discourse.

Further reading

McLeod, John, *Beginning Postcolonialism* (Manchester: Manchester University Press, 2000).

Said, Edward, *Orientalism: Western Conceptions of the Orient* (London: Penguin, 1978).

Said, Edward, *The Question of Palestine* (New York: Vintage, 1979).

Said, Edward, *Covering Islam* (New York: Vintage, 1981).

Said, Edward, 'Travelling Theory', and 'Criticism between Culture and System', in *The World, the Text and the Critic* (Cambridge, MA: Harvard University Press, 1983).

Said, Edward, *After the Last Sky* (New York: Random House, 1986).

Said, Edward, *Al-Ahram Weekly* (2003, August 7–13, Issue 650 online: www.weekly.ahram. org.eg/2003/650/op11.htm (weekly.ahram.org.eg/2003/652/op1.htm).

Speaking about or for Others

For readers and critics alike, making a suitable critical response is an important way to articulate and negotiate engagement and communication, and to move on. If we are ourselves from these historically marginalised groups, it is crucial to recognise their powerful voice and ensure it speaks for us and those like or unlike us. If we are from the historically marginalising groups, then sanitisation through merely responding critically can just continue a form of silencing, letting a generalised critical statement take over from investigating and celebrating individuality, exposing different terrible histories, and different developments. Standing back in shocked silence unable to comment also disempowers postcolonial writers. Writing about the writing of others hitherto marginalised, hidden and silenced raises the issue of potential appropriation, and possibly arrogant liberal assumptions that our (possibly white, European, Western, possibly male) recognition of texts by postcolonial writers puts them on the reading and studying map. These responses can replicate the kind of cultural imperialism against which many postcolonial authors write:

> The problems of speaking *about* people who are 'other' cannot, however, be a reason for not doing so. The argument that it's just too difficult can easily become a new form of silencing by default . . . But whites can never speak *for* Blacks.
>
> Spivak and Gunew, 1986, p. 137.

Interestingly, postcolonial critics themselves have intervened in this complex position and feminist postcolonial critic Gayatri Chakravorty Spivak offers a speaking position for white audiences reading texts by Black, Asian and postcolonial writers, suggesting that there is a kind of silencing going on, one of guilt and paralysis, because of potentially emerging as the victimiser rather than the victim, and asking: 'Why not develop a certain degree of rage against the history that has written such an abject script for you that you are silenced?' (Spivak and Gunew, 1986, p. 137). We all need to engage; on the other hand, merely celebrating and recording, without critical response, is insulting because the engagement is crucial for dialogue and development, while 'speaking for' other people's experiences should also be avoided. From different subject positions how can we ever really know what others' lives have been like or their points of view and comments? Identifying, enabling, reading and engaging in a dialogue with writing from a postcolonial context is fraught with delicate issues like this, and readers, students and critics from colonised, marginalised, or coloniser, marginaliser or neutral positions (there are not really any neutral positions) need to take their own subject position and history into account before responding, but they also need to respond, bring the work into a shared space to speak about history and moving on.

Similarly problematic is a critical approach which essentialises post-colonial writing as if the variety of experiences of these diverse people was largely a product of being Other than European (and specifically Other than British) and, additionally, somehow always characterised by speaking out against oppression. Some writers, Glaswegian Nigerian Jackie Kay for instance, have articulated their irritation at being expected only to write about their difference, their blackness, their marginalised subject position which consistently places the white interlocutor or critic in the superior position, and suggests that the ex-colonised Other has no other identity than that of oppressed and ex-victim. Many writers, Cypriot women for instance, do not seem to need to identify themselves *against* a monolithic British or European identity, nor do they write from positions of colonial oppression. Rather they tend to concentrate on identity, relationships and women's roles. So, too, many writers from other cultural contexts might write about their lives avoiding the subject of their story of colonisation, whether seen as oppressive, or (rarely, if ever) enabling. Such issues of postcolonial critical practice – avoiding essentialising and Otherising, avoiding seeing postcolonial writers solely in terms of speaking from a subaltern position, speaking out against oppression, among others, can form an important part of the discussion of such texts and their challenges.

See also *Texts*: Recuperating and Rewriting History.

Further reading

Spivak, Gayatri Chakravorty, and Sneja Gunew 'Questions of Multiculturalism', in *Hecate*, 12 (1986).

Spivak, Gayatri Chakravorty (1942–)

Gayatri Chakravorty Spivak is known for her engagement with issues of nationality, language and expression, intermixed with gender. Trained in the theory of Derrida, Spivak deliberately refuses homogenous argument. She uses atypical discourses, such as interviews, to deliver her ideas, and avoids insisting on a single argument, deferring signification in her work, preferring to explore issues, raise questions and use journalism and talk as modes of exploration. Another tension in her work is her postcolonial – and feminist – inspired wish to find a way of giving a voice to the oppressed other or the Gramscian notion of the 'subaltern', meaning 'of inferior rank'. 'The subaltern' is a term used by Antonio Gramsci to indicate groups in society subject to the control of ruling classes. While subaltern classes traditionally include peasants, workers and others denied access to controlling power, Gramsci, interested in politics and the state, focused on their historiography. Spivak specifically linked the notion of the subaltern to that of eastern women, silenced, marginalised and disenfranchised economically and socially.

'The subaltern' would involve some indication and acceptance of individual subjectivity, while also refusing the notion of the subject itself, since we are all constructs and results of time, place and influences rather than bourgeois subjects. These tensions make her work difficult to read but also dialogic and inspirational.

Spivak, in her famous essay 'Can the Subaltern Speak?' (1988), asks whether postcolonial studies can help to give a voice to suppressed peoples. She argues that the construction of the subaltern group by other groups essentialised the people so defined, who were silenced by the elite who so defined them, and so should they try to speak, they could never escape using the language which itself constructed them as secondary, subordinate. She points out that anyone who has achieved the literacy and sophistication to produce writing which is defined widely by others is almost certainly actually not themselves as subordinated or subaltern in position and so disqualified from speaking for the people they are supposed to represent.

Ashcroft *et al.* comment that silencing can be overcome, arguing that Spivak's point is that 'no act of dissent or resistance occurs on behalf of an essential subaltern subject entirely separate from the dominant discourse that provides the language and the conceptual categories with which the subaltern voice speaks. Clearly, the existence of postcolonial discourse itself is an example of such speaking, and in most cases the dominant language or mode of representation is appropriated so that the marginal voice can be heard.' In other words, they suggest that the subaltern, ironically, can employ the dominant colonial discourse to articulate the very silence that it has created (Ashcroft *et al*, *Post-Colonial Studies*, 2000, p. 219).

See also *Contexts*: Postcolonialism and feminism; *Texts*: Patriarchy and colonised women.

Further reading

Spivak, Gayatri Chakravorty, 'Can the Subaltern Speak?' in C. Nelson and L. Grossberg (eds), *Marxism and the Interpretation of Culture* (London: Macmillan 1988).

Chronology

No chronology can cover every moment of history. What follows is a chronology of key moments in postcolonial history but also of texts and authors that engage, at some level, with postcolonial issues. The intention is to suggest ways in which the political and the textual inform the shifting dimensions of the postcolonial in terms of both resistance to and dialogue with the West. References to non-postcolonial texts, and authors such as Virginia Woolf, D.H. Lawrence, T.S. Eliot and William Golding are included because they address postcolonial issues and have a postcolonial attitude.

1492 Columbus, on travelling to India in the attempt to discover a new trade route, arrives in the Americas and calls the islands now known as the islands of the Caribbean the 'West Indies'

1611 William Shakespeare, *The Tempest*

1719 Daniel Defoe, *Robinson Crusoe*

1776 The 13 original colonies of the United States declare independence from Great Britain a year after their armed revolt begins

1783 The British Crown recognises the independence of the United States

1803 The last French territories in North America are handed over to the United States, via the Louisiana purchase

1804 Haiti, in declaring independence from France, becomes the first non-white nation to emancipate itself from European rule

1808 End of the slave trade in the British Empire

Brazil, the largest Portuguese colony, achieves independence, following the exiled king of Portugal, establishing his residence there. Once he has returned home (1815), his son and regent declares an independent 'Empire' (in 1822)

1813 Paraguay becomes independent from Spain

1816 Argentina declares independence from Spain. Uruguay, then included in Argentina, achieves its independence in 1828

1818 Second and final declaration of independence of Chile from Spain

1819 Colombia (New Granada) gains independence from Spain; Panama secedes from it in 1901 and becomes an independent nation

1821 The Dominican Republic (Santo Domingo), Nicaragua, Honduras, Guatemala, El Salvador and Costa Rica all declare independence from Spain. Venezuela and Mexico also achieve independence from Spain

1822 Ecuador gains independence from Spain (and from Colombia in 1830)

1824 Peru and Bolivia gain independence from Spain

1833 Slavery Abolition Bill in Britain

1857 The Indian Mutiny or First War of Independence

1865 The Dominican Republic gains its final independence from Spain

Morant Bay Uprising

1867 Independence of Canada

1868 Cuba declares independence from Spain and is reconquered. It is taken by the United States in 1898 and governed under US military administration until 1902

1899 Outbreak of the South African or Second Anglo–Boer War

Joseph Conrad, *Heart of Darkness*; Thomas Hardy's Boer War poems; Rudyard Kipling, *The White Man's Burden*

1900 Nigeria becomes a British Protectorate

Relief of the besieged cities of Ladysmith and Mafeking (in South Africa)

Joseph Conrad, *Lord Jim*; W.E. Henley, *For England's Sake*

1901 Australian federation (Aboriginals are not counted in the federal census)

Queen Victoria dies

Britain annexes the Asante Kingdom as part of the Gold Coast in Africa

Miles Franklin, *My Brilliant Career*; Rudyard Kipling, *Kim*; Alice Perrin, *East of Suez*

1902 The South African Second Boer War ends

Cecil John Rhodes (founder of Rhodesia) dies

Joseph Conrad, *Youth*; J.A. Hobson, *Imperialism: A Study*; W.B. Yeats, *Cathleen ni Houlihan*

1903 Joseph Furphy, *Such is Life*; G.A. Henty, *With Kitchener in the Soudan*; Alice Perrin, *The Stronger Claim*; Rabindranath Tagore, *Binodini*

1904 Joseph Conrad, *Nostromo*

1905 Curzon begins work towards the Partition of Bengal and the Swadeshi movement of Indian resistance follows

1906 In South Africa the Zulu (Natal) the Bambata Rebellion

1907 Self-governing (white) colonies are declared Dominions

Pablo Picasso, *Les Demoiselles d'Avignon*

1908 Robert Baden-Powell, *Scouting for Boys*

1909 Morley-Minto reforms in India

Maud Driver, *The Englishwoman in India*

1910 John Buchan, *Prester John*; E.M. Forster, *Howards End*

1912 Formation of the South African Native National Congress (later the African National Congress)

Stephen Leacock (Canada), *Sunshine Sketches of a Little Town*; Claude McKay, *The Dialect Poetry*; Rabindranath Tagore, *Gitanjali*

1913 Rabindranath Tagore wins Nobel Prize for Literature

Solomon T. Plaatje, *Native Life in South Africa*; Sidney and Beatrice Webb, *Indian Diary*; Leonard Woolf, *The Village in the Jungle*

1914 Outbreak of First World War

Northern and Southern Nigeria unite

W.B. Yeats, *Responsibilities*

1916 Easter rising in Ireland

W.B. Yeats 'Easter 1916'

Battle of the Somme

James Joyce, *A Portrait of the Artist as a Young Man*; Katherine Mansfield, *The Aloe*

1917 October Revolution in St Petersburg

V.I. Lenin, *Imperialism: The Highest Stage of Capitalism*

1918 The Allies and Germany sign the Armistice on 11 November

Declaration of the Irish Republic

1919 Montagu-Chelmsford reforms (permitting partial self-government)

Rowlatt Acts and Amritsar massacre in India

Peace Conference at Versailles creates the League of Nations

The Dominions achieve more autonomy within the British Empire

The Austro–Hungarian Empire is divided following the First World War

1919
cont
Outbreak of Anglo-Irish War (–1921)

End of the UK protectorate over Afghanistan; Britain accepts the presence of a Soviet ambassador in Kabul

1920 Britain gives mandate control over Iraq, Transjordan, Palestine

Marcus Garvey's Back-to-Africa movement

Government of Ireland Act is passed

Katherine Mansfield, *Bliss, and Other Stories*

1921 Non-Cooperation movement in India begins, led by Mahatma Gandhi (–1922)

The Anglo-Irish Treaty followed by the outbreak of Civil War in Ireland (–1923)

Chinese empire loses control over Outer Mongolia (retaining Inner Mongolia), which (along with Tibet) has been granted autonomy in 1912, and now becomes a popular republic

W.B. Yeats, *Michael Robartes and the Dancer*

1922 The Irish Free State is declared

T.S. Eliot, *The Waste Land*; James Joyce, *Ulysses*; D.H. Lawrence, *Aaron's Rod* and *Fantasia of the Unconscious*; Virginia Woolf, *Jacob's Room*

1923 End of the 'de facto' protectorate of the UK over Nepal

D.H. Lawrence, *Kangaroo*; E.J. Pratt (Canada), *Newfoundland Verse*

1924 E.M. Forster, *A Passage to India*; Kenneth Slessor, *Thief of the Moon*

1925 Thomas Molofo, *Chaka*; Frederick Philip Grove, *Settlers of the Marsh*; Virginia Woolf, *Mrs Dalloway*

1926 D.H. Lawrence, *The Plumed Serpent*

1927 Frederick Philip Grove, *A Search for America*; D.H. Lawrence, *Mornings in Mexico*

1928   Morley Callaghan, *Strange Fugitive*; Dorothy Livesay (Canada), *Green Pitcher*; Claude McKay, *Home to Harlem*; W.B. Yeats, *The Tower*

1929   Claude McKay, *Banjo*; Virginia Woolf, *A Room of One's Own*

1930   Civil Disobedience Movement in India

The United Kingdom returns the leased port territory at Weihaiwei to China, the first episode of decolonisation in East Asia

Una Marson, *Tropic Reveries*; Solomon T. Plaatje, *Mhudi*; Henry Handel Richardson, *The Fortune of Richard Mahony*

1931   Statute of Westminster creates the British Commonwealth of Nations and establishes the constitutional parity of the Dominions with Britain. Britain grants virtually full independence to Canada, New Zealand, Newfoundland, the Irish Free State, the Commonwealth of Australia and the Union of South Africa, when it declares the British parliament incapable of passing law over these former colonies without their own consent

Una Marson, *Heights and Depth*; Naomi Mitchison, *The Corn King and the Spring Queen*; George Orwell, *A Hanging*; Edward Thompson, *A Farewell to India*; Virginia Woolf, *The Waves*

1932   The United Kingdom ends the League of Nations Mandate over Iraq. Britain continues to station troops in the country and influence the Iraqi government until 1958

J.R. Ackerley, *Hindu Holiday*; Joyce Cary, *Aissa Saved*; Kenneth Slessor, *Cuckooz Contrey*; Evelyn Waugh, *Black Mischief*

1933   T.S. Eliot, *After Strange Gods*; Frederick Philip Grove, *Fruits of the Earth*; Claude McKay, *Banana Bottom*

1934   The United States makes the Philippines a Commonwealth. The Abrogates Platt Amendment gives it direct authority to intervene in Cuba

Morley Callaghan, *Such Is My Beloved*; George Orwell, *Burmese Days*; Jean Rhys, *Voyage in the Dark*; Christina Stead, *Seven Poor Men of Sydney*; Evelyn Waugh, *A Handful of Dust*

1935 Italian invasion of Abyssinia

Government of India Act

Mulk Raj Anand, *Untouchable*; Rex Ingamells (Australia), *Gum Tops*; R.K. Narayan, *Swami and Friends*

1936 The Spanish Civil War breaks out

British poets such as Stephen Spender and W.H. Auden go to fight in Spain.

Mulk Raj Anand, *Coolie*; Joyce Carey, *The African Witch*; Graham Greene, *Journey Without Maps*; C.L.R. James, *Minty Alley*; Jawaharlal Nehru, *An Autobiography*; George Orwell, *Shooting an Elephant*; Frank Sargeson, *Conversation with my Uncle*, Nella Larson, *Passing*

1937 Eire becomes a republic

Congress assumes power in most Indian provinces

Mulk Raj Anand, *Two Leaves and a Bud*; Karen Blixen, *Out of Africa*; Zora Neale Hurston, *Their Eyes Were Watching God*; R.K. Narayan, *The Bachelor of Arts*; George Orwell, *The Road to Wigan Pier*

1938 C.L.R. James, *The Black Jacobins*; Jomo Kenyatta, *Facing Mount Kenya*; Raja Rao, *Kanthapura*; Evelyn Waugh, *Scoop*; Virginia Woolf, *Three Guineas*

1939 German invasion of Poland and outbreak of Second World War

Provincial governments resign in India

Leonard Barnes, *Empire or Democracy?*; Joyce Cary, *Mister Johnson*; Aimé Césaire, *Cahier d'un retour au pays natal*; Graham Greene, *The Lawless Roads*; Kenneth Slessor, *Five Bells*

1940 Fall of France to German army

George Orwell, *Inside the Whale*; Christina Stead, *The Man Who Loved Children*

1941 Lebanon declares independence, ending the French mandate (previously with Syria) and is recognised in 1943

1941 Ethiopia, Eritrea & Tigre (appended to it), and the Italian part of
cont Somalia are liberated by the Allies after occupation by Italy since
1935–6, no longer joined as one colonial federal state, while the
Ogaden desert (disputed by Somalia) remains under British military
control until 1948

Rudyard Kipling, *A Choice of Kipling's Verse*, edited by T.S. Eliot;
Virginia Woolf, *Between the Acts*

1942 Quit India movement

Louise Bennett, *Dialect Verse*

1944 Jamaica achieves self-government

Louise Bennett, *Anancy Stories and Poems*; Dorothy Livesay, *Day
and Night*

1945 VE day (Victory in Europe): end of war in Europe

Atomic bombs fall on Hiroshima and Nagasaki, Japan, followed
by Japanese surrender

Labour government in Britain committed to speeding up Indian
independence

Fifth Pan-African Congress in Manchester calls for 'the right of
all colonial peoples to control their own destiny'

Korea independent after 40 years of Japanese rule but splits into
communist North Korea and capitalist South Korea. Formal
recognition of Mongolia

R.K. Narayan, *The English Teacher*; George Orwell, *Animal Farm*;
Leopold Sedar Senghor, *Chants d'ombre*

1946 First Assembly of the United Nations

The former emirate of Transjordan (now Jordan) becomes an
independent Hashemite kingdom when Britain relinquishes UN
trusteeship

Postwar division of Berlin and East and West Germany between
Allies and USSR; start of Cold War

Peter Abrahams, *Mine Boy*; Evelyn Waugh, *When the Going Was
Good*; Judith Wright, *The Moving Image*

1947 India wins independence from the British Empire

The Partition of India and the creation of Pakistan

Birago Diop (Senegal), *Les contes d'Amadou Koumba*; Malcolm Lowry (Canada), *Under the Volcano*

1948 Independence of Burma and Ceylon (Sri Lanka)

Burma and Eire leave the Commonwealth

Nationalist Party wins elections in South Africa on Apartheid issue

Israel becomes independent less than a year after the British government withdraws from the Palestine Mandate. The remainder of Palestine becomes part of the Arab states of Egypt and Transjordan

SS Empire Windrush arrives at Tilbury, London bringing first postwar Caribbean immigrants to Britain

Graham Greene, *The Heart of the Matter*; Alan Paton, *Cry, the Beloved Country*; Jean-Paul Sartre, *Orphee noir*

1949 Communist takeover followed by People's Republic of China proclaimed under Mao Tse-tung

Laos independent from France

Independence of Indonesia is recognised

Eire gains independence from British Empire

George Orwell, *1984*; V.S. Reid, *New Day*

1950 India proclaimed a republic

The Korean War begins (–1953)

Mau Mau meetings held in Kenya

1951 China occupies Tibet

Libya becomes an independent kingdom

Nirad C. Chaudhuri, *The Autobiography of an Unknown Indian*; E.M. Forster, *Two Cheers for Democracy*; Rex Ingamells, *The Great South Land*

1952 The African National Congress in South Africa organises the anti-Pass Law Defiance Campaign

Mau Mau resistance in Kenya intensifies leading to declaration of a State of Emergency

Puerto Rico in the Antilles becomes an overseas Commonwealth of the United States, not independent

First British atom bomb tested

Frantz Fanon, *Peau noire, masques blancs*; E.J. Pratt, *Towards the Last Spike*; Amos Tutuola, *The Palm-Wine Drinkard*

1953 France recognizes Cambodia's independence

Camara Laye (Guinea), *L'Enfant noir*

Bernard Binlin Dadie (Ivory Coast), *Legendes africaines*; E.M. Forster, *The Hill of Devi*; Nadine Gordimer, *The Lying Days*; George Lamming, *In the Castle of My Skin*

1954 Beginning of anti-colonial nationalist uprising in Algeria led by Ahmed Ben Bella

Vietnam's independence from France recognised, but the nation is partitioned

The Pondicherry enclave incorporated into India

The United Kingdom withdraws from the last part of Egypt it controls, the Suez Canal zone

Peter Abrahams, *Tell Freedom*; Camara Laye, *Le regard du roi*; William Golding, *Lord of the Flies*; George Lamming, *The Emigrants*; Amos Tutuola, *My Life in the Bush of Ghosts*

1955 Bandung Conference of independent Asian and African countries

Final withdrawal of British troops from Egypt

Congress of the People in South Africa

Patrick White, *The Tree of Man*

1956 Independence of Sudan

Suez crisis.

1956
cont

Anglo-Egyptian Sudan becomes independent

Hungarian revolution and Soviet invasion

Castro lands in Cuba

Tunisia and the sherifian kingdom of Morocco in the Maghreb achieve independence from France

Peter Abrahams, *A Wreath for Udomo*; Mongo Betu (Cameroon), *Le pauvre Christ de Bomba*; Mavis Gallant (Canada), *The Other Paris*; Sembene Ousmane (Senegal), *Le Docker Noir*; Ferdinand Oyono (Cameroon), *Une vie de Boy*; Sam Selvon, *The Lonely Londoners*

1957
Ghana becomes the first sub-Saharan state to achieve independence from Britain

Independence of Malaya, which becomes Malaysia

Mongo Beti, *Mission Terminal*; Naguib Mahfouz (Egypt), *Thalathiyy*; Kwame Nkrumah, *Autobiography*; Patrick White, *Voss*

1958
The All-African Peoples Conference meets in Accra, Ghana

Guinea (West Africa) is granted independence from France

Signing of the Alaska Statehood Act by Dwight D. Eisenhower grants Alaska possibility of equal rights of statehood

UN trustee Britain withdraws from Iraq, which becomes an independent Hashemite Kingdom (like Jordan, but soon becoming a republic through the first of several coups d'état)

West Indies Federation

Chinua Achebe, *Things Fall Apart*; George Lamming, *Of Age and Innocence*; R.K. Narayan, *The Guide*

1959
Castro gains power in Cuba

Nirad C. Chaudhuri, *A Passage to England*; Ezekiel Mphahlel, *Down Second Avenue*; Ian Mudie, *The Blue Crane*

1960
Harold Macmillan's 'winds of change' speech

Sharpeville Massacre in South Africa

Nigeria wins independence

1960 Aboriginals recognised as Australian citizens for the first time
cont

British Somaliland (present-day Somalia), and most of Cyprus become independent, though the UK retains sovereign control over Akrotiri, Episkopi and Dhekelia as British bases

Benin (then Dahomey), Upper Volta (present-day Burkina Faso), Cameroon, Chad, Congo-Brazzaville, Côte d'Ivoire, Gabon, the Mali Federation (split the same year into present-day Mali and Senegal), Mauritania, Niger, Togo and the

Central African Republic (the Oubangui Chari) and Madagascar all gain independence from France

The Belgian Congo (Congo-Kinshasa, later renamed Zaire and later again the Democratic Republic of the Congo), becomes independent

Chinua Achebe, *No Longer at Ease*; Wilson Harris, *Palace of the Peacock*; George Lamming, *The Pleasures of Exile*; Sembene Ousmane, *Les bouts de bois de Dieu*; Raja Rao, *The Serpent and the Rope*; Wole Soyinka, *A Dance of the Forests* performed

1961 Bay of Pigs invasion and Cuban missile crisis

Berlin Wall built

Tanzania wins independence

Sierra Leone, Kuwait and British Cameroon become independent from the UK

South Africa declares independence

Former Portuguese coastal enclave colonies of Goa, Daman and Diu taken over by India

Cyprian Ekwensi (Nigeria), *Jagua Nana*; Frantz Fanon, *Les damnes de la terre* (The Wretched of the Earth); Cheikh Hamidou Kane (Senegal), *L'Aventure ambigue*; V.S. Naipaul, *A House for Mr Biswas*

1962 Algeria, Jamaica, Trinidad and Tobago, Tanganyika and Uganda win independence

Civil Rights movement in the United States develops following bus protest by Rosa Parks

Indo-Chinese border dispute

1962 Zambia and Malawi (formerly Northern Rhodesia and
cont Nyasaland) become independent from the UK

Rwanda and Burundi (then Urundi) attain independence through ending Belgian trusteeship

The South Sea UN trusteeship over the Polynesian kingdom of Western Samoa (formerly German Samoa, now called just Samoa) handed over

Commonwealth Immigration Act introduced; Commonwealth citizens no longer have right to free entry to Britain

Kenneth Kaunda, *Zambia Shall Be Free*; Christopher Okigbo, *Heavensgate*

1963 Martin Luther King gives 'I have a dream' speech

Kenya gains independence

Treason trials involving Nelson Mandela, Walter Sisulu and seven others begin in South Africa

Singapore, and Sarawak and Sabah in North Borneo form Malaysia with the pensinsular Federation of Malaya

Margaret Laurence, *The Prophet's Camel Bell*; Wole Soyinka, *The Lion and the Jewel*

1964 Malawi and Zambia gain independence

Vietnam War breaks out (–1973)

Malta gains independence from the UK

Chinua Achebe, *Arrow of God*; Margaret Lawrence, *The Stone Angel*; Gabriel Okara, *The Voice*; Christopher Okigbo, *Limits*; Leopold Sedar Senghor, *Poemes*; Ngugi wa Thiong'o, *Weep Not, Child*

1965 Southern Rhodesia (Zimbabwe) declares independence from the UK as Rhodesia, a second apartheid regime, but is not recognized. Gambia is recognised as independent. The British protectorate over the Maldives archipelago in the Indian Ocean ends

In Britain the Race Relations Act is passed, leading to creation of Race Relations Board

1965 Ama Ata Aidoo, *Anowa*; Mudrooroo (Colin Johnson), *Wild Cat*
cont *Falling*; Wole Soyinka, *The Interpreters* and *The Road*; Ngugi wa
Thiong'o, *The River Between*

1966 Australia sends troops to Vietnam

In the Caribbean, Barbados and Guyana, and in Africa,
Botswana (then Bechuanaland) and Lesotho become independent from the UK

Chinua Achebe, *A Man of the People*; Elechi Amadi, *The
Concubine*; Margaret Atwood, *The Circle Game*; Louise Bennett,
Jamaica Labrish; Seamus Heaney, *Death of a Naturalist*; Robert
Kroetsch, *The Words of my Roaring*; Flora Nwapa, *Efuru*; Okot
p'Bitek, *Song of Lawino*; Jean Rhys, *Wide Sargasso Sea*; Paul
Scott, *The Jewel in the Crown*; Francis Selormey (Ghana), *The
Narrow Path*

1967 Secession of Biafra and outbreak of Nigerian civil war (–1970)

Six day Arab–Israeli War

On the Arabian peninsula, Aden becomes independent from the
UK, as South Yemen, to be united with formerly Ottoman North
Yemen (1990–1)

Edward Kamau Brathwaite, *Rights of Passage*; Wilson Harris,
Tradition, the Writer and Society (essays); Thomas Keneally, *Bring
Larks and Heroes*; Alex La Guma, *A Walk in the Night*; Gabriel
Garcia Marquez, *One Hundred Years of Solitude*; V.S. Naipaul,
The Mimic Men; Wole Soyinka, *Idanre, and Other Poems* and
Kongi's Harvest; Efua Sutherland, *The Marriage of Anansewa*;
Ngugi wa Thiong'o, *A Grain of Wheat*

1968 Martin Luther King shot and murdered

Student uprising in Paris

'Prague Spring' uprising

Mauritius and Swaziland achieve independence from the UK

After nine years of organised guerrilla resistance to Portuguese
rule, most of Guinea-Bissau comes under native control

Equatorial Guinea (Rio Muni) made independent from Spain

1968
cont
Australia relinquishes UN trusteeship (nominally shared by the United Kingdom and New Zealand) of Nauru in the Pacific

Mass demonstration in London and elsewhere against Vietnam War

Enoch Powell makes racist 'rivers of blood' speech against immigration

Edward Kamau Brathwaite, *Masks*; Bessie Head, *When Rain Clouds Gather*; Earl Lovelace, *The Schoolmaster*; Alice Munro (Canada), *Dance of the Happy Shades*; Yambo Onologuem (Mali), *Le Devoir de Violence*

1969
Elechi Amadi, *The Great Ponds*; Ayi Kwei Armah, *The Beautyful One Are Not Yet Born*; Edward Kamau Brathwaite, *Islands*; Robert Kroetsch, *The Studhorse Man*; Toni Morrison, *The Bluest Eye*; V. S. Naipaul, *The Loss of El Dorado: A History*

1970
Maya Angelou, *I Know Why the Caged Bird Sings*; Margaret Atwood, *The Journals of Susanna Moodie*; Nuruddin Farah, *From a Crooked Rib*; Oodgeroo Noonuccal (Kath Walker), *My People*; Flora Nwapa, *Idu*; Okot p'Bitek, *Song of Ocol*

1971
Civil war erupts in East Pakistan with a declaration by Sheikh Mujibir Rahman of the independent state of Bangladesh

Two-week India-Pakistan War ends in defeat for West Pakistan

Fiji and Tonga in the South Sea gain independence from the UK

Bahrain, Qatar, Oman and six Trucial States (federating as United Arab Emirates) become independent Arab monarchies in the Persian Gulf as British protectorates are lifted

Expulsion of Asians from Uganda by President Idi Amin; many sought refuge in Britain

Kofi Awoonor (Ghana), *This Earth, My Brother*; George Bowering, *Touch*; Northrop Frye, *The Bush Garden*; Bessie Head, *Maru*; George Lamming, *Water With Berries*; Alice Munro, *Lives of Girls and Women*; V. S. Naipaul, *In a Free State*; Wole Soyinka, *Madmen and Specialists*

1972
Margaret Atwood, *Surfacing* and *Survival*; Buchi Emecheta, *In the Ditch*; Thomas Keneally, *The Chant of Jimmie Blacksmith*; Wole Soyinka, *The Man Died: Prison Notes*

1973   Australian Aborigines granted the vote

Patrick White wins Nobel Prize for Literature

The Bahamas granted independence from the UK

Britain joins European Economic Community

Guerrillas unilaterally declare independence from Portugal in the Southeastern regions of Guinea-Bissau

Ceasefire announced in Vietnam

Ayi Kwei Armah, *Two Thousand Seasons*; Kamala Das, *The old playhouse and other poems*; J.G. Farrell, *The Siege of Krishnapur*; Athold Fugard, John Kani and Winston Ntshona, *The Island;* Witi Ihimaera, *Tangi*; Robert Kroetsch, *Gone Indian*; Derek Walcott, *Another Life*; Ruby Wiebe (Canada), *The Temptations of Big Bear*

1974   Pakistan recognises Bangladesh

The Labour Prime Minister of Australia, Gough Whitlam, is forced to resign

Grenada in the Caribbean gains independence from the UK

Guinea-Bissau on the coast of West Africa is recognised as independent by Portugal

Buchi Emecheta, *Second-Class Citizen*; Nadine Gordimer, *The Conservationist*; Bessie Head, *A Question of Power*; Margaret Laurence, *The Diviners*; Konai Helu Thaman, *You the Choice of My Parents*

1975   Indira Gandhi, the Prime Minister of India, found guilty of election fraud. State of emergency declared (–1977)

The Comoros archipelago in the Indian Ocean off the coast of Africa is granted independence from France

Angola, Mozambique and the island groups of Cape Verde and São Tomé and Príncipe, all four in Africa, achieve independence from Portugal. East Timor also declares independence, but is subsequently occupied and annexed by Indonesia nine days later

Surinam (Dutch Guiana) gains independence from the Netherlands

1975 Papua New Guinea gains independence from Australia
cont

Amilcar Cabral, *Unite et lutte*; Patricia Grace, *Waiariki*; Seamus Heaney, *North*; Linton Kwesi Johnson, *Dread, Beat an' Blood*; Bharati Mukherjee, *Wife*; Charles Mungoshi (Zimbabwe), *Waiting for the Rain*; V.S. Naipaul, *Guerillas*; Ntozake Shange, *Shange Play: One*

1976 Students revolt in Soweto, South Africa

Seychelles archipelago in the Indian Ocean off the African coast gains independence (one year after granting of self-rule) from the UK

Colonial rule by Spain terminated over the Western Sahara (Rio de Oro), but is partitioned between Mauritania and Morocco (which annexes the entire territory in 1979), rendering ineffective the declared independence of the Saharawi Arab Democratic Republic

Les Murray, *The Vernacular Republic*; Ngugi wa Thiong'o and Micere Mugo, *The Trial of Dedan Kimathi*; Wole Soyinka, *Death and the King's Horseman*

1977 French Somaliland (Afar and Issa-land after its main tribal groups), later called Djibouti, is granted independence from France

Ama Ata Aidoo, *Our Sister Killjoy*; Faith Bandler, *Wacvie*; Bessie Head, *The Collector of Treasures*; Ngugi wa Thiong'o, *Petals of Blood*

1978 Dominica in the Caribbean, and Solomon Islands and Tuvalu (the Ellice Islands) in the Pacific, gain independence from the UK

Ayi Kwei Armah, *The Healers*; Patricia Grace, *Mutuwhenua*; Dambudzo Marachera (Zimbabwe), *The House of Hunger*; Timothy Mo, *The Monkey King*; Edward Said, *Orientalism*; Wole Soyinka, *Myth, Literature and the African World* (essays)

1979 United States returns the Panama Canal Zone (held under a regime sui generis since 1903) to the republic of Panama

The Gilbert Islands (present-day Kiribati) in the Pacific as well as Saint Vincent (and the Grenadines) and Saint Lucia in the Caribbean become independent from the UK

1979 Mariama Ba (Senegal), *Une si longue lettre*; Buchi Emecheta, *The*
cont *Joys of Motherhood*; Nuruddin Farah, *Sweet and Sour Milk*;
Nadine Gordimer, *Burger's Daughter*; Festus Iyayi, *Violence*;
Mazisi Kunene, *Emperor Shaka the Great*; Alex La Guma, *Time of
the Butcherbird*; Mudrooroo, *Long Live Sandawara*; V.S. Naipaul,
A Bend in the River; Paul Scott, *Staying On*; Aminata Sow Fall
(Senegal), *La greve des battu*

1980 Zimbabwe wins independence

Quebec referendum on secession from Canada

The joint Anglo-French colony of the New Hebrides becomes the
independent island republic of Vanuatu

George Bowering, *Burning Water*; Anita Desai, *Clear Light of Day*;
Les Murray, *The Boys who Stole the Funeral*; Stanley
Nyamfukedza (Zimbabwe), *The Non-Believer's Journey*; Miriam
Tlali, *Amandla*; Derek Walcott, *Remembrance and Pantomime*

1981 Belize (British Honduras), Antigua and Barbuda gain independence from the UK

J.M. Coetzee, *Waiting for the Barbarians*; Nadine Gordimer, *Judy's
People*; Robert Kroetsch, *Field Notes*; Salman Rushdie, *Midnight's
Children*; Wole Soyinka, *Ake*; Ngugi wa Thiong'o, *Detained* and
'Writers in Politics' (essays); Archie Weller, *The Day of the Dog*

1982 Falklands War

Valerie Bloom, *Touch Me, Tell Mi*; Buchi Emecheta, *Double Yoke*;
Janet Frame, *To the Is-Land*; Julia Kristeva, *Powers of Horror*;
Catherine Lim, *The Serpent's Tooth*; Earl Lovelace, *The Wine of
Astonishment*; Timothy Mo, *Sour Sweet*; Ngugi wa Thiong'o, *Devil
on the Cross*

1983 Saint Kitts and Nevis (an associated state since 1963) gain independence from the UK

J.M. Coetzee, *The Life and Times of Michael K*; Wilson Harris, *The
Womb of Space* (essays); Mudrooroo, *Doctor Wooreddy's
Prescription for Enduring the Ending of the World*; Njabulo
Ndebele, *Fools*; Grace Nichols, *I Is a Long Memoried Woman*;
Michael Ondaatje, *Running in the Family*; Salman Rushdie,
Shame; Ngugi wa Thiong'o, *Barrel of a Pen*; Alice Walker, *The
Color Purple*

1984   Anglo–Chinese Hong Kong agreement

Brunei sultanate on Borneo becomes independent

Nicole Brossard (Canada), *Double Impression*; David Dabydeen, *Slave Song*; Janet Frame, *An Angel at My Table*; Seamus Heaney, *Station Island*; Jackie Kay, *A Dangerous Knowing*; V.S. Naipaul, *Finding the Centre*; Grace Nichols, *The Fat Black Woman's Poems*

1985   Neil Bissoondath, *Digging up the Mountain*; Merle Collins, *Because the Dawn Breaks*; Anita Desai, *In Custody*; Keri Hulme, *The Bone People*; Amryl Johnson, *Long Road to Nowhere*; Jamaica Kincaid, *Annie John*; Ellen Kuzwayo, *Call Me Woman*; Joan Riley, *The Unbelonging*; Nawal el Saadawi (Egypt), *God Dies by the Nile*; Nayantara Sahgal, *Rich Like Us*; Ken Saro-Wiwa, *Sozaboy*

1986   Wole Soyinka wins Nobel Prize for Literature

US bombing of Libya

Buchi Emecheta, *Head Above Water*; Nuruddin Farah, *Maps*; Amitav Ghosh, *The Circle of Reason*; Lorna Goodison, *I am becoming my mother*; Festus Iyayi, *Heroes*; Robert Kroesch, *Excerpts from the Real World*; B. Kojo Laing, *Search Sweet Country*; Mudrooroo, *The Song Circle of Jacky*; Ben Okri, *Incidents at the Shrine*; Caryl Phillips, *A State of Independence*; Olive Senior, *Summer Lightning*; Ngugi wa Thiong'o, *Decolonising the Mind*; Derek Walcott, *Collected Poems*

1987   Chinua Achebe, *Anthills of the Savannah*; Thea Astley, *It's Raining in Mango*; Witi Ihimaera, *The Whale Rider*; Sally Morgan, *My Place*; Toni Morrison, *Beloved*; V.S. Naipaul, *The Enigma of Arrival*; Michael Ondaatje, *In the Skin of a Lion*; Caryl Phillips, *The European Tribe*; Zoë Wicomb, *You Can't Get Lost in Cape Town, A Clearing in the Bush*

1988   Jean Breeze, *Riddym Ravings and Other Poems*; Erna Brodber, *Myal*; Peter Carey, *Oscar and Lucinda*; Upamanyu Chatterjee, *English, August*; Michelle Cliff, *No Telephone to Heaven*; J.M. Coetzee, *Foe*; David Dabydeen, *Coolie Odyssey*; Tsitsi Dangarembga, *Nervous Conditions*; Amitav Ghosh, *The Shadow Lines*; Lorna Goodison, *Heartsease*; Seamus Heaney, *The Government of the Tongue* (essays); Chenjerai Hove, *Bones*; Jamaica Kincaid, *A Small Place*; Ruby Langford, *Don't Take Your*

1988 *Love to Town*; R.K. Narayan, *A Writer's Nightmare* (essays); B.P.
cont Nichol, *Selected Organs*; Ben Okri, *Stars of the New Curfew*;
Salman Rushdie, *The Satanic Verses*; Glenyse Ward, *Wandering Girl*

1989 Ayatollah Khomeini pronounces death sentence (fatwa) on Salman Rushdie

The Berlin Wall comes down and Communist regime collapses in Eastern Europe

Tiananmen Square student demonstration in China crushed

Chinua Achebe, *Hopes and Impediments*; Nadine Gordimer, 'The Essential Gesture' (essays); M. Nourbese Philip, *She Tries Her Tongue*; Nayantara Sahgal, *Mistaken Identity*; Shashi Tharoor, *The Great Indian Novel*; Ngugi wa Thiong'o, *Matigari*; Miriam Tlali, *Soweto Stories*; M.K. Vassanji, *The Gunny Sack*; Derek Walcott, *Omeros*

1990 Nelson Mandela walks free from prison

The break-up of the former Soviet Union decolonised Eastern Europe and central Asia. Newly independent states of Armenia, Azerbaijan, Belarus, Estonia, Georgia, Kazakhstan, Kyrgyzstan, Latvia, Lithuania, Moldova, Russian Federation, Tajikistan, Turkmenistan, Ukraine and Uzbekistan result. The three Baltic republics – Estonia, Latvia and Lithuania – argue they could not be granted independence at the dismemberment of the Soviet Union because they never joined, but were militarily annexed by Stalin, and thus illegally colonised.

Reunification of East and West Germany

Namibia gains independence from South Africa

The UN Security Council gives final approval to end the US Trust Territory of the Pacific (dissolved in 1986), finalising the independence of the Marshall Islands and the Federated States of Micronesia (prior to US trusteeship and colonial possession of the empire of Japan)

Alan Duff, *Once Were Warriors*; Hanif Kureishi, *The Buddha of Suburbia*; Sindiwe Magona, *To My Children's Children*; Mudrooroo, *Writing from the Fringe* (essays)

1991 The Gulf War

Apartheid ends in South Africa

The constituent republics of the former Yugoslavia: Slovenia, Croatia, Macedonia, and Bosnia and Herzegovina started breaking away. After the initial Yugoslav wars, the process ends in 1992.

Jewelle Gomez, *The Gilda Stories*; Ben Okri, *The Famished Road*; Caryl Phillips, *Cambridge*; Salman Rushdie, *Imaginary Homelands* (essays)

1992 Nadine Gordimer wins Nobel Prize for Literature

Michael Ondaatje, *The English Patient*

1993 Derek Walcott wins Nobel Prize for Literature

Eritrea effectively decolonises itself from Ethiopia

Vikram Seth, *A Suitable Boy*; Ngugi wa Thiong'o, *Moving the Centre* (essays)

1996 Martha Nussbaum, *For Love of Country*

1997 The sovereignty of Hong Kong is returned to China, ending Britain's 99-year lease over the territory

Arundhati Roy, *The God of Small Things*; Meera Syal, *Anita and Me*

1998 Nalo Hopkinson, *Brown Girl in the Ring*

1999 East Timor achieves independence from Indonesia

The sovereignty of Macau is returned to China from Portugal, as the lease period has expired. It is the last coastal enclave that militarily stronger powers had obtained through treaties from the Chinese Empire. Like Hong Kong, it is guaranteed a semi-autonomous system of government within the People's Republic of China

Conflict in former Yugoslavia leads to ethnic cleansing

J.M. Coetzee, *Disgrace*; Salman Rushdie, *The Ground Beneath Her Feet*

2000   Zadie Smith, *White Teeth*

2001   9/11: the attack on the Twin Towers in Manhattan, New York (believed to have been directed by Osama Bin Laden).

Tananarive Due, *The Living Blood*

2002   The remainder of Yugoslavia, Serbia and Montenegro, formed the Federal Republic of Yugoslavia in 1992, which in 2002 was reformed and renamed Serbia and Montenegro

East Timor formally achieves independence from Indonesia after a transitional UN administration, three years after Indonesia ended its quarter-century military occupation of the former Portuguese colony

US and British military put on standby for war against Iraq, where Saddam Hussein is believed to be stockpiling 'weapons of mass destruction'

2003   Military invasion of Iraq by US and British forces after UN efforts to ensure Iraq has no weapons of mass destruction prove inconclusive

Monica Ali, *Brick Lane*

2004   Anthony Kwame Appiah, *The Ethics of Identity*; Andrea Levy, *Small Island*

2005   Lebanon's decolonisation from Syria is still ongoing

Salman Rushdie, *Shalimar the Clown*; Zadie Smith, *On Beauty*

References

Abraham and Torok, *The Shell and the Kernel: Renewals of Psychoanalysis, Volume 1* (Chicago: University of Chicago Press, 1994).

Ahmed, A., *In Theory,* (London: Verso, 1992).

Anderson, B., *Imagined Communities: Reflections on the Origin and Spread of Nationalism* (London: Verso, 1983).

Andrade, Susan Z., 'Rewriting History, Motherhood, and Rebellion: Naming and African Women's Literary Tradition', in *Research in Africa Literature,* 21, 1 (1990).

Angelou, Maya, *I Know Why the Caged Bird Sings* (London: Virago, 1970).

Appiah, Anthony Kwame, 'Cosmopolitan Patriots', in Martha Nussbaum and Joshua Cohen (eds), *For Love of Country* (Boston: Beacon Press, 1996).

Ash, Ranjana Sidhanta, 'Writers of the South Asian Diaspora in Britain: A Survey of Post-War Fiction in English', *Wasafiri,* Spring 21 (1995).

Ata Aidoo, Ama, *Anowa* (Harlow: Longman, 1965).

Atwood, Margaret, *Survival* (Toronto, ON: House of Anansi Press, 1972).

Bakhtin, Mikhail, *Rabelais and His World* [1965] (Cambridge MA: MIT Press, 1968).

Bandler, Faith, and Len Fox, Introduction, *Marani in Australia* (Adelaide: Rigby/Opal, 1980).

Baynton, Barbara, *Bush Studies* (London: Duckworth, 1902).

Belsey, Catherine, *Critical Practice* (London: Methuen, 1980).

Bennett, Louise, *Selected Poems* (Kingston: Sangsters Book Stores, 1982).

Bethel, Lorraine, in Barbara Smith *et al.,* (eds), *But Some of Us Are Brave: Black Women's Studies* (London: The Feminist Press, 1982).

Bhabha, Homi K., 'Of mimicry and man: the ambivalence of colonial discourse', in Philip Rice and Patricia Waugh (eds), *Modern Literary Theory: A Reader* (London: Edward Arnold, 1992).

Bodelsen, C. A., *Studies in Mid-Victorian Imperialism* (London: Heinemann, 1960).

Bradley [1788], cited in Jennings, K. and Hollingsworth, D. *Sly Maidens and Wanton Strumpets in Hecate* (1987–8) (pp. 113–33; p. 129).

Brathwaite, Edward Kamau, *Other Exiles* (Oxford: Oxford University Press, 1975).

Brathwaite, Edward Kamau, *Black + Blues* (Havana: Casa de las Américas, 1976).

Brathwaite, Edward Kamau, *Mother Poem* (Oxford: Oxford University Press, 1977).

Brathwaite, Edward Kamau, *Soweto* (Mona, Jamaica: Savacou, 1979).

Brathwaite, Edward Kamau, *Sun Poems* (Oxford: Oxford University Press, 1982).

Brathwaite, Edward Kamau, *Third World Poems* (Harlow, Essex: Longman, 1983).

Brathwaite, Edward Kamau, *X Self* (Oxford: Oxford University Press, 1987).

Brathwaite, Edward Kamau, *Middle Passages* (Northumberland: Bloodaxe Books, 1992).

Brown, David Maughan, *Land, Freedom and Fiction: History and Ideology in Kenya* (London: Zed Books, 1985).

Brown, Lloyd (ed.), *Women Writers in Black Africa* (Westport, Conn.: Greenwood Press, 1981).

Brown, Toni, 'Immunity', in Victoria A. Brownworth (ed.), *Night Bites: Vampire Stories by Women* (Seattle, WA: Seal Press, 1996).

Buck, Claire (ed.), *Bloomsbury Guide to Women's Literature* (London: Bloomsbury, 1992).

Butcher, K. F, 'Black Immigrants in the United States: A comparison with native blacks and other immigrants', *Industrial and Labor Relations Review*, 47 (1994).

Campbell Praed, Rosa, *Affinities: A Romance of To-day* (London: Richard Bentley & Son, 1885).

Carr, Helen, *Jean Rhys* (Tavistock: Northcote House, 1996).

Césaire, Aimé, 'Cahier d'un retour au pays natal' [1939] (Paris: Présence Africaine, 1983).

Chatterjee, Debjani, 'Animal Regalia', in *I Was That Woman* (Somerset: Hippopotamus Press, 1989).

Cixous, Hélène, *The Laugh of the Medusa* [1975], in Elizabeth Abel and Emily K. Abel (eds), *The Signs Reader: Women, Gender, and Scholarship* (Chicago: University of Chicago Press, 1976).

Clare, Monica, *Karobran: The Story of an Aboriginal Girl* (Sydney: APCOL, 1978).

Cliff, Michelle, *No Telephone to Heaven* (New York: Plume Books, 1996).

Coetzee, J.M., *Boyhood* (London: Secker & Warburg, 1997).

Coetzee, J.M., *Youth* (London: Secker & Warburg, 2002).

Cooper, C. quoting Zora Neale Hurston from *Their Eyes Were Watching God* (London: Virago, 1993), p. 7.

Cooper, 'The Word Unbroken by the Beat: The Performance Poetry of Jean Binta Breeze and Mikey Smith', in *Wasafiri*, no. 11 (1993).

Dabydeen, David, *Literature in the Modern World*, A316, BBC and Open University television production, 1991.

Daniels, Kay, and Mary Murnane, *Uphill All the Way* (Brisbane: University of Queensland Press, 1980).

Davidson, Basil, *The Black Man's Burden* (New York: Three Rivers Press, 1992).

Davis, Angela, *Women, Race and Class* (London: The Women's Press, 1982).

Davis, Jack *et al.*, (eds), *Paperbark, an Anthology of Black Australian Writing* (St. Lucia, QLD: University of Queensland Press, 1990.)

Deleuze, Gilles and Felix Guattari in David Punter, *Postcolonial Imaginings: Fictions of a New World Order* (Edinburgh: Edinburgh University Press, 2000)

Derrida, Jacques (1993) in David Punter, *Postcolonial Imaginings: Fictions of a New World Order* (Edinburgh: Edinburgh University Press, 2000).

Desai, Anita, *Cry, the Peacock* (New Delhi: Vision Books, 1963).

Desai, Anita, *Voices in the City* (London: Peter Owen, 1965).

Desai, Anita, *Bye, Bye Blackbird* (Delhi, India: Orient Paperbacks, 1968).

Desai, Anita, *Where Shall We Go This Summer?* (Delhi, India: Orient Paperbacks, 1975).

Desai, Anita, *Fire on the Mountain* (London: William Heinemann, 1977).

Desai, Anita, *In Custody* (London: William Heinemann, 1984).

Desai, Anita, *Baumgartner's Bombay* (London: Vintage, 1988).

Desai, Anita, *Journey to Ithaca* (London: William Heinemann, 1995).

Desai, Anita, *Fasting Feasting* (London: Vintage, 2000).

Devanny, Jean, *Sugar Heaven* (Sydney: Modern Publishers, 1926).

Devanny, Jean, *The Butcher Shop* (Sydney: Modern Publishers, 1926).

Devy, G.N., *After Amnesia: Tradition and Change in Indian Literary Criticism* (London: Sangam Books, 1992).

Dickens, Charles, *Great Expectations* [1861] (Glasgow: Blackie, 1961).

Dirlik, Arif, 'The Post Colonial Aura: Third World Criticism in the Age of Global Capitalism', in *Critical Inquiry*, 20, 2 (Winter) (1994).

Donga, *Makeba Muse,* Feb. (1977).

Driver, Dorothy, 'Transformation through Art; Writing, Representation and Subjectivity in Recent South African Fiction', in *World Literature Today: South African Literature in Transition*, 70, 1 (Winter) (1996).

Du Bois, W.E.B. (ed.), *Crisis,* the magazine of the NAACP (National Association for the Advancement of Coloured People) (New York: 1910).

Du Bois, W.E.B, *The Souls of Black Folks* [1903] (New York: Signet Classics, 1995).

Due, Tananarive, *The Between* (New York: HarperCollins, 1995).

Due, Tananarive, *My Soul to Keep* (New York: HarperCollins, 1997).

Due, Tananarive, *The Black Rose* (Madison: Turtleback Books, 2001).

Due, Tananarive, *The Living Blood* (New York: Washington Square Press, 2001).

Duff, Alan, in interview in *Meanjin,* C. Thompson (1993).

Duff, Alan, *Once Were Warriors*, in C. Thompson (ed.), *Talanoa: Contemporary Pacific Literature,* Thompson (Honolulu: University of Hawai'i Press, 1994).

Eagleton, Terry, *Ideology: An Introduction* (London and New York: Verso, 1991).

Eilersen, Gillian Stead, *Tales of Tenderness and Power* (Oxford, Heinemann, 1989).

Emecheta, Buchi, *Second Class Citizen* (London: Heinemann, 1974).

Emecheta, Buchi, *The Bride Price* (London: Allison & Busby, 1976).

Emecheta, Buchi, 'Feminism With a Small 'f'!.', in Kirsten Holst Petersen (ed.), *Criticism and Ideology: The Second African Writers Conference*, Stockholm, 1986, ed. Kirsten Holst Petersen (Upsala: Scandinavian Institute of African Studies, 1998).

Emecheta, Buchi, *Gwendolen* (London: Heinemann, 1989).

Evans, Raymond, 'Don't you remember Black Alice, Sam Holt? Aboriginal Women in Queensland History', in *Hecate,* 11, 2 (1982).

Faludi, Susan, *Backlash* (London: Pluto Press, 1992).

Fanon, Frantz (1967) quoted in Ania Loomba (ed.), *Colonialism/Post Colonialism* (London: Routledge, 1998).

Fee, Margery, 'Why C K Stead Didn't Like Keri Hulme's *The Bone People*: Who Can Write as Other?', in *Australian and New Zealand Studies in Canada* 1 (1989), in Sandra Tawake, 'Transforming the Insider–Outsider Perspective: Postcolonial Fiction from the Pacific', in *The Contemporary Pacific*, 12.1 (2000).

Ferrers, Kay, *A Time to Write* (Sydney: Penguin, 1984).

Franco, Jean, 'Beyond Ethnocentrism: Gender, Power and the Third-World Intelligentsia', in Cary Nelson and Lawrence Grossberg (eds), *Marxism and the Interpretation of Culture* (Basingstoke: Macmillan, 1988).

Franklin, Miles, *My Brilliant Career* [1901] (Melbourne: Georgian House, 1946).

Fugard, Athol, *Sizwe Bansi Is Dead* (New York: Viking, 1976).

Garvey, Marcus, *The Negro World* (New York: 1922).

Gilman, Sander, 'Black Bodies, White Bodies: Towards an Iconography of Female Secularity in Late Nineteenth-Century Art, Medicine and Literature', in J. Donald and A. Rattansi (eds), *Art, Culture and Difference* (London: Sage Publications, in association with the Open University, 1992).

Gilroy, Paul *et al.*, *The Empire Strikes Back: Race and Racism in 70s Britain* (Birmingham: Centre for Contemporary Cultural Studies, Birmingham University, 1982).

Gomez, Jewelle, *The Gilda Stories* (Ithaca, NY: Firebrand Books, 1991).

Goodison, Lorna, 'I Am Becoming my Mother', in *I Am Becoming My Mother* (London: New Beacon Books, 1986).

Gramsci, A., *Selections from the Prison Notebooks*, eds. and trans. Quintin Hoare and Geoffrey Nowell Smith (London: Lawrence & Wishart, 1971).

Guha, R. (ed.), *Subaltern Studies 1: Writings on South Asian History and Society* (7 vols) (Delhi: Oxford University Press, 1982).

Hacker, Andrew, *Two Nations: Black and White, Separate, Hostile, Unequal* (New York: Bantine Books, 1992).

Haggard, Rider, *She* [1887] (Washington DC: Regnery Publishing, 1999).

Hardy, Thomas, *Tess of the D'Urbervilles* [1891] (London: Penguin Classics, 2003).

Head, Bessie, *The Collector of Treasures* (London: Heinemann, 1977).

Head, Bessie, 'Life' in *Tales of Tenderness and Power* (London: Heinemann, 1989).

Head, Bessie, 'Portrait of a Wedding' in *Tales of Tenderness and Power* (London: Heinemann, 1989).

Head, Bessie, *Tales of Tenderness and Power* (London: Heinemann, 1989).

Henderson, Mae Gwendolen, in Laura Chrisman and Patrick Williams (eds), *Colonial Discourse and Post-Colonial Theory* (Hemel Hempstead: Prentice-Hall, 1993).

Holquist Michael and Katerina Clark, *Mikhail Bakhtin* (Cambridge, MA: Harvard University Press, 1984).

Hopkinson, Nalo, *Brown Girl in the Ring* (New York: Time Warner International, 1998).

Hopkinson, Nalo, 'A Habit of Waste', David Hartwell and Glenn Grant (eds), *Northern Suns* (New York: Tor Books, 1999).

Hopkinson, Nalo, *Skin Folk* (New York: Aspect, 2001).

Huggins, Jackie, 'Firing on the Mind: Aboriginal Women Domestic Servants in the Inter-War Years', in *Hecate*, 13, 2 (1987/8).

Hulme, K., *Te Kaihau/The Windeater* (Brisbane: University of Queensland Press, 1986).

Ihimaera, Witi, *Tangi* (Auckland: Heinemann, 1973).

Ihimaera, Witi, *Nights in the Gardens of Spain* (Auckland: Secker and Warburg, 1995).

Innes, C.L., in Bruce King (ed.), *New National and Post Colonial Literatures: An Introduction* (Oxford: Clarendon Press, 1996).

Irigaray, Luce, *This Sex Which is Not One* [1977] (New York: Cornell University Press, 1985).

Jacobs, Harriet, *Incidents in the Life of a Slave Girl* [1861] (London: Penguin, 2000).

James, C.L.R., *The Black Jacobins* [1938] (New York: Vintage, 1989).

Jameson, Frederick, *Marxism and Form: Twentieth-Century Dialectical Theories of Literature* (Princeton: Princeton University Press, 1971).

Jan Mohamed, Abdul R., 'Worldliness-without-World, Homelessness-at-Home: Toward a Definition of the Specular Border Intellectual', in Michael Sprinker (ed.), *Edward Said: A Critical Reader* (Oxford: Blackwell, 1992).

Johnson, Amryl, *Long Road to Nowhere* (London: Virago, 1985).

Jones, Eldred and E. Palmer, 'Locale and Universe', in *Journal of Commonwealth Literature*, 3 (1967).

Karodia, Farida, *Daughters of the Twilight* (Oxford: Heinemann, 1986).

Karodia, Farida, *Coming Home and Other Stories* (Oxford: Heinemann, 1988).

Keeffe, Kevin, 'Aboriginality: Resistance and Persistence', in *Australian Aboriginal Studies*, 1 (1988).

Keesing, R., 'Creating the Past: Custom and Identity in the Contemporary Pacific', in *Contemporary Pacific*, 1/2 (1989).

Koebner R. and H. Schmidt, *Imperialism: The Story and Significance of a Political Word, 1840–1960* (Cambridge: Cambridge University Press, 1964).

Kristeva, Julia, *Des Chinoises* (Paris: Éditions des Femmes, 1974).

Kristeva, Julia, 'Stabat Mater' (1976) in K. Oliver, *The Portable Kristeva* (New York: Columbia University Press, 1997).

Kristeva, Julia, *Desire in Language: A Semiotic Approach to Literature* (New York: Columbia University Press, 1980).

Kumar, Amitava, 'Introduction', in Amitava Kumar (ed.), *Away: The Indian Writer as an Expatriate* (London: Routledge, 2004).

Kunene, Mazisi, *Emperor Shaka the Great* (Portsmouth, NH: Heinemann, 1979).

Kuzwayo, Ellen, *Call Me Woman* (Johannesburg: Ravan Press, 1985).

Lacan, Jacques, *Écrits: A Selection*, trans. Alan Sheridon (London: Tavistock, 1977).

Langford, Ruby, 'Singing the Land', *Hecate*, 17, 2 (1991).

Larson, Charles, *The Emergence of African Fiction* (London: Macmillan, 1973).

Larson, Nella, *Passing* (New York: Knopf, 1929).

Lazarus, Neil, *Resistance in Post-Colonial African Fiction* (New Haven and London: Yale University Press, 1990).

MacKenzie, Craig, *Bessie Head: A Woman Alone – Autobiographical Writing* (Oxford: Heinemann, 1990).

Maes-Jelinek, Hena, *et al.*, *A Shaping of Connections: Commonwealth Literature Studies – Then and Now* (Sydney, Coventry, Aarhus: Dangaroo Press, 1989).

Maugham, Somerset, *The Moon and Sixpence* (London: Heinemann, 1919).

McConnel, Ursula, *Myths of the Munkan* (Carleton, Victoria: Melbourne University Press, 1957).

McGuinness, Bruce, in J. Davis and Bob Hodge (eds), *Aboriginal Writing Today* (Canberra: AIAS, 1985).

Memnott, Paul and Robin Horsman, Preface to Elsie Roughsey, *An Aboriginal Mother Tells of the Old and the New* (Ringwood: Penguin, 1984).

Meston, Archibald, *First Report on Western Aborigines*, 16 June, col/140 (1897).

Meyer, Susan L., 'Colonialism and the Figurative Strategy of *Jane Eyre*', in *Victorian Studies*, 33 (1990).

Mongia, Padmini, in Anna Rutherford, Lars Jensen and Shirley Chew, *Into the Nineties: Post-Colonial Women's Writing* (Armidale, New South Wales: Kunapipi, Dangaroo Press, 1994).

Moreton-Robinson, Aileen, *Talkin' Up to the White Woman* (Brisbane: Queensland University Press, 2000).

Morris, Mervyn, *Shadowboxing* (London: New Beacon, 1979).

Morris, Mervyn, 'Gender in Some Performance Poems', in *Critical Quarterly,* vol. 35, no. 1 (1988).

Morris, Mervyn, *Examination Centre* (London: New Beacon, 1992).

Morrison, Toni, *The Bluest Eye* (New York: Henry Holt, 1969).

Murray, Elizabeth, *Ella Norman or a Woman's Perils*, MICROFILM (Microform) 1 reel (35mm) (London: British Library, 1864).

Naipaul, V.S., *A House for Mr Biswas* (London: Andre Deutsch, 1961).

Naipaul, V.S., *The Middle Passage* (London: Andre Deutsch, 1962).

Naipaul, V.S., *In a Free State* (London: Andre Deutsch, 1971).

Naipaul, V.S., *Among the Believers: An Islamic Journey* (London: Penguin, 1981).

Naipaul, V.S., *The Enigma of Arrival* (London: Viking, 1987).

Naipaul, V.S., *A Way in the World* (London: Viking, 1994).

Naipaul, V.S., *The Mimic Men* (New York: Vintage, 2001).

Naipaul, V.S., *Half a Life* (London: Picador, 2001).

Naipaul, V.S., *Magic Seeds* (London: Picador, 2004).

Narayan, R.K, *The Guide* (London: William Heinemann, 1958).

Ngcobo, Lauretta, *Cross of Gold* (London: Longman, 1981).

Nichols, Grace, 'Winter Thoughts', in *Purple and Green: Poems by Women Poets* (London: Rivelin Grapheme, 1985).

Nichols, Grace, *Whole of a Morning Sky* (London: Virago, 1986).

Nwapa, Flora, *Idu* (London: Heinemann, 1970).

Nwapa, Flora, *This Is Lagos and Other Stories* (London: Heinemann, 1971).

Nwapa, Flora, *Never Again* (London: Heinemann, 1975).

Nwapa, Flora, *Wives at War and Other Stories* (London: Heinemann, 1980).

Nwapa, Flora, *Women Are Different* (London: Heinemann, 1986).

Ogungbesan, Kolawole, 'The Cape Gooseberry Also Grows in Botswana: Alienation and Commitment in the Writings of Bessie Head', in *Journal of African Studies*, 6 (1979).

Ondaatje, Michael, *Coming Through Slaughter* (Toronto: House of Anansi, 1976).

Ong, Walter, quoted in Gay Wilentz, *Binding Cultures* (Bloomington, IN: Indiana University Press, 1992).

Orwell, George, *Burmese Days* (San Diego, CA: Harvest/HBJ Book, 1974).

Oxford English Dictionary (Oxford University Press, 1989).

Peterson, Kirsten Holst and Anna Rutherford, *A Double Colonisation: Colonial and Post-Colonial Women, Writing* (Mundelstrop, Denmark: Dangaroo Press, 1986).

Pettman, Jan, *Living in the Margins* (New South Wales: Allen & Unwin, 1992).

Phillips, Mike and Trevor Phillips, *Windrush: The Irresistible Rise of Multi-Racial Britain* (London: HarperCollins, 1998).

Pritchard, Katherine Susannah, *Coonardoo* [1929] (Sydney: Harper & Collins, 2002).

Pule, John Puhiatau, *The shark that ate the sun: Ko e mago ne kai e la* (New York: Penguin, 1992)

Qabala, A. in Ari Sitas (ed.), *Black Mamba Rising: South African Worker Poets in Struggle* (Durban: Worker Resistance and Culture Publications, 1986).

Rao, Raja, *The Serpent and the Rope* [1960] (New York: Overlook Hardcover, 1986).

Reddy, Jayapraga, *On the Fringe of Dream-Time and Other Stories* (Johannesburg: Skotaville, 1987).

Rice, Anne, *Queen of the Damned* (New York: Alfred A. Knopf, 1988).

Rushdie, Salman, *Grimus* (London: Gollancz, 1975).

Rushdie, Salman, *The Satanic Verses* (London: Viking, 1988).

Said, Edward, *Joseph Conrad and the Fiction of Autobiography* (Cambridge, MA: Harvard University Press, 1966).

Said, Edward, *Beginnings: Intention and Method* (New York: Basic Books, 1975).

Said, Edward, *Covering Islam: How the Media and the Experts Determine How We See the Rest of the World* (London: Routledge, 1985).

Said, Edward, *Peace and Its Discontents* (New York: Random House, 1995).

Said, Edward, *Out of Place* (New York: Vintage Books, 1999).

Said, Edward, *Reflections on Exile* (Cambridge, MA: Harvard University Press, 2000).

Said, Edward, *Freud and the Non-European* (London: Verso, 2003).

Sam, Agnes, *Jesus is Indian and Other Stories* (Denmark: Dangaroo Press, 1989).

Scammell, G. V., *The First Imperial Age: European Overseas Expansion c. 1400–1715* (London: HarperCollins, 1989).

Schmidley, Dianne 'Profile of the Foreigh-Born Population' United States Bureau of the Census (2001) www.census.gov/prod/2002pubs/p23-206-pdf.

Sheshadri-Crook, Kalpana (1994) quoted in Loomba, Ania, *Colonialism/Post Colonialism* (London: Routledge, 1998).

Singh, Khushwant, *Train to Pakistan* (New York: Grove Press, 1956).

Slemon, Stephen, 'The scramble for post-colonialism' (1994) in Bill Ashcroft, Gareth Griffiths and Helen Tiffin, *Post-Colonial Studies: The Key Concepts* (London: Routledge, 2000).

Smith, Shirley C., with Bobbi Sykes, *Mumshirl: An Autobiography* (Richmond, Victoria: Heinemann, 1981).

Soyinka, Wole, *The Interpreters* (London: Heinemann, 1965).

Soyinka, Wole, *Season of Anomy* (London: Rex Collings Ltd, 1973).

Soyinka, Wole, *Opera Wonyosi* (Bloomington: Indiana University Press, 1981).

Spence, Catherine, *Clara Morrison: A Tale of South Australia during the Gold Fever* (London: John W. Parker & Son, 1854).

Spivak, Gayatri Chakravorty, *In Other Worlds: Essays in Cultural Politics* (London: Routledge, 1988).

Stead, C.K., 'Keri Hulme's *The Bone People* and the Pegasus Award for Maori Literature', in *Ariel: A Review of International English Literature* (New York: Modern Languages Association, 1985).

Sulter, Maud, 'As a Black woman' (1985), in Gina Wisker, *Post-Colonial and African American Women's Writing: A Critical Introduction* (Basingstoke: Macmillan, 2000).

Sutherland, Efua, *The Marriage of Anansewa* (Harlow: Longman, 1967).

Tasma, *Tasma's Diaries: The diaries of Jessie Couvreur with another by her young sister Edith Huybers* (Canberra: Mulini Press, 1995).

Tawake, Sandra, 'Transforming the Insider-Outsider Perspective: Postcolonial Fiction from the Pacific', in *The Contemporary Pacific*, 12.1 (2000).

Thiong'o, Ngugi Wa, *Detained: A Writer's Prison Diary* (London: Heinemann, 1981).

Threadgold, Terry, *Stories of Race and Gender: An Unbounded Discourse* (London: Pinter, 1988).

Tiffin, Helen, 'Post-Colonial Literatures and Counter Discourse', in *Kunapipi* 9 (1987).

Tlali, Miriam, *Muriel at the Metropolitan* (Johannesburg: Ravan Press, 1975).

Tlali, Miriam, *Amandla, a Novel* (Johannesburg: Ravan Press, 1980).

Tlali, Miriam, 'Dimomona', in *Footprints in the Quag: Stories and Dialogues from Soweto* (Cape Town: Clyson Printers, 1989).

Tlali, Miriam, *Soweto Stories* (London: Pandora Press, 1989).

Tutuola, Amos, *My Life in the Bush of Ghosts* (London: Faber & Faber, 1954).

Umeh, Marie, 'African Women in Transition in the Novels of Buchi Emecheta', in *Présence Africaine*, 116, 4 (1980).

Vervoerd, Hendrik, on the creation of the South African Department of Bantu Education in 1958, cited in William J. Pomeroy, *Apartheid Axis* (New York: International Publishers, 1971).

Ward, Glenyse, *Wandering Girl* (Broome, Western Australia: Magabala Books Aboriginal Corporation, 1988).

Ward, Glenyse, *Unna You Fullas* (Broome, Western Australia: Magabala Books Aboriginal Corporation, 1991).

Waters, M.C., *Black Identities: West Indian Immigrant Dreams Arm American Realities* (Cambridge, MA: Harvard University Press, 1999).

Wilentz, Gay, *Binding Cultures* (Bloomington, Ind.: Indiana University Press, 1992).

Willetts, Kathy, 'In Search of the Authentic Voice', in *Hecate*, 16, 1/2 (1990).

Wilson-Tagoe, Nana, 'Towards a Theorization of African Women's Writing', in Stephanie Newell (ed.), *Writing African Women* (London: Zed Books, 1997).

Woodcock, George (ed.), 'Possessing the Land' (1977) in *Canadian Literature*, Vol. 1 (Vancouver, BC: 1959).

Yulal-Davis, Nira and Floya Anthias in G. C. Spivak and S. Suleri, *Woman–Nation–State* (London: Macmillan, 1989).

Filmography

An Angel at My Table, dir. Jane Campion, 1990.

Anita and Me, dir. Meera Syal, 2002.

Bhaji on the Beach, dir. Meera Syal, 1992.

Cry Freedom, dir. Oliver Stone, 1987.

East is East, dir. Damien O'Donnell, 1999.

Literature in the Modern World, Lit A306, Open University film (with Linton Kwesi Johnson), 1991.

Once Were Warriors, dir. Lee Tamahori, 1994.

The Piano, dir. Jane Campion, 1993.

Whale Rider, dir. Niki Caro, 2003.

Music

Johnson, Linton Kwesi, *Dread, Beat an' Blood* (Island, 1978).
Johnson, Linton Kwesi, *Bass Culture* (Island, 1980).
Johnson, Linton Kwesi, *Tings an' Times* (LKJ Records, 1991).
Johnson, Linton Kwesi, *LKJ A Cappella Live* (LKJ Records, 1996).
Mbuli, Mzwakhe, 'The Spear Has Fallen', on *Change is Pain* (Rounder Records, 1992).

TV

Goodness Gracious Me, dir. Nick Wood, BBC2, 1998.
Life Isn't All Ha Ha Hee Hee, Meera Syal, 2005.
Warrior Marks, dir. Pratibha Parmar, with Alice Walker, Arena TV, 1993.
Windrush, dir. Celina Smith, BBC TV, 1998.

Websites accessed

Due, Tananarive, in interview 17 March 2002: www.tananarivedue.com/interview.htm
Hall, Stuart (1999) www.mediaed.org.uk/posted_documents/Hybridity/html
Hanania, Ray online: www.hanania.com/col11149.htm
Said, Edward, interview with David Barsamian, *The Progressive Interview* online: www.progressive.org/0901/intv1101.html
Said, Edward, *The Palestine Monitor online:* www.palestinemonitor.org/Special%20Section/Edward%20Said/The_edward_said_cover.htm
Wood, Michael, online: www.lrb.co.uk/v25/n20/wood01_.html

General Index

(Main references for specific topics are given in **bold type**)

Abbott, Diane, 68
Aboriginal, **9–10**, 128
  land rights, **47–8**, 68
  oral tradition, 117, 122, 130, 143;
    performance poetry, 132
  silenced or misinterpreted, 40, 114, 183;
  'third class citizens', 5, 129
  and the vote, 6, 201, 219
  women's experiences, 78–80, 158, 165,
    173
  writers, xiii, 63–4, **74–80**, 134, 138,
    164–5
Achebe, Chinua, 6, 10, 20, 43, 50, 55, 108,
  117, 159, **161–2**, 175, 178
  publication chronology, 218, 219, 220,
    221, 226, 227
  on story-tellers, 131; *Things Fall Apart*,
    72, 110
Adisa, Opal Palmer, 149
adoption, 126
Africa, 52–3, **112–18**
  ANC, 6, 15, 24, 45; colonialism, effects of,
    19, 44, 45, 55, 59, 161–3
  cultural roots/language, 43, 50, 93, 109,
    120–21, 149–55, 186–8, 191
  decolonisation, 21, 25; diaspora, 26, 27,
    49, 97, 182
  oral tradition, 75, 122, **130–38**;
    performance poetry, **139–46**
  women's experiences, 57, 81, 83, 86–7,
    101–6, 152, 164–75
African-American, 44, 57
  performance poetry, 138; race/gender
    perspectives, 108, 124, 148, 164, 183,
    188
  writing, 100, 121, 131, 133, 149–50, 163,
    187
  see also Négritude
Afrikaner/Afrikaans, 11
Aidoo, Ama Ata, 101, 106, 188
  legend, use of, 118, 132
  publication chronology, 221, 224
Ali, Monica, 32, 134
Alvi, Moniza, 32, 97
America, x, 3–7, 23, 152, 186–8
  diaspora, 27; indigenous peoples, 10–11,
    128, 133
  land rights, 47–8, 68; nationalism, 50 (*see
    also* Pan-Africanism)
  slavery, experiences of, 93, 121, 133, 182
  see also colonialism, decolonisation,
    independence
Amin, Idi, 28, 222
Angelou, Maya, 164, 222

Apartheid, 3, **11–16**, 84, 87, 154, 165–7,
  183
  protest and protest writers, 13, **80–3**, 132,
    145
Appiah, Anthony, 187–8
Arab, *see* orientalism
Armah Ayi Kwei, 55
Ash, Ranjana, 115
Ashcroft, Griffiths and Tiffin *et al.*, 10, 16,
  25, 175, 177, 178, 206–7
Asian, 86, 99
  immigrant experiences, **25–34**, 39
  women's experiences, 38, 57, 79–80, 97,
    98, 124, 134, 155–6
  writers, 43, 93, 100, 130, 133, 144,
    169–70, **179–91**
assimilation, 29, 30, 33, 36, 43, 45, 74, 169,
  186
Astley, Thea, 64
Atwood, Margaret, xiii, 5, 54, 58, 108
  Alias Grace, 61, 63, 157
  publication chronology, 221, 222
Australia, xiii, 4
  diaspora, 27; globalisation, 6;
    perceptions of, 147
  writers, 127, 148, 153, **156–8**, 175
  see also Aboriginal and colonisation
Auden, W.H., 1, 159
autobiography, 14, 75, 85, 103
  semi-fictionalised, 71, 77, 127, **164–8**

Ba, Mariama, 113
Bakhtin, Mikhail, 131, 133, 176
Bandung conference, 69
Bangladesh, 22
Barnard, Marjorie, 158
Bantustans, 12–13
Beat poets, 120, 133, 138
Bennett, Louise (Miss Lou), xv, 25, 46, 110,
  117, **121–2**, 140, 143, 193
Bermuda, 5
Bhaba, Homi, xii, 29, 50, 98, 176, 177, **179**,
  186, 187, **190**, 192
  cosmopolitanism, 56, 91; mimicry, 173
Biko, Steve, 14
Bloom, Valerie, 132–3, **143–4**
Boehmer, Elleke, 39, 45, 54, 133, 175
Brah, Avtar, 29
Brathwaite, Edward Kamau, xv, 110,
  120–1, 134, 143, 177, 193, 196
  publication chronology, 221, 222
Breeze, Jean 'Binta', 46, 108, 120, 132,
  140–2, 181
  Brighteye, 31–2, 66

239

British Commonwealth, 5, **22–3**, 24, 44, 63, 127, 178
British Empire, 4, 18, 22, 23, 44, 45, 61, 178, 190
  chronology, 208, 211, 216
Brodber, Erna, 46, 100, 131, 133
  Myal, 152–3, 196
Brontë, Charlotte, 60, 160, 200
Burford, Barbara, 124–5

Cabral, Amilcar, 11, 24, 43, 49, 50, 54, 60, 69
Caliban, 89–90, 135
Campion, Jane, 147, 237
Canada, xii, xiii, 14, 62, 117, 154
  chronology, 209, 213, 225 (*see also* Commonwealth)
  decolonisation, 4, 5, 23, 27, 156
  First Nation writers, 9, 74, 117, 127, 132
  women's expriences, 54, 58, 61, 63, 149, 151, 157
cannibalism, 16
canonical texts, xi, 61, 72, **89–90**, 107, 134, 143, 173, 200
Carey, Peter, 64, 158
carnival, 6, 68, **176**
Caribbean, xiv, xv, 4, **17**, 44, 45, 47, 69, 84
  immigrant experiences, 25, 27, 28, **31–2**, 34–5, 63, 78, 93, 108, 169, 180, 183, 191, 193 (*see also* SS Empire Windrush)
  language, 35, 36–7, **120–1**, 193
  poets/performance poets, 25, 35, 73, 121–2, 132–3, **138–45**, 177, 178, 180, 193–4
  and slavery, 35, 55, 117, 160–61
  women's experiences, 21, 36, 60, 97, 115, 124, 126, 148–9 (*see also* Hopkins, Nalo)
  see also colonialism
Carter, Angela, 54
Castro, Fidel, 50
Cesaire, Aime, 185, 194–5
Chatterjee, Debjani, 32, 98
Cixous, Helene, 54
Coetzee, J., xiii, 13, 14–15, **81**, 90, 100, 108, 111, 168
Cohen, Patsy, 76
Collins, Merle, 35, 93–4, 108, 117–18, 120, 132–3, 141, 181, 192
colonial, **3–9**, 10, 37, 39, 122, 175, 182, 186, 196, 200, 207
  anti-colonialism, **10–11**, 44–6, 50, 55, 59–60, 63, 69, 87–8, 156, 217
  colonialism, xi, xiii, xiv, 15, **17–22**, 26, 50, 57, 72–3, 82, 100, 112, 127, 147, 162–3, 171, 178, **185–90**, 202; and cultural inequality, 89–90, 98, 100, 108, 110–11, 124, 136, 152–5, 156–8, 160–1, 169, 204
  colonisation, 26, 28, 39, 205; colonised, viewpoint of the, 55, 102, 105
  decolonisation, **23–6**, 174; discourse, **177–8**; 'mimicry', xii, 192

neo-colonialism, **51–2**, 162
rule/influence, x, xi, xii, xv, xvi, 1–3, 10, 16, 28, 40, 44, 47–9, 51, 54, 62, 69, 71–3, 81, 95, 98, 108, 110, 130, 157, 159, 166, 174, 176–7, 184, 190, 201, 203; on language, **55–6**, 123, 174–5; stereotyping, **41–2**
  texts, xi, xiv, 61, 72, 81, 118, 134
Columbus, Christopher, 16, 17, 47
Commonwealth, 4–5, **22–3**, 44
  decolonisation within, 24
  Games, role of, 23,
  independence from, 45
  literature, 127, **178**; writers, 21
Communist influence, 45
Conrad, Joseph, 10, 20–1, 88
Cooper, Caroline, 141
Cosmopolitanism, 174, **179–82**
  global citizenship and, **186–8**
Creole, 60–1, **120, 122**, 160–1, 190, 196
Cyprus, xii, 4, 5, 45, 59, 157

Dabydeen, David, 25, 63
Dangarembga, Tsitsi, **21–2**, 58
Dark, Eleanor, 158
Defoe, Daniel, 81, 89–90
Derrida, Jacques, 206
Desai, Anita, xiii, 2, 24, 47, **94–7**, 114, 115, 123, 131, 132, **135–8**, 143
  publication chronology, 225, 226
Devanny, Jean, 158
dialect, viewed as 'substandard', 34–5, 120, 193
  reclaimed, 121, 143–4
dialogue
  and difference, **36–9**; between identities, 93; with diaspora, 27, 32, 34, 35
  with culturally mixed origins, 28; history, 30–1, 33, 34; homeland/s, 29–31, 33
diaspora, **24–35**, 36–9, 66, **92–9**, 101, 108, 116, 142, 144, 169–70, 180, 181–2, 194
  and musical forms, 121
Dickens, Charles, 64, 158
discourse, xii, xv, 8, 36, 38, **39–42**, **107–9**, 131, 134
  analysis, 202; atypical, 206; colonial, **177–8**, 192; colonialist, 45; and diaspora, 99, 181
  of disempowerment and challenge, 59, 101–2, 109–10, 123, 134, 135, 172, 179, 185, 195, 201
disenfranchisement, 7, 48
dispossession, 2, 48, 68, 79, 97, 98, 143, 145, 150, 164–5
Douglas, Marcia, 149
Dreaming, the, 10, 47, 75
Dub, 37, 73, 140, 143, 196
Du Bois, W.E.B., 52, 53, 149
Due, Tanarive, 149
Duff, Alan, 119, **128–9**

Egypt, 69
  chronology of independence, 216, 217, 218

Eldershaw, Flora, 158
Emecheta, Buchi, 29, 101, **103–6**, 108, 110,
    113, 115–16, 117, 133, 138, 143, 188
empire, 3–4, 7, **17–22**, 23, 25, 40, 44, 45,
    46, 48, 54, 58, 60, 61, 63, 159, 171, 190,
    194
  challenges to, **87–9**
  former British, 178
  myth of, 98
Enlightenment, 19, 84, 90, 159, 181, 186
  'enlightenment', 20–1, 94, 97
essentialism, 15, 57, 81, **184**
Eurocentric, 25
exile, 13, 25, 38, 89, 115, 156, 158, 169, 181,
    191

Fanon, Frantz, 11, 21, **43**, 45, 49, 50, 60, 69,
    184, **185–6**, 201
  see also Négritude
female circumcision (clitoridectomy), 101,
    188
feminism, xii, xiii, 54, 79, 80, 100, 102, 103,
    105, 106, 113, 119, 124, 131, 171,173,
    184, 195, 206
  and postcolonialism, **56–8**, 126, **155–6**
Ferrier, Carole, 75, 77, 78
Fiji, 16, 26, 42, 54
  Fijian writers, xiii
First Fleet, 59
First Nations, 6, **9**, 74
Forster, E.M., xvi, 21, 87–9, 172, 192, 199
Foucault, Michel, 55, 107, 110, 173, 177,
    202
Frame, Janet, 165
Franklin, Miles, 158
free trade, 23
Freire, Paulo, 109, 173
Freud, Sigmund, 185
  Freudian influence, 61, 131, 157, 169, 195
Fugard, Athol, 14

Gandhi, Mahatma, 46, 60
Garvey, Marcus, 60, 194
Gaza strip, 48, 50
genocide, 40, 62, 64, 68, 183
Ghana, 24, 45, 51, 69, 118, 120
ghettoisation, 30, 37, 97
Ghosh, Amitav, 29
ghosts, 150, 153
Gilroy, Paul, 30, 49, 67
global citizenship, 91, 179, **186–8**
global imperialism, 18, 19
globalisation, 5, 6
Goodison, Lorna, 115
Gordimer, Nadine, 11, 13
Govinden, Betty, 15, 164
Grace, Patricia, xiii, 119
Gramsci, Antonio, 201, 206
Guevara, Che, 69
Guinea-Bissau, 53
Gunew, Sneja, xiv, 173, 204, 205

Haggard, Rider, 112

Hall, Stuart, 30, 67, 181
Hardy, Thomas, 166
Harlem Renaissance, 52, 84, 125, 194
Head, Bessie, 14, 54, **83–7**, 115, 133, 134,
    138, 143, 165, 188
  publication chronology, 222, 223, 224
Henderson, Gwendolen Mae, 108, 173
Henry, Lenny, 68
Herk, Aritha van, 58
Hereniko, Vilsoni, xiii, 42, 128
Hindu, 2, 24, 40, 47, 49, 89, 118, 180
Hobsbawm, Eric, 49
Hobson, John A., 88, **189**
homelands, 4, 12, 14, 26, 27, 29, 31, 32, 34,
    35, 36, 54, 62, 91, 97
  idealised, 37, 93
  rewriting the colonisers', **168–70**
Homer, xiv
Hopkinson, Nalo, 117, 148–9, **151–2**, 154–5
Howe, Darcus, 65, 67
Hulme, Keri, 129
Hurston-Neale, Zora, 134
hybridity, x, 27, 36, 39, 71, 74, 170, 174,
    177, **189–91**, 198
  new expressions of, 182; positive, 29, 34,
    91, 98; redefining Britishness, 180

identity, xii, xv, xvi, 5, 7, 10, 27, 30, 36, 47,
    63, 67, 74, 84, 87–9, 93–4, 103, 115, 136,
    142, 163, 171–5, 179–81, 184, 187, 196,
    199
  asserting, 151; autobiography and, 14;
    control of, 12, 92, 205
  cultural, 6, 26, 97, 132, 185–6, 190, 196;
    deconstruction of, 101; diasporan, 98
  difference as component of, 169; gaps in,
    31; hybrid, 31, 39, 170
  through language, **120–22**, 141, 193;
    loss of, 116, 150
  national, 48–51, 56, 98–9, 110, 112–3,
    120, 127, 156, 201
  new versions of, 38, 102, 122, 124, 158,
    177; sexual/gendered, 28, 83, 85,
    160, 195
  and writing, 100, 107–9, 114, 164
Imperial, *see* Empire
Independence, **44–6**, 49–51, 59, 63, 115,
    124, 156–7
  of India and Pakistan, 24–5, **46–7**;
    nationhood and, 51, 56; removal of,
    104
India, 2, 4, 6, 19, 45, **46–7**, 48, 49, 56, 59,
    87–8, 94–5, 114–15
  Indian mutiny, 2, 59
indigenous peoples, 9, 10, 36, 59, 62, 68,
    71, 101, 117, **127–9**, 150, 159, 174,
    189
  languages of, 110, 172
  seen as savages, 20, 90, 185
  writers, 74, 100, 123, 129, 134, 168
Ireland, xii, 27, 46, 63, 107, 156, 178
  Irish uprising, 2
Israel, 45, 48–50, 201

Jamaica, xii, 7, 22, 31–2, 45, 122, 139, 141–3, 151–2, 161–2, 193–4
  see also Caribbean
James, C.L.R., 11, 44, 51
Jewish, 26, 49, 95
Jhabvala, Ruth Prawer, 123
Jinnah, Muhammad Ali, 2, 46
Johnson, Amryl, 132, **144–5**
Johnson, Linton Kwesi, 29, 32, 73, 111–12, 132, 140, 142, **143**, 145, 168

Karodia, Farida, 14, 165
Kay, Jackie, 116, 126, 205
Keneally, Thomas, 156
Kenya, xv, 22, 24, 28, 45, 51, 55, 59, 114, 162, 191
Kincaid, Jamaica, 17, 133, 149
  Annie John, 17, 133
Kipling, Rudyard, 159, 192
Klerk, F.W. de, 15
Kok, Ingrid de, 13, 81, **82–3**, 165
Kristeva, Julia, 131, 198
Kureishi, Hanif, 29, 32, 43, 170, 181, 191
Kuzwayo, Ellen, 14
Kwazulu, Natal, 15

Lacan, Jacques, 185, 195
Lahiri, Jumpna, 131
land rights, 2, **47–8**, 68, 150, 164
Langford, Ruby, 54, 63, 75, 76, **78–9**, 100, 129, 134, 168
Lenin, 18, 45, 189
lesbian, 30, 126
Levy, Andrea, 34, 66, **162**, 168
life writing, 54, 77, 83, 84, 100, 130, 148, 149, **164–8**
Lim, Catherine, 110, 116, 148
Liverpool, 35, 160
Lorde, Audre, 173, 187
Lovelace, Earl, 6, 177
Lyotard, Jean-Francois, 61

Macaulay's Minute, 25
Makarios, Archbishop, 59
Malange, Nise, 132, 139, 142, **145–6**
Malaya, 19, 45, 111, 153, 199
Malaysia, 10, 111, 148–9, 153, 154, 199
Malta, 4, 5
Mandela, Nelson, 3, 13, 15, 44
Mandela, Winnie, 14
Mansfield, Katherine, 63, 169
Maori, xiii, xvi, 8, 23, 40, 48, 114, 117, **118–19**, **127–8**, 132, 172
marginalisation, xii, 22, 54–5, 93, 109, 119, 128, **133–8**, 155, 161, 168, 171, 187, 204–5, 206
Marquez, Gabriel Garcia, 4
Marley, Bob, 139
Marsh, Selina Tusitula, 41–2
Marson, Una, 121, 178
Marxism, xiii, 45, 162
Maugham, Somerset, 41–2
Mau Mau, 45, 51, 59, 110, 162

Mauritius, 26
Mbuli, Mzwakhe, 13, 122, 132, 139, 142, **145**, 146
metamorphosis, 153, 154
metropolitanism, 174
Mew, Charlotte, 88
Mhlope, Gcina, 165, 188
middle passage, 93, 121, 182
migration, **25–36**, 49, 63, 74, 97–9, 121, 141, 159, 162, 168–70, 172, 174, 181–2, 187, 189, 191, 193
mimicry, xii, 63, 136, 171, 172–3, 177, 190, **192**
Minh, Ho Chi, 50, 69
Minh-ha, Trinh, 57
Mistry Rohinton, 29
Mitchinson, Naomi, 87, **159–60**
Morgan, Sally, xiii, 10, 54, 75, **77–81**, 132, 134, 138, 143, 165, 168
Morris, Mervyn, 134, 139
Morrison, Toni, 84, 93, 100, 131, 133, **148–9**, 150, 161, 163
Mother Africa, 101, 105–6, **112–16**
Mother India, **112–16**
motherhood, 56, 74, **101–6**, **113–16**, 126
  under apartheid, 82–3
motherlands, 7, 115, 116, 123
Mountbatten (division of India and Pakistan), 2, 46
Mozambique, 53
Mukherjee, Bharati, 29, 32
multiculturalism, 36, 49, 74, 169, **179–80**, 189–90
Munro, Alice, 58
Murray, Les, 5
Muslim, 2, 24, 46–7, 49, 137, 203
myths, xiv, 10, 72, 74, 75, 91, **117–19**, 121–2, 137–8, 148–9, 154, 169–70
  and historical links, 110, 129, 131–2, 143, 150–1; questioning, 106
  reviving, 103, 107, 108, 127, 159

Naipual, V.S., xiii, 6, 138, 192
Naryan, R.K., 6, 118
Narrogin, Mudrooroo (Colin Johnson), 10, 168
Nasta, Susheila, 25, 30, 38, 57, 98–9, 123, 124, 179
National Front, 67
nationhood, 28–9, 45, 59, 60, 63, 66, 172, 185
  nation language, 71, 110, **120–2**, 139, **193–4**
  national identity, 100, 105, 110, 112–3, 127, 196
  nationalism, 34, 43, 45, 46, **49–51**, 57, 92, 195; nationalist myths, 25, 98
  and women's equality, **123–6**
Ngcobo, Lauretta, 14, 83, 146, 183
Négritude, 11, 43, 50, 52, 125, 184–6, **194–6**
Nehru, Jawaharlal, 2, 46, 60
neocolonialism, x, 6, 7, **51–2**

New Zealand, xii, 5, 8, 19, 23, 27, 54, 62–3, 68, **118–19**, 147, 156–8, 169, 172
see also Maori
Nichols, Grace, 32, **36–7**, 55, 93, 108, 110, 115, 138, 181–2
Nigeria, xii, xiii, 45, 93, 104–6, 205
    Nigerian writers, 6, 55, 103, 108, 110–11, 143, 159–61, 205
Nkrumah, Kwame, 3, **44**, 50, 51–2, 59–60
Njau, Rebekah, 114
Nussbaum, Martha, 56, 186–7, 188
Nwapa, Flora, **101–3**, 106, 114–16, 118, 133, 188

Okigbo, Christopher, 117
oral traditions, xv, 74, 117, 120–2, 152, 172, 193
    oral literature, xi, xiii, xv, 2, 54, 71, 74–6, 79, 101–2, 106–8, **130–4**, 143, 159, 178
    oral storytelling, 73, 75, 91–2, 95, 100, 117–19, 135, **140–2**, 149–50, 153, 168
Orang Asli, 10
Orientalism, x, 27, 109, 173, 177, 200, **201–3**
Other/Otherise/Othering, xiii, 16, 27, 29, 54–5, 57, 59, 81, 87–8, 90, 109–10, 112, 124, 130, 134, 147, 150, 155, 160–1, 164, 184, **195–9**, 201–3, **204–5**

Pacific Islands, 40, 129
Pacific Rim, 41,
Pakistan, xii, 2, 24–5, **46–7**, 48, 49, 95, 97, 115
Palestine, 48, 49, 201
Pan Africanism, 24, 45, **52–3**
Pass Laws, 12, 13, 15
patriarchy, 51, 88, 106, 114, 116, 123, 134, **135–8**
performance poetry, xv, 13, 31, 35, 46, 54, 73–4, 107–8, 117, 121–2, 130–34, **138–46**, 168, 177, 180, 193–4, 196
Phillips, Caryl, 28, 29
Phillips, Marlene Nourbese, 110
Pilkington, Doris, xiii
postcolonial Gothic, **147–55**, **196–9**
postmodernism, 81, 100, 202
primitive, 10, 20, 47, 73, 84, 89, 119, 124, 147, 159, 161, 185, 197
Pritchard, Katherine Susannah, 158
Punter, David, 72, 95, 147, 150, 155

Queen Victoria, 17, 18
'queer theory', xiii

Race Today, 67, 143
Racism, 34–5, 40, 64–7. 73, 77, 81–2, 84, 154, 158, 169, 173, 183, 191
    politically legitimised, 12
Raj, 4, 38, 40, 172
Randhawa, Ravinder, 33
Rao, Raja, 55
Rastafarian, 133, 139, 140, 143, 193, 196

reggae, 73, 139–41, 196
resistance, x, 2, 7, 10, 24, 43, 44–5, 51, 53, 54–5, **59–60**, 135, 156, 174, 195, 206
Rhys, Jean, 21–22, 60–61, 159, **160–1**, 168–9
Robinson Crusoe, 6, 15, 81, **89–90**
Roots movement, 194
Roughsey, Elsie, 76
Roy, Arundhati, 32, 91, 131, 133
Rushdie, Salman, xiii, 2, 24, 28, 32, 47, 91, 94, 118, 149, 168, 181, 191

Said, Edward, 18, 60, 109, 173, 177, 200, **201–3**
Salkey, Andrew, 67
Schreiner, Olive, 15
Selvon, Sam, 90
semi-fictionalised autobiography, 14, 71, 74, 77, 127, 134, **164–8**
Senghor, Leopold, 44, 53, 194
Senior, Olive, 148, 149, 151
Sepamla, Sipho, 13
Seroet, Wally Mongane, 13
settler, xi, xii, 5, 27, 36, 48–50, 197
    invader, 10
    societies, **62–4**
    writing, **156–8**
Shakespeare, xi, 89, 135, 200
Sharpeville, 13
Sikh, 2, 24, 38, 40, 49, 92
silencing, xi, xii, xiv, 19, 21, 42, 54–5, 58, 67, 73, 76–7, 83, 90, 93, 100, 101–2, 107, 109, 123–5, 127, 130, 135–6, 138, 142–4, 147, 150, 155–6, 161–3, 164, 167–8, 172, 187, 193–4, 196, 201–2, **204–7**
slavery, 4, 19–20, 35, 49, 55, 72, 89–90, 108, 110, 114, 116, 120, 125, 132–3, 150, 160
    anti-slavery, 61; and diaspora, **26–7**; narratives, 164; reversed, 17
    social legacy of, 67, 117, 148, 154, 183
Slemon, Steven, x, 8, 63–4
Slovo, Gillian, 15
Smith, Mikey, **139**, 142, 143, 147, 193
Smith, Zadie, 28, 34, 43, 46, 180, 191
Soga, Tiyo, 52
Somerville, Margaret, 76–7
South Africa, 6, 11–15, 24, 27, 45, 53, 183, writers, 54, 90, **80–7**, 90, 108, 121–2, 127, 132–4, 138–9, 142–3, 145–6, 164–7
    see also Apartheid
Soweto, 6, 12–13, 145
Spare Rib, 125
Spivak, Gayatri Chakravorty, xiv, 21, 40, 60, 123, 135, 173, 187, 200, 204–5, **206–7**
storytelling, *see* oral traditions
subaltern, 40, 101, 135–6, 138, 164, 173, 187, 205, **206–7**
Suleri, Sara, xiv, 57–8, 60, 100, 133–4, 173
Sulter, Maud, 125–6
Sutherland, Efau, 118
Syal, Meera, 29, 32, 98, **169–70, 180–1**, 191

Sykes, Bobbi, 74–5

Teaiwa, Teresia, 42, 54
terra nullius, 47, **68**, 147
Thaman, Helu Konai, xiii
Thiong'o Ngugi Wa, xv, 46, 51, 55, 108–9, 110, **162–3**
Third World, 6,7,63, 68–9, 85, 121
Tlali, Miriam, 12, 13, 165
Tricontinentalism, **68–70**
Tunisia, 24
Tutuola, Amos, 118
Twin Towers (9/11), 203

vampire, 148, 150–1, 154
vernacular, 37, 46, 73, 108, 117, 121–2, 132, 187, 193–4
Vervoerd, Henrik, 12–13, 167

Waitangi, Treaty of, 48
Walcott, Derek, xiii, xiv, xv, 1, 17, 55, 90
Walker, Alice, 57, 79, 86, 93, 131, 188

Ward, Glenyse, 54, 75, 77, 78, 138, 143, 165
Washington, Booker T., 194
werebeast,148–9
West Indies, 17, 19, 26, 47, 52, 67, 121, 139, 141, 169
Wicomb, Zoe, 12, 14, 81, 84, 134, 165, **166–8**
Windrush, SS Empire, 28, 31, **65–8**, 74, 141, 162
Woolf, Virginia, 54, 87, 88, 107–8
Wordsworth, xi, xiv, xv, 63
World War II, 18, 23, 27, 45, 46, 48, 52, 65–6, 91–2, 111, 153, 162, 189

Yahp, Beth, 111, 148, **153**, 199
Yeats, W.B., 2, 44, 50, 72, 88
Yoruba, 111, 118, 132

Zambia, 45
Zephaniah, Benjamin, 29, 112, 177
Zimbabwe, 21, 51, 53, 57–8
Zulu, 51, 84

Index of Works Cited

(Main references for specific works are given in **bold type**)

Aboriginal Mother, An (Labumore/Roughsey), 76
'Aboriginal Women's Narratives' (Ferrier), 80
Aboriginal Writing Today (Mudrooroo Narrogin), 80
Adoption Papers (Kay), 126
African Novel in English: An Introduction, The (Booker), 22
African Societies in Southern Africa: Historical Studies (Thompson), 53
After the Last Sky (Said), 203, **204**
Alias Grace (Atwood), **61–2**, 63, 157
'All Wat Kind Is' (de Kok), 82, **83**
Amandla, a Novel (Tlali), 13, 225, **237**
Anansi and Miss Lou (Bennett), 121, **122**
Angel (Collins), 34–5
Angel at My Table, An (Frame), 165, **168**, 226
'Angel of Progress: Pitfalls of the Term "Colonialism", The' (McLintock), 9
Anita and Me (Syal), 32, **169–70**, 180, 228
Annie John (Kincaid), **17**, 133, 135, 226
Anthills of the Savannah (Achebe), 162, **163**, 226
Anticolonialism in British Politics: The Left and the End of Empire, 1918–1964 (Howe), 46
'Arrival of Brighteye, The' (Breeze), **31**, **35**, 142
Arrow of God (Achebe), 55, **56**, 161, 220
Aspects of South African Literature (Heywood), 16
Away: The Indian Writer as an Expatriate (Kumar), 39

Bacchae of Euripides, The (Soyinka), 111, **112**
Baumgartner's Bombay (Desai), 95
Because the Dawn Breaks: Poems Dedicated to the Grenadian People 99, 135
Beginning Postcolonialism (McLeod), 204
Beloved (Morrison), 133, **135**, 150, 226
Bessie Head: A Woman Alone – Autobiographical Writing (MacKenzie), 86, **87**
Bewitched Crossroad, A (Clayton), 87
Black Atlantic, The (Gilroy), 44, **51**, 67
Black British Feminism (Mirza), 126
Black Exercise Book, The (Rhys), 62
Black Jacobins, The (James), 51, 214, **234**
Black Mamba Rising: South African Worker Poets in Struggle (Sitas), 147
Black Man's Burden, The (Davidson), 24
Black Revolutionary: Padmore's Path from Communism to Pan-Africanism (Hooker), 53

Black Skin, White Masks (Fanon), 43, **185–6**, 195
Bondmaid, The (Lim), 110, **112**
Bone People, The (Hulme), 129, **130**, 226
Border Traffic (Humm), 146
Born a Half Caste (Kennedy), 75, **80**
Brick Lane (Ali), 34, **35**, 229
Brown Girl in the Ring (Hopkinson), 228
Buddha of Suburbia, The (Kureishi), 170, **181–2**, 227
'Butterfly' (Collins), 94, **99**

'Cahier d'un retour au pays natal' (Cesaire), 231
Call Me Woman (Kuzwayo), 14, 226, **234**
Cambridge Guide to Women's Writing (Sage), 99
'Can the Subaltern Speak?' (Spivak), 40, 135, **206–7**
Canadian Imagination: Dimensions of a Literary Culture, The (Staines), 65
Canadian Literature (Woodcock), 63, 156, **237**
'Chant Me a Tune' (Collins), 93, **99**
Clear Light of Day (Desai), 2, 24, 47, 94, 95, 96, 115, 116, 132, 136, **137–8**, 225
Clearing in the Bush, A (Wicomb), 166–7, **168**, 226
Cloud Cuckoo Land (Mitchison), 159, **163**
Collected Poems (Walcott), **74**, 226
Collected Poems of W.B. Yeats, The, **9**
Colonial Discourse and Post-Colonial Theory (Chrisman and Williams), 9
Colonial & Postcolonial Literature (Boehmer), **9**, 175
Colonialism and Culture (Dirks), 42
Colonialism/Post Colonialism (Loomba), **22**, 39, 175
Coming Home and Other Stories (Karodia), 14
Conquered, The (Mitchison), 159, **163**
Conservationist, The (Gordimer), **11**, 223
Contemporary African Literature and the Politics of Gender (Stratton), 107
Corn King and the Spring Queen, The (Mitchison), 159, **163**, 213
Cosmopolitanism (Appiah), 189
Covering Islam (Said), 203, **204**
Crick Crack Monkey (Collins), 118, 132–3, **135**, 151, 192
Critical Perspectives on Chinua Achebe (Innes and Lindfors), 74
Crocodile Fury, The (Yahp), 111, 153, **155**, 199
Cross of Gold (Ngcobo), 14

Cry Freedom, 14
Culture and Imperialism (Said), 22
Cultivating Humanity (Nussbaum), 186, **189**

Dark Matter: A Century of Speculative Fiction from the African Diaspora (Thomas), 149, **155**
Dark Side of the Dream: Australian Literature and the Postcolonial Mind (Hodge and Mishra), 64
Daughters of the Twilight (Karodia), 14
Decolonising the Mind (Ngugi), **163–4**, 226
Destination Biafra (Emecheta), 103, **105–6**, 110
De-scribing Empire (Tiffin and Lawson), 175, **176**
Dialect Verse (Bennett), 121, **122**, 215
Dialogic Imagination, The (Bakhtin), 133, **135**
'Dimomona' (Tlali), 12
Don't Take Your Love to Town (Langford), 63, 75, 78–9, **80**, 129
Dragon Can't Dance, The (Lovelace), 6, **177**
Dread, Beat an' Blood (Johnson), **74**, 143, 224
Drum, 15
Dusklands (Coetzee), 15, **16**, 81

East is East, 32
'Easter 1916' (Yeats), 2, **9**, 211
Efuru (Nwapa), **101–7**, 114, 221
Emperor Shaka the Great (Kunene), 51, 225, **234**
Empire Strikes Back, The (Gilroy), 67
Empire Writes Back, The (Ashcroft, Griffiths and Tiffin), **7–9**, 175
'Empire Writes Back with a Vengeance, The' (Rushdie), 35
English Auden: Poems, Essays, And Dramatic Writings, 1927-1939, The, 9
English Patient, The (Ondaatje), **91–2**, 228
Ethics of Identity, The (Appiah), 187, **189**, 229
Evonne! On the Move (Goolagong), 74, **80**
Expansion of England, The (Seeley), 19, **22**
Extravagant Strangers (Phillips), 28, **35**

Fasting Feasting (Desai), 95, 96–97, **99**, 115, 136, 137
Fat Black Woman's Poems, The (Nichols), 36–7, **39**, 138, 226
Female Novelists of Modern Africa (Taiwo), 117
Feminist Review 1988, 56, **59**, 79
'Five Nights of Bleeding' (Johnson), 73, **74**, 112
Foe (Coetzee), 15, **16**, 81, 90, 226
Footprints in the Quag: Stories and Dialogues from Soweto (Tlali), 12
For Love of Country: Debating the Limits of Patriotism (Nussbaum), 186, **189**
'From Victims to Survivors: The Anti-hero as a Narrative Strategy in Asian Immigrant Writing with Special Reference to *The Buddha of Suburbia*', (Seema), 35

Gender, Politics and Fiction (Ferrier), 80
Gilda Stories, The (Gomez), 228
God of Small Things, The (Roy), 32, **35**, 91, 228
Grain of Wheat, A (Thiong'o), 51, 55, **56**, 110, 162, 221

Harmony Silk Factory, The (Aw), 111, **112**, 153, 154
Healers, The (Armah), 55, **56**, 224
Heart of Darkness (Conrad), 10, **11**, 20, 88, 90, 209
Hecate, 80
History of Negro Revolt, A (James), 44, **46**
History of Sexuality, Volume 1, An Introduction, The (Foucault), 56
History of the Voice, The (Kamau Brathwaite), xv, **17**, 120, 177
Home Truths (Nasta), 25, **35**
House for Mr. Biswas, A (Naipaul), 6, 138, 219, **235**

I Is a Long-Memoried Woman (Nichols), 55, **56**
I Know Why the Caged Bird Sings (Angelou), 222
'I, the Unemployed' (Malange), **145–7**
Idu (Nwapa), 101, 114, 222, **235**
Imagined Communities: Reflections on the Origins and Spread of Nationalism (Anderson), 49
Imperial Leather: Race, Gender and Sexuality in the Colonial Contest (McLintock), 201
Imperialism: A Study (Hobson), **189**, 210
Inglan is a Bitch (Johnson), 143, **147**
In the Heart of the Country (Coetzee), 81, **83**
Ingelba and the Five Black Matriarchs (Cohen and Somerville), 76, **80**
Insights into Black Women's Writing (Wisker), 176
Introduction to Post-Colonial Theory, An (Childs and Williams), **35**, 175
Inventing Ireland (Kiberd), 56
'Irish Airman Foresees his Death, An' (Yeats), 44, **46**
Islands (Brathwaite), 121, **122**, 222
It's Raining in Mango (Astley), 64, 226

Jack Maggs (Carey), **64**, 158
Jamaica Dialect Poems (Bennett), 121, **122**
Jamaica Labrish (Bennett), **17**, 121, 221
Jane Eyre (Brontë), 60, **62**, 90, 160, 161
Jean Rhys (Howell), 62
Journal and Selected Writings of the Rev. Tiyo Soga, The (Soga), 53
Joys of Motherhood, The (Emecheta), 103, 104, **106**, 225

Kanthapura (Rao), 55, **56**, 214
Kehinde (Emecheta), 104–06

Last Virgin in Paradise (Teiawa and Hereniko), 42

Lava of This Land: South African Poetry, 1960–96, The (Hirson), 83
'Learning Myself Anew', (Govinden), 16
Let It Be Told (Johnson), 146
Let It Be Told: Black Women Writers in Britain (Ngcobo), 184
'Let Them Call It Jazz' (Rhys), 21, **22**
Life and Times of Michael K (Coetzee), 15, **16**, 81, 225
Life and Works of Bessie Head, The (Ola), 87
'Life(H)istory Writing: The Relationship between Talk and Text', (Somerville), 80
Life Isn't All Ha Ha Hee Hee (Syal), 169, **170**, 191
Like a House on Fire (COSAW), 15, **16**, 165
Lion and the Jewel, The (Soyinka), 111, **112**, 220
Living Blood, The (Due), 229
Location of Culture, The (Bhaba), 192
Long Road to Nowhere (Johnson), 144, **146**, 226

Madwoman in the Attic, The (Gilbert and Gubar), 160, **163**
Man for the People, A (Achebe), 162, **163**
Maori: The Crisis and the Challenge (Duff), 128, **130**
Maru (Head), 86, **87**, 115, 222
Marxism and the Interpretation of Culture (Nelson, and Grossberg), 127
Mask (Brathwaite), 121, **122**
Me Cyaan Believe It (Smith), 147
'Message to the Tricontinental', (Guevara), 69, **70**
Mi Revalueshanary Fren (Johnson), 143, **147**
Midnight's Children (Rushdie), 2, **9**, 24, 47, 118, 225
Mimic Men, The (Naipaul), 192, 221, **235**
'Modernism's Last Post' (Slemon), 9
Modernity and Its Future (Hall), 182
Moon and Sixpence, The (Maugham), 42
Moses Ascending (Selvon), 90, **91**
Motherlands: Black Women's Writing from Africa, the Caribbean and South Asia, 'Introduction' (Nasta), 59
Moving the Centre (Ngugi), 163, **164**, 228
'Mummy and Donor and Deirdre' (Kay), 116, **126**
Muriel at the Metropolitan (Tlali), 13
My Beautiful Laundrette (Kureishi), 170
My Place (Morgan), **10**, 75, 77, 132, 165, 226
Myal (Brodber), 118, **119**, 133, 152, 196, 226

Nation and Narration (Bhabha), 51
Nationalism in Asia and Africa (Kedourie), 53
Nations and Nationalism since 1780: Programme, Myth, Reality (Hobsbawm), 51
Neo-Colonialism: The Last Stage of Imperialism (Nkrumah), 51, **52**
Nervous Conditions (Dangarembga), **21–2**, 226

New National and Post Colonial Literatures: An Introduction (Innes), 50
New Statesman (Howe), 68
New Statesman and Society (Alibhai), 39
No Longer at Ease (Achebe), 162, **163**, 219

'Omeros' (Walcott), **17**, 55
On the Fringe of Dream-Time and Other Stories (Reddy), 14
Once Were Warriors (Duff), 119, **128–30**, 227
One Hundred Years of Solitude (Garcia Marquez), 4, **9**, 221
One is Enough (Nwapa), 101, 103, **107**, 114
Orientalism: Western Conceptions of the Orient (Said), **112**, 201
Oscar and Lucinda (Carey), **64**, 158, 226
Other Britain, Other British: Contemporary Multi-cultural Fiction (Lee), 35

Painter of Signs, The (Narayan), 6, **9**
Palm-Wine Drinkard, The (Tutuola), 118, **119**, 217
Pan Africanism: The Idea and Movement 1976–1963 (Olisanwuche), 53
Pantomime (Walcott), 90, **91**, 225
Part of My Soul Went with Him (Mandela, W.), 14, **16**
Passage to India, A (Forster), xvi, 87, **89**, 172, 199, 212
'Passages' (Nasta), 38, **39**
Passing (Larson), 84, 214, **234**
Past the Last Post: Theorizing Post-colonialism and Post-modernism (Adam and Tiffin), 9
Pedagogy of the Oppressed (Freire), 109, **112**
Pond, The (Morris), 140, **147**
'Possessing the Land' (Woodcock), 63, **65**, 156
Possessing the Secret of Joy (Walker), 188, **189**
Postcolonial and African American Women's Writing: A Critical Introduction (Wisker), 176
Postcolonialism: An Historical Introduction (Young), 3, **9**
Postcolonial Imaginings (Punter), 72, **74**, 150
Post-Colonial Literatures in English (Walder), **9**, 175
Postcolonial Studies: An Essential Glossary (Thieme), 9
Post-Colonial Studies: The Key Concepts (Ashcroft, Griffiths, and Tiffin), 16
Postmodern Condition: A Report on Knowledge, The (Lyotard), 62
Powers of Horror (Kristeva), 198, **200**, 225
Prelude (Mansfield), 63, **64**
'Problems of a Creative Writer in South Africa' (Moyana), 16
Psychology of Jingoism, The (Hobson), 189
Purple and Green: Poems by Women Poets, 39

Question of Palestine, The (Said), 203, **204**
Question of Power, A (Head), 84, 85, 87, 115, 165, **168**, 223

'Questions of Multiculturalism' (Spivak and Gunew), 206

Rabelais and His World (Bakhtin), 177
Reading Chinua Achebe: Language and Ideology in Fiction (Gikandi), 74
'Red Indians in England' (Hyder), 39
'Reinventing Britain' (Bhabha), 182
Rich Estate, A (Ravenscroft), 87
Riddym Ravings and Other Poems (Breeze), 141, **146**, 226
Rights of Passage (Brathwaite), 121, **122**, 221
Ripples in the Pool (Njau), 114, **117**
'Rise of Colonial Nationalism: Australia, New Zealand, Canada and South Africa First assert Their Nationalities, The' (Fieldhouse), 22
Robinson Crusoe (Defoe), 6, **9**, 15, 81, 89, 90, 208
Room of One's Own, A (Woolf), 54, **56**, 213

'Schooner Flight, The' (Walcott), xiv, 74
'Search for Freedom in Indian Women's Writing, The' (Ash), 115, **117**
Selected Poems (Bennett), 121, **122**
Serowe, Village of the Rain Wind (Head), 86, **87**
'She was so quiet' (Collins), 93, **99**
Sizwe Bansi Is Dead (Fugard), 14
'Skin Teeth' (Nichols), 110, **112**
Small Acts (Gilroy), 51
'Small Passing' (de Kok), 82, **83**
Small Island (Levy), 34, **35**, 66, 162, 168, 229
Soweto Stories (Tlali), 13, **147**, 227
'Spain 1937' (Auden), 1, **9**
'Spear Has Fallen, The' (Mbuli), 145, **147**
Spring Cleaning: Poems (Breeze), 146
Strangers to Ourselves (Kristeva), 198, **200**
Surfacing (Atwood), 5, **9**, 222
'Survival' (Atwood), 5
Swamp Dwellers, The (Soyinka), 111, **112**

Tales of Tenderness and Power (Head), 86
Talking Back: Thinking Feminist, Thinking Black (hooks), 100, **101**
Te Kaihau/The Windeater (Hulme), 16
Tempest, The (Shakespeare), 5, **9**, 89, 90, 135, 208
Textual Politics from Slavery to Postcolonialism: Race and Identification (Plasa), 62
Things Fall Apart (Achebe), 55, **56**, 72–3, 74, 110, 131, 161, 218
This Is Lagos and Other Stories (Nwapa), 101
'Three Women's Texts and a Critique of Imperialism' (Spivak), 201
Tigers are Better Looking (Rhys), 21, **22**
Tings an' Times (Johnson), 143, **147**
'Toilet, The ' (Mhlope), 165, **168**
Touch Mi, Tell Mi (Bloom), 143, **146**
Towards a Black Feminist Criticism (Smith), 109

Towards International Government (Hobson), 189
Tricontinental, 69, **70**
True History of the Kelly Gang (Carey), **64**, 158

'Under Western Eyes: Feminist Scholarship and Colonial Discourse' (Talpade Mohanty), 59
'Unity and Struggle' (Cabral), 54
'Unsettling the Empire Resistance Theory' (Slemon), 64

'Vercingetorix and Others' (Mitchison), 159, **163**
View of the Art of Colonisation, A (Wakefield), 22
Vision of Order: A Study of Black South African Literature in English, A (Barnett), 87
Voyage in the Dark (Rhys), 169, **170**, 213

Wacvie (Bandler), 75, **80**, 224
Waiting for the Barbarians (Coetzee), 81, **83**, 225
'Walking with mih brother in Georgetown' (Nichols), 39
Wandering Girl (Ward), 75, 77, 78, 227, **237**
War in South Africa: Its Causes and Effects, The (Hobson), 189
Whale Rider, The (Ihimaera), **118–19**, 226
When Rain Clouds Gather (Head), 85, 86, **87**, 115, 222
Whispers from the Cotton Tree Roots: Caribbean Fabulist Fiction (Hopkinson), 149, **155**
White Teeth (Smith), 34, **35**, 180, 191, 229
Wicked Old Woman, A (Randhawa), 33, **35**
Wide Sargasso Sea (Rhys), 60, 61, **62**, 160, 161, 221
Wild Cat Falling, (Johnson, (Mudrooroo), 10
Windrush, 31
Windrush: The Irresistible Rise of Multi-Racial Britain (Phillips and Phillips), 66
'Winter Thoughts' (Nichols), 37, **39**
"Wintering: Making Home in Britain" (Innes), 35
Woman, Native, Other (Minh-Ha), 57, **59**
'Women's Liberation' (Noonuccal), 80
World Literature Written in English (Slemon), 64
Wretched of the Earth, The (Fanon), 21, **22**, 43, 45, 185, 195, 219

You Can't Get Lost in Cape Town (Wicomb), 12, 14, **16**, 166, 226
'Young Gifted and Brown' (Srivastava), 39
Youth (Coetzee), 81

Zabat: Poetics of a Family Tree (Sulter), 125, **127**